To My Dearest Wife, Lide

MARITIME CURRENTS: HISTORY AND ARCHAEOLOGY

To My Dearest Wife, Lide

Letters from George B. Gideon Jr. *during* Commodore Perry's Expedition to Japan, 1853–1855

Edited by M. PATRICK SAUER and DAVID A. RANZAN

The University of Alabama Press
Tuscaloosa

The University of Alabama Press
Tuscaloosa, Alabama 35487-0380
uapress.ua.edu

Typeface: Garamond and Aquiline Two

Cover images: *Above*, unknown Chinese artist, "Whampoa Reach," Library of Congress; *below*, example of Gideon's letters
Cover design: Michele Myatt Quinn

Library of Congress Cataloging-in-Publication Data

Names: Gideon, George B., 1827–1863, author. | Gideon, Eliza, 1827–1871, correspondent. | Sauer, M. Patrick (Michael Patrick), 1972– editor. | Ranzan, David A., editor.
Title: To my dearest wife, Lide : letters from George B. Gideon Jr. during Commodore Perry's expedition to Japan, 1853–1855 / edited by M. Patrick Sauer and David A. Ranzan.
Description: Tuscaloosa : The University of Alabama Press, [2019] | Series: Maritime currents : history and archaeology | Includes bibliographical references and index.
Identifiers: LCCN 2018054794| ISBN 9780817320232 (cloth) | ISBN 9780817392376 (ebook)
Subjects: LCSH: Gideon, George B., 1827–1863—Correspondence. | United States Naval Expedition to Japan (1852–1854) | Perry, Matthew Calbraith, 1794–1858. | United States. Navy—Officers—Correspondence. | Marine engineers—United States—Correspondence. | United States. Navy—History—19th century—Sources. | Seafaring life—History—19th century—Sources. | Japan—Description and travel—Sources. | East Asia—Description and travel—Sources.
Classification: LCC DS881.8 .G53 2019 | DDC 952/.025—dc23
LC record available at https://lccn.loc.gov/2018054794

Contents

Illustrations

Preface

George Gideon's letters had been in the possession of Gideon's great-great-grandniece, the mother-in-law of one of the editors. Discovered after her death, the letters resided in her attic wrapped up in manila paper like a badly wrapped present, and tied with a small string. The letters were written on extremely thin paper, in minuscule writing, and more often than not the words bled through the paper. Not one square inch of the paper was wasted. One four-page letter contained over seventy-five hundred words. Gideon wrote around the margins and in some cases in between the existing lines.

We have aimed to transcribe the text as accurately and literally as possible in the hopes of preserving the style of the nineteenth-century writing. In the interests of consistency and clarity, however, we have made a few changes in punctuation and spelling. Gideon used capitalizations very freely and was not consistent in their use. We have altered his usage to make sentences more intelligible, while retaining his capitalizations where appropriate, especially if the context was forgiving. We have standardized the datelines at the start of each entry as follows: place (when given), day of the week (when given), month, date of the month, and year (when given). Any errors in dates have been kept as they were, followed by our corrections in brackets. Interlineations were brought down to the line of text at the place indicated, as were additions in the margin.

Gideon used quotation marks around ship names. We have followed current style in italicizing names of ships, and we have done the same for book titles. When an incomplete or incorrect word could be expanded or corrected by a bracketed insertion, we have done so. However, if this seemed too awkward, we placed the full correct word in brackets, following the incorrect word. If there was no confusion, or if the word added flavor, it was left unaltered. All the underlined passages in the manuscript were done by Gideon.

The chapters of the manuscript cover six-month periods in the correspondence. Due to limitations of space, the text had to be considerably shortened. To accomplish this, we decided to remove mostly passages pertaining to Gideon's thoughts and concerns involving his family and associates back home, and those concerning mundane and repetitive ship duties that do not contribute to the overall story.

We are humbled that the University of Alabama Press has seen fit to publish this volume. We are indebted to series editor Gene A. Smith and the Press's director Linda Manning, editor-in-chief Dan Waterman, marketing coordinator Blanche Sarratt, and their colleagues who assisted with the preparation of this book for publication. A special thanks to James C. Bradford, former series editor, for his much-needed advice and assistance.

Chronology

1852

May 15	Ordered to report on board the *Powhatan*

1853

February 13	"We're off for Japan!" Leaves Norfolk
March 2	Arrival at Madeira
April 1–4	At island of Saint Helena
April 14–28	At Cape Town
May 10–27	At Mauritius
May 21	Promoted to first assistant engineer
June 12	Straits of Malacca
June 15–July 3	Singapore
July 7	At Labuan
July 9	At Borneo
July 12–19	At Labuan coal depot
July 25–August 6	At Hong Kong
August 10–20	Anchored in harbor of Nappa Kaing Island (Naha-Okinawa)
August 25–September 4	At Hong Kong
September 6	Anchored in Cumsingmoon, China. Commodore Perry visits ship at 11:30 AM
November 3–5	Macao, Canton, Whampoa
November 5–December 1	At Whampoa anchorage near Canton
November 26	Perry and party come aboard

December 2	At Macao
December 3	At Hong Kong
December 17	Arrival of *Mississippi*

1854

January 10	Receives 2 charts of Ryukyu Islands and a chart of Jedo Bay and islands to the south
January 22	Back to Naha
February 14	Arrival in Jedo Bay
February 18	Hoists Perry's broad pennant. Perry meets Japanese authorities
February 27	Anchored off Yokohama
March 8	Perry leaves for negotiations
March 13	Captain Abbott sent ashore with 14 boats full of presents for emperor of Japan
March 27	Receipt of Japanese presents
March 31	Treaty signed
April 9	Anchored at American Anchorage
April 18	At Shimoda (first treaty port)
May 18	At Hakodate (second treaty port)
June 8–20	Return to Shimoda
July 1–18	Naha
July 20	Off Yung River
July 27	Off Min River
August 3	At Amoy
August 8	At Hong Kong
September 6–16	Cruise between Macao, Hong Kong, and Whampoa
September 28	At Shanghai
October 16–November 11	Off Pei-ho River. Dr. Parker of U.S. legation visits China authorities
November 17	Return to Shanghai
November 26	Goes ashore to see rebel chief Chen Alin but is denied

November 27	Visit of the Taou-Tai and lieutenant governor of the province
December 1	At Hong Kong
December 3	Anchored in Macao Roads
December 5	At Whampoa
December 10–13	At Hong Kong
December 14	Whampoa
December 26	At Hong Kong

1855

January 2	Commander Adams visits with ratified treaty
January 26–February 21	At Shimoda to provide aid to shipwrecked Russians
March 8–20	At Shanghai
May 24	At Amoy
May 28	At Hong Kong
June 8	Macao
June 18	Cutter sent to *Caroline Dow* to quell mutiny
June 25	Hong Kong
July 1	At Whampoa
July 7	Back to Hong Kong
August 4	British and U.S. forces defeat piratical fleet of junks in Ty-ho Bay
November 13	Departure from Singapore
December 2–11	At Mauritius
December 23	Cape Town

1856

February 18	Detached from USS *Powhatan* and granted three-month leave

To My Dearest Wife, Lide

Introduction

On March 31, 1854, George B. Gideon Jr., a second assistant engineer serving aboard the USS *Powhatan*, excitedly wrote to his wife Lide: "About five o'clock we [. . .] were invited in the Cabin by the Commodore to see the treaty, and I have seen it signed and sealed! We get the Ports of Matsmay [Hakodate], Shumuda [Shimoda] and all the Ports of the Lou Chou [Ryukyu Island or Okinawa]. But this is not a commercial treaty. The only things stipulated are that vessels can visit these and trade as they can at present. We are allowed to go ashore at them and go anywhere within a circuit of 14 miles. Perry appeared to be very much pleased with his success."

A remarkable and historic nineteenth-century initiative that altered the course of U.S. and Japanese history, the Japanese Expedition of 1853–54 was "the first comprehensive statement of the basis of an American policy for the Pacific."[1] Conceived and implemented by Commodore Matthew Calbraith Perry, the expedition had as its principal goal the negotiation of a treaty that would provide for the protection of American seamen, permit American vessels to safely acquire provisions in Japanese waters, and open Japanese ports for trade. Perry's supreme achievement brought "a highly civilized but rigidly secluded people into the comity of nations."[2]

In February 1853, under the command of Captain William J. McCluney, the USS *Powhatan* embarked from Hampton Roads, Virginia, for the East Indies via the Cape of Good Hope. The replacement for the USS *Princeton*, which had suffered mechanical issues, the *Powhatan* was attached to the East India Squadron until the latter part of 1855. One of the "black ships of the evil mien,"[3] the *Powhatan* accompanied Commodore Perry on his second visit to Japan in February 1854 and served as his flagship at the time the treaty with the Japanese was signed, on the last day of March 1854.

During the expedition to Japan, George Gideon penned fifty-one known letters that provided a personal commentary throughout the voyage between

1. Portrait of George B. Gideon Jr.

February 13, 1853 and December 23, 1855. Each letter, consisting of journal-like entries written over several days, was part of Gideon's attempt to stay connected to his bride of three years while he performed his duties during this momentous U.S. diplomatic mission in the Pacific Rim. His letters present a unique perceptive that will interest not only antebellum naval, military, and maritime historians, but also historians of technology, of diplomacy, and of social history and gender. Throughout his writings, his explanation of his duties as assistant engineer offers insights into the gradual adoption and embrace of steam technology in the antebellum era. Perry, a big supporter of the implementation of steam technology in the antebellum navy, oversaw the construction of the *Mississippi* and suggested several alterations while on the *Powhatan*. In his prideful words, Gideon proclaims the *Powhatan* the "Fastest as well as the best and most sea worthy sea Steamer afloat."

The letters provide a fascinating window into the nature of gender, marriage, and sexuality. Far from his wife and unable to care for her within the normal rules established by American society, Gideon was not shy to express his sense of loneliness and longing for his wife Lide. Occasionally his letters express a tone of self-doubt and helplessness to support his family or of his eagerness to keep her interest in him. His increasing disdain about his time overseas, which in his opinion was stifling his career, is an interesting look into the position of an antebellum middle-class white man. Regrettably, Lide's letters did not survive.

His concern in reforming his own alcohol consumption while on tour reflected a societal movement that was blanketing antebellum America and perhaps influenced him into sobriety. On New Year's Day, 1854, Gideon took a pledge to abstain from alcohol except for medicinal purposes. "The reasons I tell them are my own. They are as follows: Rum costs money, it affects the mind as well as the body, its influence in action is a false energy and an impure irrational excitement."

When he wasn't on duty in the engine room, he would escape to his cabin and spend his time reading. Through his correspondence, he would share his booklist with his wife, even suggesting some that would interest her to read. The topics ranged from the scientific (Pambour) to the spiritual (the Holy Bible) to the dramatic (Shakespeare) to the entertaining (Bulwer-Lytton).

George B. Gideon Jr., born on January 27, 1827, in Pennsylvania, was the eldest son of George B. Gideon Sr. (1810–49) and Anna Gertrude Lex (1808–57). He spent much of his adolescence in the Spring Garden District of Philadelphia, where he graduated from the prestigious Central High School of Pennsylvania in July 1845. On February 6, 1848, Gideon left Philadelphia for New York to take a job with J. P. Morris & Company. Eight months later, he decided to enter the U.S. Navy and on October 31, 1848, he received a commission as a third assistant engineer.

On February 1, 1849, Gideon received his first assignment, to the Erie Naval Station, to serve on board the USS *Michigan*, the first iron ship built by the U.S. Navy. The *Michigan* would be the sole naval force of the United States on the Great Lakes until her decommissioning in 1912. While stationed in Erie, Pennsylvania, Gideon met Eliza (Lide) Ward, the daughter of William Ward (1795–1852) and Eliza Mayberry Harner (1801–87). Eliza was born on June 5, 1827, in Bellefonte, Centre County, Pennsylvania. Her father served as sheriff of Centre County for three nonconsecutive terms between 1830 and 1845. In 1832, William Ward participated in the Democratic Jackson Committee of Correspondence. He relocated his family to Erie

County in 1848.[4] On February 27, 1850, Gideon married Eliza in Centre County, Pennsylvania.

On January 3, 1851, Gideon was ordered to examination and on February 26 he was promoted to second assistant engineer. He was detached from the *Michigan* on April 16, 1852, and ordered to report on board the *Powhatan* May 15, with a salary of eight hundred dollars a year. He left Erie on April 30. In October 1852 the *Powhatan* sailed from New York for Vera Cruz with the U.S. minister to Mexico, Alfred Conkling. Upon returning to the United States, the ship was laid down at Norfolk, Virginia.

From June 15 to August 6, the *Powhatan* made calls at several ports (Singapore, Labuan, Borneo, and Hong Kong) before coming to anchor at Nappa Kaing Island (Naha-Okinawa). While the *Powhatan* was under repair at the port of Naha, Gideon described for his wife the islanders' apprehension toward the Americans. "On our approach, the girls, boys and women would run like deers [*sic*], and in the neighborhood of shops [. . .] 'twas closed [. . .] and the owners out of sight!" When Gideon went ashore at Naha to engage in trade relations with the Loo Chooans, he was refused service. To procure any goods on the island, one had to use the Dutch or missionaries as middlemen.

By August 30, 1853, Gideon learned of Commodore Perry's successful diplomatic interaction with the Japanese at Uraga and the agreed arrangement that "Commodore Perry had allowed the Emperor until next May to make up his mind." On July 14, 1853, Perry delivered President Millard Fillmore's letter and his own credentials to the Japanese commissioners. He left Edo Bay and sailed to Hong Kong for winter quarters.[5]

Perry's reasoning for allowing the emperor one year to deliberate stemmed from multiple situations occurring around him. The Japanese accepted the president's letter in opposition to the Japanese laws. The Japanese officials informed Perry that "business relating to foreign countries cannot be transacted here in Uraga, but at Nagasaki." The squadron was low on provisions, fresh water, and coal, which limited the length of Perry's stay in Japanese waters. In addition, the presents for the Japanese had not arrived yet. Finally, some of the ships in his squadron were needed to secure American interests in China. In Shanghai, for example, Chinese officials repeatedly instructed foreigners to protect themselves.[6]

While Commodore Perry was negotiating with the Japanese, China was being torn apart by a theocratic civil war. The Taiping Rebellion involved the established Qing dynasty and the Christian millenarian movement of the Heavenly Kingdom of Peace. The conflict would last fourteen years (1850–64) and amass twenty million dead. According to Gideon, "[t]his Chinese War may occupy as much if not more of our attention than Japan." Presenting a rare and extraordinary glimpse into America's expanding interests in the Pacific, Gideon reports on the ongoing relationship with China in commerce. He provides a perspective into the Taiping Rebellion, brief views on the Crimean War, and quite cynical views of the navy's role in supporting American economic interests in East Asia.

The Taiping Rebellion would spark additional uprisings throughout China. One such insurgency involved the Small Knife or Dagger Society, conspiring against the imperial dynasty in Shanghai, China. For the Americans on leave in Shanghai, it proved to be a dangerous event. In October 1854, Lieutenant Henry Rolando of the *Powhatan* and Lieutenant Alphonse Barbot of the *Vandalia* had dinner with one of the rebel chiefs, Chen Alin, when "an onset was made on Alin's house." Both Americans returned to their ships unharmed. It was concluded that the attack was from a party of rebels who resented Alin's popularity among foreigners. Later, in November, even Gideon entered the "Rebel City" against orders and attempted to see Alin, but was denied by the rebels. "I did not care to be humbugged or beg to see Alin." But even with the rebels' refusal, Gideon expressed sympathy toward them, especially the rebel chief. "A reward of three hundred thousand dollars is offered for the Rebel Chief, Alin's head. He escaped, and well for him." With the start of infighting among the rebels, the imperialists put down the insurrection and retook Shanghai.

In February 1854, the USS *Powhatan* was ordered to Japan. On February 12, Gideon first viewed the land of the shogun. "The landscape of the island of Nyphon [Nippon] presented itself most beautifully. The land is mountainous and from its appearance volcanic. The peaks and top sides were covered with snow and the air felt like home!" The next day, Mount Fuji "loom[ed] up in magnificent grandeur. Its peaks extending into the clouds gave it the appearance of the [frustum] of a cone, and covered with snow. It looked like an immense pearl. This silvery streak of moonlight playing at bo peep on its slant sides perfectly enraptured me. How grand! How beautiful!" The *Powhatan* came to anchor in the Bay of Jeddo (Yedo or Tokyo Bay) at three o'clock in the afternoon about twenty miles from Uraga. Perry sent his trusted chief of staff, Captain Henry Adams, to receive the Japanese delegation, headed by the governor of Uraga.

On February 18, Perry transferred his broad pennant to the *Powhatan*. During Perry's first trip to Japan, he had used the *Susquehanna* as his flagship.

Unfortunately, the *Susquehanna* was put at the service of Robert McLane, minister plenipotentiary to China, to deal with the Chinese.[7]

Four days later, Gideon mentioned that tension arose among the officers and the commodore. One such altercation involved Perry and *Powhatan*'s chief engineer, George Sewell. "Sewell and he had a row today about condensed water pipes. He suggested a plan to Sewell and sent to know if he had done it. Sewell told him that he did not order him to do it. Com. said a suggestion of his was as good as an order and he [Sewell] replied that he could not obey suggestions. Perry then intimated that he would have to get someone else in his place. He is the greatest humbug extant. He can't bluff Sewell though!" Officers continued to share their opinions of Perry on the *Powhatan*. "Everyone on board seem disgust[ed]. The Commodore has created a moroseness and disquietude all over. He is like an evil genius. Whenever he makes his appearance, everybody leaves as if scared to death. 'There's Old Perry' one will exclaim and in an instant the decks will be deserted." Gideon even shared Perry's response to the officers' aversion. "He [Perry] says (so I have heard) that if he had known there was so much dissatisfaction he would not have come on board and intends to leave as soon as possible. We are all glad of this. He is a mighty big humbug and we are all sick of him. He can go willingly."

When Perry left Japan six months earlier, he had been a pleased and confident man, and his accomplishment on the first visit had exceeded his expectations. During the winter quarters, Perry grew tense and even pessimistic. His differences with U.S. commissioner and consul to China Humphrey Marshall, the rumors of French and Russian maneuvers, and recent correspondence from the Navy Department had unsettled his disposition.[8]

The *Powhatan* was handicapped by poor morale, sickness and disease, petty squabbles of honor, and wardroom personalities. The officer corps was given to broad alcohol abuse and poor behavior on liberty, and the enlisted men to chronic desertion. Gideon painted a more comprehensive picture of the dysfunction rampant in the navy in the 1850s. The *Powhatan* was reported as having "no order or system." The "crew is completely disorganized, almost mutinous and the ship is generally in a nasty condition." In 1850, the U.S. Congress enacted its annual naval appropriations bill, which contained a provision abolishing flogging in the U.S. Navy. Concerned about discipline in the absence of flogging, Perry advised his commanders to recruit landsmen and young men rather than tough, savvy veteran seamen, in hopes that they would be easier to handle. Furthermore, Congress was unable to enact a new navy code of regulations before the squadron sailed to Japan. To punish the offenders, Perry utilized deprivation of liberty, confinement in irons, ship assignment transfers, reduction of ranking, withholding of salary and discharge from service.[9]

On February 26, the *Vandalia* arrived from Uraga with news. "The Japanese are willing to come to term! They say that for 200 years they have had no intercourse with other people than the Dutch, but the Imperial Council had abrogated that law with respect to the Americans and they were prepared to enter into arrangements for concluding a commercial treaty." After several days of preparation, the "Commodore left our ship at twelve o'clock [on March 6] and received a salute of 17 guns from the *Macedonian*, as acting Minister Plenipotentiary. The boats numbered 27 and the launches had the brass field pieces in the bow from them a salute of 21 guns was fired in honor of the Japanese Flag and followed by one of 17 guns in honor of the Japanese Commissioner. It was a beautiful sight." Gideon relayed to his wife the culinary details of the menu of cold soup and candy red with white streaks that was served at the Reception House.

On March 13, all the presents intended for the Japanese were taken ashore. They included a miniature locomotive and a telegraph machine. Engineers Jesse Gay and Robert Danby (for the locomotive) and telegraphers John Williams and William Draper (for the telegraph) were ordered to leave the ship to prepare the presents. On March 24, a sumo wrestling match was given for Commodore Perry. "An exhibition . . . consisted in gymnastic exercises by the largest men in Japan. A body of immense fellows numbering over fifty and averaging in weight over two hundred pounds! They were naked all but the bag containing their 'dusenberries.' They wrestled and but[t] each other on the shoulder and the shocks are so violent as to split the skin on the forehead in many instances." Three days later, Gideon had the honor to start a marine engine of the *Powhatan* in the presence of the commodore, the prince, and his commissioners, and then attended a party on the quarterdeck.

The last day of March was a special day for both the United States and George Gideon. For the United States, the commercial treaty was signed by the Japanese officials. For Gideon, his first footsteps on Japanese soil or on the "Islands of Nippon" were planted that day. He was part of the landing party that assembled on the beach to receive Perry. Following Perry, he marched into the building erected for the reception. "The floors of the building are thickly covered with white straw mat and the sides are covered with wall paper and paintings of birds resembling cranes or storks." Perry entered a private room, while Gideon took a seat at a table in the outer room and was served cups of tea, candy, and cake. After taking a walk to see the miniature locomotive, Gideon returned to the festive hall and partook of a second course that consisted of oysters, nuts, vegetables, omelets, and different types of soups. After a third course consisting of shrimp, lobster, fish, rice, and a kind of paste on a board, he returned to the *Powhatan*. At five o'clock that evening, he was called to Perry's cabin and saw the signed treaty. "Perry appeared to be very much pleased with his success." Then Gideon added his own two cents' worth about the arrangement: "My opinion is that it will never be of any service to the United States than trade [and] from all I can learn about it consists principally in the export of Copper and of that we can spare them some from Lake Superior." Sadly enough, the first purchase made by the Americans after the treaty was signed occurred while burying the first American in Japan. They paid eighty cents for a Japanese priest to officiate at the burial service of Seaman William Board.

After the Japanese affair, there were discussions among the officers aboard the *Powhatan* speculating which ships would "take the Commodore from Jeddo [Tokyo] to Bonin Islands and from thence to the Sandwich Islands and California." Most agreed that it would be the *Mississippi*. "It was very well known that it will not be the *Susquehanna* for he is afraid of her." The *Susquehanna* was an inferior ship that needed major overhaul.[10] On June 19, at eight o'clock in the morning, speculation became reality. The "Broad Pennant of Commodore Perry—Special Ambassador from the United States to the Court of Jedo and Commander in Chief of the U.S. Naval Force in the East India, China and Japan Seas—was hoisted on board of the *Mississippi*. [. . .] Our men really cheered. Never has a man made himself so unpopular as Commodore Perry. He was emphatically driven out of the ship!" The *Mississippi* sailed to Hong Kong, where on September 11, 1854, Perry and his flag lieutenant Silas Bent left the USS *Mississippi* for the Peninsular & Oriental mail steamer *Hindostan* and traveled overland through Europe via the Isthmus of Suez to Trieste, Vienna, Dresden, Berlin, and Holland.[11]

After Perry's departure, the USS *Powhatan* participated in another diplomatic mission, this one to China. President Franklin Pierce sent Dr. Peter Parker to China to negotiate a revision of the Wanghia treaty of 1844 that would include some new concessions and would provide for "the establishment of a United States diplomatic resident in Peking, the free extension of foreign trade throughout China, and the removal of restrictions to the personal liberty of United States citizens."[12] By November 3, 1854, Parker with ministers Sir John Bowring and Robert M. McLane went to the mouth of the Pei-ho River, where tents were pitched for the occasion at Teen Tsin Hae Kow Forts, to meet the Chinese commissioners from Peking and to begin conversation. The negotiations failed.

Early in January 1855, Captain Adams returned from the United States to continue negotiations with the Japanese, "[s]ome additions and alterations having been made in the original paper." While Adams was there, Gideon contemplated resignation when he learned that the USS *Powhatan* had not been ordered to sail home. "I was so angry yesterday when Capt. Adams stated that he had not orders for us to return home that I immediately wrote my resignation and consulted Sewell about it. Faron agrees to send his in with mine but he backed out. I went ashore to see about a passage to California which will cost two hundred dollars and no ship to sail for a month or more. I would have to run, and the next mail may bring something." Gideon decided to stay on, but unfortunately for him, he would have to wait another nine months to return to the United States.

At the end of January, Gideon visited shipwrecked Russians near Shimoda. On December 23, 1854, Shimoda had suffered a catastrophic event: an earthquake leading to a tsunami that nearly wiped out the local population. Gideon went ashore and reported on the devastation and the resilience of the people: "out of more than one thousand houses only sixteen were saved. 200 lives were lost! S[h]imoda is now one mess of ruins! I was on shore yesterday and was completely lost. They are building very rapidly and in a year the town will be as large as ever."

On February 14, the commissioners of Japan promised to sign the treaty ratification and deliver it in a week. Taking a page from Commodore Perry's playbook, Captain Adams strongly insisted that "in case it was not finished in seven days this ship would return to the United States and report the refusal which would induce the President to send a large fleet out here to destroy all their towns and cities. This threat had the desired effect and the promise was made to 'hurry up the cakes.'" Gideon also agreed that this course of action would "frighten these humbugs into measures." A week later, Gideon informed his wife about the subdued festivities surrounding the signing of the ratified treaty. Instead of a grand celebration, such as the one that accompanied Perry's treaty signing, the inclement weather only permitted "one boat [to bring ashore] Capt Adams and another with several other officers [. . .] to finish the business."

Gideon's letters also highlighted another event that occurred during the

Japanese Expedition—Chinese piracy. While lying at anchor in Macao Roads in December 1853, Gideon expressed his first thought about the news of pirates. "The whole river between Whampoa and Canton was infested by Pirates. Several boats had been attacked and robbed. We never saw the shadow of one either going or coming and I hold that the Pirate affair is a humbug." Vessels' orders were issued to patrol the navigable waters near Canton and Hong Kong to protect the "American interests." On Christmas day, 1853, Gideon noted that the "HMS *Hermes* [had] been successful in arresting Chinese pirates out . . . near Hong Kong."

In early August 1855, the *Powhatan* participated in a key allied engagement against the Chinese pirates. On August 3, "[a]t about two o'clock [. . .] the *Rattler* and small steamer *Eaglet* with 93 of our men [that] composed the party" left Hong Kong. Three days later, he conveyed to his wife the engagement at Ty-ho Bay. "Last evening the *Rattler* returned from the Pirate grounds bringing with her our three boats and those that were left after the attacks." The *Rattler*

> proceeded about five miles when she had to stop on account of the shallowness of the water. The boat then pulled away in the direction of some junks which were under way and firing shot. These junks soon ran aground when they opened broadsides on our first launch under command of Lieut. Rolando with Mr. Craig as his aid. Rolando pulled towards them firing his howitzer and making every shot tell. He soon silenced the guns of one, then another and a third. He then boarded them, and whilst on board, the boat containing Capt. Fellows also boarded and then at the time when the two boats crews and officers were on board, some secreted Chinese piratical miscreant fired the magazine and blew up the junk! Three of our men were killed and eleven wounded. Mr. Rolando being wounded in the hand and blown overboard, but saved. Capt. Fellows was blown overboard without being injured. He could not swim but was saved by one of our men named Taylor who was badly wounded.
>
> Now must have commenced a general fight. The Chinamen throwing stink pots, spears, and firing guns loaded to the very muzzle and our men with the Englishmen fighting like demons showing no quarter. Seventeen junks were destroyed and some 300 Chinamen killed. The *Rattler* lost 4 men killed, six wounded. The Englishmen pay the Americans the highest compliments, and those of our officers who saw the

> slaughter say that the Englishmen fought like very devils. It was neck or nothing. I hear men talk of taking deliberate aim and shooting Chinamen in the water, of knocking their brains out with cutlasses and muskets. In all, three junks were blown up by pirates themselves.

Also during the Japanese Expedition, a military conflict between Russia and an alliance consisting of France, the British empire, the Ottoman empire, and Sardinia peppered Gideon's letters from July 3, 1854, to September 22, 1855. As he heard news from Sebastopol of the devastation ("a loss to the Russians of 12,000 killed and 3000 of the Allies!"), Gideon lamented, "If this is true, what a sacrifice of human life!" In November 1854, Gideon received the stunning news of the allied English and French engagement against the Russians at Petropaulski in the southern part of Kamchatka, where "the English and French were defeated with a serious loss and both admirals killed."

At the end of his service, Gideon became disillusioned with the U.S. Navy, especially developing a feeling of hatred toward Secretary of the Navy Dobbin, for not ordering the USS *Powhatan* home in 1855. "If ever a man made me an enemy, that man is John C. Dobbin. [. . .] He is a heartless unfeeling wretch, a tyrant and an ass! Excuse me Lide, but my resentment must find vent somewhere, for that North Carolina hog I detest, abhor, hate!"

After a laudable service in the East Indies Squadron, the USS *Powhatan* headed home, traveling the same route it had sailed almost three years before, via Mauritius and Cape of Good Hope. On February 18, 1856, Gideon was detached from the *Powhatan* and granted a three-month leave. On April 24, he was ordered to examination. In May 1856, as his leave was expiring, it was reported that he was living in Walker Township, Centre County, Pennsylvania. On July 10, 1856, Gideon received a master of arts diploma from the Central High School of Pennsylvania. On August 26, he was ordered to the USS *Merrimack*, and on September 8 the vessel sailed from New York for Europe, visiting France and Spain, and returning to the United States in March 1857.

On March 18, 1857, Gideon was ordered to examination. On April 14, he was detached from the *Merrimack* and ordered to the Office of Engineer in Chief. On May 2, 1859, he received a commission of chief engineer beginning from April 23. On September 28, he was ordered to the *Narragansett*. Two days later, he forwarded a doctor's report on his condition to the department and requested a medical survey at the Navy Yard, Boston. On October 7, he was detached from the *Narragansett* for sickness and placed on waiting orders. On October 20, he advised the department that he was residing at 775 North 24th Street, Philadelphia, Pennsylvania.

Gideon was ordered to the USS *Pawnee* on March 3, 1860. The *Pawnee* was present at the bombardment of Fort Sumter by the Confederates. It assisted in the destruction of government property at the Norfolk Navy Yard during the night of April 20 and 21, 1861, and towed the *Cumberland* to Fortress Monroe. On July 2, 1860, Gideon was recommissioned chief engineer. On May 18, 1861, he was transferred to the *Colorado* of the Gulf Squadron. The *Colorado* was for a time the flagship of that squadron. On June 28, 1862, he was detached and granted two weeks' leave. On August 20, he was appointed a member of the Board of Examiners.

On June 16, 1863, Gideon died in Philadelphia. The cause of death was given as edema of the glottis, a swelling caused by fluid accumulation in the soft tissues of the larynx. The condition, usually inflammatory, can result from infection, injury, or inhalation of toxic gases. Three days later, he was interred in Odd Fellows Cemetery. In 1874, his remains were moved to Mount Lebanon Cemetery in Lebanon, Pennsylvania to be placed near his wife.

Five years after George Gideon passed away, his wife Eliza remarried on November 10, 1868, to Benjamin Bringhurst Lehman (1818–91). She died on January 7, 1871, in Dayton, Montgomery County, Ohio, and was interred at Mount Lebanon Cemetery.

Chapter One
February 13–April 19, 1853

Powhatan,[1] [February 13, 1853][2] 10 O'clock PM

My Dearest Devoted Lide,

We're off for Japan! We may remain in the Roads[3] tonight, but I think not however, of this I'll inform you before I close. [. . .] *Don't fret.* I'll keep you as well aware of the progress of the Japanese squadron as I can be made aware myself. *I don't think anyone of us will regret the cruise.* I think I will kiss you again before the collapse of two years!

I'll write to you from Madeira.[4] [. . .] Kellogg[5] and I are on watch together. He is a fine fellow. He has been on Steamers before too! He was in Collins Line. I didn't think to tell the Post Master to forward the letters. [. . .] Direct as I did in the envelope, it makes no difference whether it goes by the Cunard Line, Collins Line, the Southampton Line or any other, it will go to London and Mr. Goodan will forward it. *You pay 28 cents.* I pay the rest. When you write tell me everything. Where you are, how they treat you and everything, but for my sake Lide, don't make any more beds. Don't clean any more chambers. *Be a Lady.* I *know* that you can be my housekeeper when necessary. We are now off Old Point, the Rip Raps[6] on our right. We do not stop, but go right to sea.

Whipple,[7] Kellogg, and *Gideon* are in *cahoots.* King[8] is disposed to take the *right side.* I think I can fix him. Farons[9] comb will be cut before he returns. *I will be ahead of him yet.* I gave up the privilege of sleeping in the mess room to *Kellogg.* Mr. Faron said that it was *my* place or Mr. Kings. I told Mr. Faron that I and I alone had to decide that matter. [. . .] Therefore as *I* preferred sleeping below I would exchange with Mr. Kellogg. [. . .] *Mr. Kellogg and Mr. Gideon are a match together* and Mr. Kellogg *is* Mr. Gideons friend. He goes just where I wanted him to go. Sewell asked me who I wanted on watch with me, I told him I wanted the man who by *right*, etiquette and *law*, was to go with me, that I can do my duty, and would *make* my assistant do his. Mr. Kellogg is the man because he outranks both Fauth[10] and Arnold.[11] My more tender feelings would prompt me to ask for Kellogg, but so far as duty is concerned I care not who it is. *I* can do mine and know how to make him do his. No doubt Mr. Fauth is huffed because he is not. He is with a *Man*, not a fool! I am glad that Mr. Kellogg is on watch with me. Nothing could have suited me better.

U.S. Ste. *Powhatan*, At Sea Lat. 32°04 Lon. 24°21,[12] Feb 28th 1853

My Dearest Lide,

We have now been at sea 15 days and have yet to run some 400 miles before reaching Madeira. The passage so far has been a very rough one indeed. The sea running tremendously the whole time, and as yet we have not had one hour smooth weather. The wind for the majority of the time has been ahead. Blowing strong. We had a gale of wind last week and such pitching and rolling as was done by the *Powhatan* I never saw before; and I hope that I may never see again. The Capt.[13] too is afraid to burn a sufficient amount of coal to make the ship run. We could easily leverage 10 miles an hour with an economical expenditure of coal, but no! We must only burn so much. The *Mississippi*[14] only burns that much. Now whether he is prejudiced in favor of the *Mississippi*, and don't want the *Powhatan* to make better time, I can't say but it looks indeed very much like it. Several times the wind has hauled so that we could use our sails, and on every such occasion the Capt. would issue an order to reduce the expenditure of coal. As it is we will make the run in just about the same time as the *Mississippi*.

I have been sea sick since the 1st day out. Though for the past 2 or 3 days I've been much better. For about 10 days I felt most horrible, and when called to take my watch I felt like one having a death sentence read to him. I couldn't eat nor could I drink, but you have been so and know the feeling. I never gave up, and as yet have never lost a watch at sea. I am hoping now that I'll get over it. I feel pretty well today though I have a dullness and swimming in the head. The Voyage has been so monotonous. A most perfect sameness around everything and everybody. We have seen only two or three vessels since we left, and have not spoken.

One Mr. Kellogg tries to make it appear that he is just as well satisfied as if he had been left attached to the *Princeton*,[15] but I openly assert that he is

2. Horace Binder, lithographer, "USS *Powhatan,*" 1880.

not. And it sometimes shows itself through his expressions, for he will say sometimes that he had nothing to do there but dress up, keep clean and visit the ladies. Now full of grease, salt, coal dust and tallow. Salt horse and hard tack[16] in place of roast beef and good biscuits. Soppy musty dirty water in place of good pure wholesome water. But he don't get sea sick and I do. Now my getting sick don't give me any better food or water than he gets for its all alike. Therefore if he should like it, that most horrible home with nothing but a crust for a daily meal to cross the Atlantic Ocean is an idiot.

Tuesday March 1st

Our mess is composed of the most uncongenial spirits that ever convened. Fauth and Stamm[17] are hand and glove with one another and judging from the sincerity with which they support each other and each other's opinions they must have taken a solemn vow for each other's mutual protection. Old Whipple, he is a queer fellow, but a good kind hearted soul as ever lived, he gets about 2/3rds drunk and then he is in an official or dignified humor. He loves power and authority.

Every evening except Sunday we have a Grand Concert in the Passed Midshipman Mess Room. Lieut. Boudinot,[18] leader of the band, Passed Mid. Selden[19] second violin, McCaul[e]y[20] and Bibby[21] on the flute. Dr. Wheelwright,[22] guitar and a Diego boy on the guitar also. Jno. Wilson[23] does the singing assisted by Schaffer (Masters Mate). They play very well together, and some evenings the steerage is full. Every Officer in the ship save the Capt. and 1st Lieut. have been in there at one time.

I think that the cruise will be a most interesting one. I think also that we will not go to Japan. But anon of this. Write according to the directions I gave you. Write at least once a month and tell me everything that happens. How you are and all you know.

I wish I could have had 3 or 4 more of those calico shirts made. They are just the thing in the Engine Room. I am in hopes that there will be an English Man of War at Madeira so that I that I can get some white flannels. They serve out the best kind of white, and we serve out that nasty blue stuff. I think of trading off some of my Canton flannel ones. They will never be of any use to me, for I will never throw off flannel such as I now wear.

I have read another novel since we left, called *Ernest Maltravers*. One of Bulwers. Oh! How horrible I feel when I first get up from a sleep. Every bone aches. Losing sleep, irregular living is the cause of it. I am not the only one either who keeps sea sick. The Capt. of Marines[24] is sick all the time. He was once sea sick 74 days!

What descriptions of our cruise are in contemplation? Faron takes his ideas from Colton's book. A description of Madeira is in it. I saw him writing from the book the other day. The two books are called *Ship and Shore* by Walter Colton and the other *Deck and Port* by Colton. Buy them and read them. I have glanced occasionally at them and I think they will be very interesting.

We were 210 miles from Madeira at noon today and in order to get there tomorrow the Capt. has issued an order to burn more coal, so we are now going along as they say in Virginia "right smart" and there is no doubt but that we will be there tomorrow, and thus be 17 days out.

There will be certainly will be an examination for promotion very soon, and the sooner the better, for I'm going to post myself up before our return and in passing the "back pay" will come in very well, and at the expiration of my leave I can do my best to get ordered to the *Michigan*.[25] That would be nice.

U.S. Ste. *Powhatan*, Funchal Roads,[26] Madeira, March 6th 1853

My Dear Lide,

We were a little over 17 days, and about 17 days from the time we discharged the Pilot off the Capes. [. . .] We stopped 3 times on our way at sea. Once to examine the wheels and once to key up the drag links. Then on the morning of the 1st (the day before we got in) fire was discovered around the smoke pipe, occasioned by the pipes being too close to the beam and hatch combing and the absence of a water jacket,[27] which the constructors of the ship neglected to put in. The fire was put out without much trouble and a watch kept over it until we got in, and as soon as we did we examined everything and found that no, or but very little damage had been done. An order was immediately given to make a jacket and prevent anything of the kind occurring again. The jacket will be finished on Tuesday morning.

The day after we got here we commenced coaling and continued until last night when we finished. Thus coaling the ship in less time, yes in less than half the time that she was ever coaled before. On the 3rd we had a Madeira dinner. We sat down to roast and boiled chickens, roast beef, good fresh bread, lettuce, green peas, tomatoes, string beans, sweet potatoes and real Irish potatoes. Then a few bottles of good old Madeira to wash it down, and a smoke of a good cigar after made me feel pretty well. Now imagine how hungry I was, what an appetite I had, and how I relished all. Having been sea sick for nearly the entire run from Norfolk, and while I was so that I could not eat all the poultry was done away with, and there was for the last week out nothing but salt horse and hams which I couldn't eat, and had to survive on hard tack and molasses. Today we have had radishes, lettuce and peas. Fine fish and excellent turtle soup. Yet I've said nothing about the oranges and bananas! I eat about 3 oranges every morning before I turn out. They are great things in the morning. The Spanish proverb says of oranges that they are "gold in the morning, silver at noon and lead at night." The bananas I don't eat. But this is all on board the ship. I must now take you ashore.

On Friday Mr. Kellogg and myself went ashore for the purpose of visiting the Grand Corral, and Mr. Kellogg said that he intends to stand on as high a peak as any man had ever been on that island. The Island itself as you view it from sea is truly grand, sublime, magnificent. A clear day it is really beautiful and on cloudy days you lose sight of the tops of peaks in the clouds. They

3. "Letter to my wife Lide while in Funchal Roads, Madeira," March 6, 1853.

look as if they were something or that a vapour or fog was rising from them. Mr. K[ellogg] and I started. In the first place as our own boats cannot land for the surf, we had to cull one of the Portuguese boats, which hover around the ship in great numbers and go ashore in that we got in the boat and was pulled to within a rod or two of the shore when suddenly they whirled the boat around, one of the men rolled up his pants as high as he could and run along the gunwale of the boat to the stern, and watching a breaker setting in they pulled or backed their oars and the one man jumped out and held her where she was, then when the sea receded we jumped out on the land. The boat is then hauled completely out of the water and remains "high and dry" until someone wants to go off. They charged us 40 cents apiece for landing us, which was an extortion, the regular price being but 20 cents, and only 5 cents to their own "kin" however the novelty of landing was worth the money, and probably the poor devils had not made as much in a long time before, and pehaps 'twill be a long time before they make as much again.

We had no sooner struck the land than we were beset by at least 50 beggars and fellows wanting to show us around, get horses for us and guide us generally so that we could see the elephants. Without paying any attention to their mixture of English and Portuguese we continued our way, somewhere. Didn't know where we in reality were going. At last we brought up in front of the stables, and we were again beset by at least 30 or 40 saddled horses and men anxious each that we should take his horse. As it was impossible to choose, after a little astonishment at such perseverance and I may say impertinence we succeeded in getting horses tail. No matter how fast we went, gallop trot or walk, these poor fools still held on, and now we come to steep and rugged ascent, and narrow paths at that, over stones and rocks, up, up, up wonderful how the horses manage to keep their footing, and as much as how these poor devils of men can stand such fatigue. At last after a most perilous passage over the stones and rocks and mountains, hills out of the question, we at last tired, sore and bruised reached the Corral. We had to go, for turn back was out of the question. The path being too narrow to turn around on, and even an attempt would probably result in tumbling horse, rider and "tail holder" to the bottom. But the Corral, it is a deep valley or gorge in the mountains, green with vegetation, wild flowers, and beautiful streamlets running down its sides and along its bottom. It is indeed a beautiful place. In fact really most grand and magnificent. Kellogg would still go on, but I was so tired and sore that I had to remain and wait for him. He saw nothing more, only stood a little higher up than I did.

After a stroll around for about an hour we prepared to return, and again mounting our horses, with the men at our "tails" we started. The going down I thought, and in fact it is more dangerous than going up. The horses would tread at times so carefully that you would think they were going to stop. But after a great deal of anxiety on at least my part we arrived on a level or pretty safe footing. All and all the ride was a great novelty, and such a one as I don't wish to repeat. After paying the fellows who followed us and held the horse's tails 50 cents we paid someone $2.00 apiece for the use of the horses.

While going, and coming from the Corral we met a great many of those women who carry bundles of brush, or a kind of hay used for fuel. These poor creatures had no shoes on, and but very little clothing. A mere wrapper of calico extending a few inches below their knees. Their legs and feet bare and rough. Awful looking shins they had, and how in the world they can withstand the travelling up and down those rugged heights over sharp rocks and stones with their enormous bundles (sometimes larger than two of their bodies) I can't understand. But they do it and without a murmur.

We took a look around the city after our return and a cleaner place I never saw. It's all "downhill" and fine pure water runs along each side of the street. We were met by cripples, beggars, sick ladies and gentlemen being carried through the street on their palankeens [palanquins]. The more you give the darned beggars the more they ask. If you give them anything they stow it away and commence begging of you again. It is also a place of profligacy. More wretchedness, pollution and degradation is met in this little city than in any other place I have ever seen. It's truly disgusting. It is said that over 3/4ths of the children here are bastards. But after taking a glass of their Madeira I came on board heartily tired and sore from my ride and without the least desire to go ashore anymore.

Today [Monday] we have taken on board several casks of wine for some of the *Mississippi's* Officers, and 2 casks for the President of the U.S. and 2 for the Secretary of the Navy. The President and Secretaries wine being presents from our Consul here, Mr. Marsh.[28] They are now watering the ship and finish this evening. Tomorrow (Tuesday March 8th) we sail. I'm glad of it, although I feel so bad when at sea, yet I want to be off. It's more expensive here than at sea, for the mess bill is more.

Commodore Perry left word for Capt. McCluney, or a letter I should say, stating that he would make the run from here to Cape Town[29] in 33 days and he expected that we ought to make it 20. We do not stop either at Ascension or St. Helena[30] if we can help it. We may carry the trade winds to 3 or 4 degrees south of the line or to the line, and during that time we will not steam any but use the sails altogether. I expect to melt crossing the line. From Cape Town we go to Madagascar[31] to look after some pirates or to chastise the inhabitants. I can't learn exactly what, but it appears that a ship called the *West Wind*[32] was wrecked and the crew that escaped from the wreck to the shore were murdered. That's one yarn. Another is that the whole neighborhood is infested with pirates and that they intercept vessels from Australia. I am of the opinion that our cruise will be confined to the China Seas and that we will see no more of Japan than you will. How I would like to know who the Sec. of the Navy is.[33] I guess Stockton.[34]

The poor devils ashore here came on board and trade oranges, bananas &c. for tobacco, and the grand trouble with them is to get the tobacco ashore. A Customs House boat is constantly hovering around the ship and every man that goes ashore from the ship is searched and if any tobacco is found on or about him he is arrested, put in jail and as soon as possible transported for 5 years. It is only the natives they search not us. Our men have not had any liberty yet. None of them been ashore, though they deserve to have liberty. But the trouble of getting them off the ship again is the reason they are not allowed to go. I have bought a very nice hat, a kind of leghorn or braid for 60 cents. It is lined well and a pretty hat. They have all kinds of feathers, flowers &c. to sell here, but I am afraid they would spoil before I get home, and more over funds are scarce.

I am afraid that we shall not meet the *Mississippi* before we get to Hong Kong. And then too, which is a thousand times worse, I can't hear from you until we get there, and when will we get there! I suppose in about 5 months. This is awful. I only soiled six shirts coming across. Washing here is 60 cents pr. dozen. Men take the clothes ashore and get them washed. We pay the men 60 cents and they pay the women who wash the clothes 10 cents. Everything is done through 2 or 3 sets of hands. We had to engage a Steward, and so did all the vessels as soon as we got here. The Steward furnishes the mess, brings things off and charges his own price for them. I suppose 4 or 5 times what he gave for them. Oh! this travelling. I am content. I've seen all of the "old world" that I wish to, and my greatest desire, my greatest wish, the consummation of all my hopes, everything, my very life soul, all, all, all are yours. To be with you is all that I can ask. May god spare us both to meet again.

We have a Masters Mate here named Schaffer from Baltimore who has taken a great fancy to me, and the Gunner Mr. City[35] appears to be kindly disposed. Jno. Butler[36] the Carpenter, Mr. Elliott's[37] friend is the fussiest, most selfish creature I have ever heard or seen. It is now growing late. They are bringing fresh beef and vegetables off, looks very much like leaving. The Steamer for England is expected in tonight or tomorrow morning and leaves the same day. We leave as I said before at 5 o'clock tomorrow afternoon. Then good bye Madeira, and in bidding good bye to Madeira I must bid good bye to you!

I have a clerk now in the office with me who writes a magnificent hand and who attends very well to everything. He does a great deal of writing for the men. That is he writes letters for them, and when they get letters from their sweet hearts he in many cases reads them for those who cannot read. He tells some rich jokes contained in them.

Again I'm with you fearing that some duty tomorrow night prevents my writing again. I have again seated myself this evening to talk a little with you. The Steamer that arrived this morning was from England and she brought news from there stating that the *Mississippi* had arrived at Cape Town 40 days from this place, thus knocking Commo. Perrys 23 days into a "cocked hat." [. . .] I am in hopes that we will get another 1st Lieut. after we join the Squadron. Mr. Glisson[38] is too kind, too easy, and in fact totally dis-qualified for his post.

The ship is in the dirtiest condition imaginable. Even our own department is very dirty. Mr. Sewell is extremely kind to me, but he does many things wrong. He has been but little at sea, and even that could be gotten over but he so repeatedly displays his ignorance and interferes with everybody's duties as to create much discontent. Every Engineer on board does his duty reluctantly. Sewell throws all responsibility off his shoulders and his assistants have to take it. He thinks they must be pitched into.

Accept a thousand kisses and my everlasting affection. Good bye. Good night. Think of me often, and may God bless and protect you shall be my daily prayer. Truly and affectionately, My Dear Lide, yours George.

Powhatan, Cape Town, Cape of Good Hope, April 17th [1853]

My Dear Lide,

Leaving St. Helena on Monday the 4th April we again soon found ourselves on the wide pathless ocean, on the broad stormy ocean of water. In my young and youthful imaginings of this great ocean I had pictured in it the maximum of trials, anxieties and misfortunes, the concentration of the trouble, the very essence of danger, but now I've seen it. I've been on it. I've crossed it, braved its dangers, drank its troubles and made myself acquainted with its anxieties. But what is it compared with the howling, wintering ocean of life!

We arrived here (Table Bay)[39] on Thursday the 14th at half past 11 o'clock in the morning. I think in my last I gave you all the news acquired at the Islands very near to the time we sailed. We were ready to sail at 6 o'clock, but seeing a vessel in the distance bound in we remained to ascertain what and who she was. She came in handsomely and passed under our stern. She proved to be the U. S[.] Brig *Perry*[40] Capt. Page. We were anxious to hear the news, so we waited anxiously to learn. We learned that she had been cruising 4 months and that she had touched here for the purpose of giving her men liberty. This was all. Some 3 or 4 of her Officers in company with Capt. Page visited us and thus we gained the valuable information. All hope as it were vanished. I really expected to hear something from home. Not that I expected a letter from you, but I really hoped that we might learn something. Well, about 8 o'clock these Officers of the *Perry* left us, and in about 20 minutes we were steaming it to sea and soon found ourselves as I opened this letter.

The Assistant Engineers changed the arrangement of their watches. That is instead of keeping the watches from Midnight to Meridian by 4 hours apiece, and from Meridian to Midnight by 3 hours apiece we divided the 24 hours into 4 parts, and each Engineer, on each watch take a part. In other words we keep 6 hour watches having the same watch every day. I take from 12 to 6 PM. Therefore I sleep in every night and have all the morning to myself. Now this having all the morning to myself admits of some discussion. I have it all to myself by right and justice, but the Chief unable to attend personally to duties out of the Engine Room, or fearing to contaminate his unsullied person by contact with a Fireman or Coal Heaver must now have an Assistant Engineer interposed between the Plebeians and his Pope like self. My turn in consequence of the new arrangement to thus make myself a medium as it were comes every 3rd day. This is called the "days duty at sea" and is dreaded more than a dozen Engine room watches.

Mr. Faron has the watch by the new arrangement from 6 in the morning to noon when I relieve him. He of course must be relieved to breakfast. At breakfast he sent to know if I would relieve him! According to my conception of just and right reliefs it was my place to do so, but in an argument just after this ship went into Commission between the Asst. Engineers I took the side that the following watch was the relief. All the rest took the opposite and we adopted the arrangement to have the previous watch relieve. This was the case up to the time the watches and dinner hour was changed. Previous to the latest change (we have had two changes) I was surprised at Faron sending for me and objected altogether or upon principle and would have broken up the new arrangement before being imposed upon had they not explained that to bring it about Faron had agreed to relieve me if I would him.

The arrangement was adopted when I was on watch, though I had proposed it, and on the statement thus made of the circumstances I agreed and so we go on smoothly.

Our ship is full of rats and I've seen several cock roaches. One night between St. Helena and this place being in a semi sleep in my bunk I felt something crawl coldly and lazily over my leg. It made me dream of snakes and eels. Coming to realize the matter I found it to be a rat amusing himself about my feet and drawing his long tail over my bare legs! Pleasant, is it not?

Another difficulty occurred between myself and Sewell some days ago. I mustered the men at morning quarters and one man being absent I reported him to the Chief Engineer. His answer to my report was "hunt him!" This occasioned a dispute with him and he asked me if I wanted him to hunt him. Now I did not consider myself a Boatswains Mate and Mr. Sewell with the whole United States Navy combined cannot make me one. I came to the conclusion after reviewing such an answer to my report to report no more men without having it noticed. [. . .] But to this case of reporting him Sewell came to me and asked me if I found that man. I told him I had sent for him. He intimated that I had not and again ordered me to hunt him. There I threw myself on my dignity and informed the Chief that I was not a Boatswains Mate, and in this case I had reported a man to him and I wanted notice taken of it. He told me I was wrong, that he didn't want a Boatswains Mate to interfere with our men! As much as to say "I'd rather you be one, for this department." Many words and severe remarks followed, when in a passion he turned from me and said "I'll hunt him myself"! Evidently this "agonized" him and kindled in his partial nature feelings of any kind but love for me. He afterwards sent for the log books, expenditures, receipts &c. fortunately everything had been posted and duty accounted for. So he missed his aim in an endeavor to find fault there, for sending for me he said that the man had been found and that he had been "pitched into." Then followed a kind of explanation in which he expostulated with me, came the pathetic, talked of kindness to the men &c. At this very moment and at all times since I first made myself acquainted with the Servicemen under me have loved me. I teach to do so and every day I receive evidence of the fact, so the indirect charge of Mr. S[ewell] to the contrary occasioned but a smile. However, the gentleman and myself by this time entertain no piqued feelings. While on this subject I may add that our Chief Engineer pleases no one, that he has shown his "cloven foot" exposed his ignorance and made no friends.

April 19th

The day was cool and reminded me of September or October at home. On barely getting anchored "Bomb Boats" [bumboats] as usual flocked around us in numbers. They contained apples, pears, cocoanuts [*sic*], bad oranges, and the most delicious white grapes. [. . .] Then the next day we had new potatoes, fresh meat of different kinds and vegetables including tomatoes. I believe this is the fall of the year here. It really feels like fall and it is the coldest weather we will experience for some time.

On Friday I remained on board and had a fine chance of viewing the land, the beach and the mountains. Table Mountain[41] is a high parallelogram. Perfectly square or level on the top, which top is generally obscured by a kind of cloud. This cloud is called the Table Cloth. Then stretching towards the bay we have the Lions Rump and other prominent or peculiar shaped projections called by different names. Mr. Kellogg's ambition to "stand on the highest peak" yet haunts him, and he intends standing on Table Rock if he can get there. For me I have no ambition that way.

On Saturday it rained very hard but in the morning it promised to clear off and in company with Mr. McCaul[e]y (a 2nd McCollum, by the way) Mr. Schaffer, Mr. Fauth, and another individual who accompanied them, not me (his name I believe is Stamm) I went on shore. [. . .] On shore I selected some stores for the Department and then the party started to the Masonic Hotel. There are many very fine Hotels here, the Masonic one of the best. We remained there about an hour, ordered dinner and then took a walk through the town. [. . .] We visited several Book stores, where I purchased a book that I've been long wanting. It is called *Alice, or the Mysteries* and is a sequel to *Ernest Maltravers* by Bulwer. As they do not have it in the cheap form as in the United States, and these being bound nicely I bought both. [. . .] We then (the others having bought some books too) returned to the hotel and had a magnificent dinner. All kinds of vegetables, fruits &c which cost us 1 dollar apiece. Taking another walk around we became tired again and returned to the Hotel. Mr. Fauth and I then took the sun down boat and came on board, leaving the others on shore.

Speaking of the days duty reminds me again of Sewell. He has established an "Order Book" in which are some of the most ludicrous orders, conflictions, repetitions and superfluities imaginable. In this book there is an order in effect that while in Port the Engineer having the days duty must not leave the Engine Room without being relieved! This he thinks is necessary in order that the Engineers presence shall keep the men busy. In other words to say "the mice can't play, when the cats in the way." Now it produces no such effect. There I go again arguing with you about Sewell's nonsense, but you will excuse me, for all these things you know effect me.

I like the look of Cape Town. I could live here had I you with me.

We learned that the *Mississippi* had been here and had remained 10 days.[42] That she had given her men "liberty" and that they had acted outrageous, having whipped the soldiers and the police. We also found a vessel here from the United States loaded with coal for us, having waited here 60 days for us. She had on board 800 tons. The most of it anthracite. We will fill up and as soon as that is done sail for Mauritius, where we expect to remain about a month.

We have also learned that Prussia, Austria, and France have demanded from England the person of Louis Kossuth.[43] This will, if true, probably lead to a war, and in that event we may be called home to be in the more immediate vicinity of our Commerce for its protection. However, this may or may not be as it is, and we are so near China, I would prefer going there. Then they may order us home as soon as they like.

I believe in one of my former letters I spoke of the leaking of our ship. Well she leaked on coming to at this place worse than ever. They called me on Thursday night to get up steam at 1 o'clock in the morning to pump out the ship. She had 30 inches of water in her! This was seriously talked of, even so far as going back home for repairs. But I'll resume tomorrow Lide, perhaps tonight. I've written so steady, and so fine that I feel tired. So good night and may you now be thinking of and framing happy hours and days for us when we meet. May you ever bear in mind that the heart that turns the hand now writing beats alone for you.

I was amused after we came to anchor at this place to hear the Officers talk and argue as to the cause of the ships making so much water. The Carpenter stated positively that it was not the ship, that it was something about the Engines, either valves, pipes, or cocks. This opinion of the Carpenter (and by the by our carpenter is a very different man from our friend George Elliott. Elliot to say the least is worth a ship load of such men) of course finds backers. And all the Officers in the ship but the Engineers firmly hold that the trouble is in our Department, and go so far as to assert that all the Engineers know it. Now what amused me was the various methods and endeavors made to pump us. We would not go on deck or within speaking of a Lieutenant without being drawn by him into some kind of a conversation which was surely bound to wind up in questions about pipes, and valves &c. that could

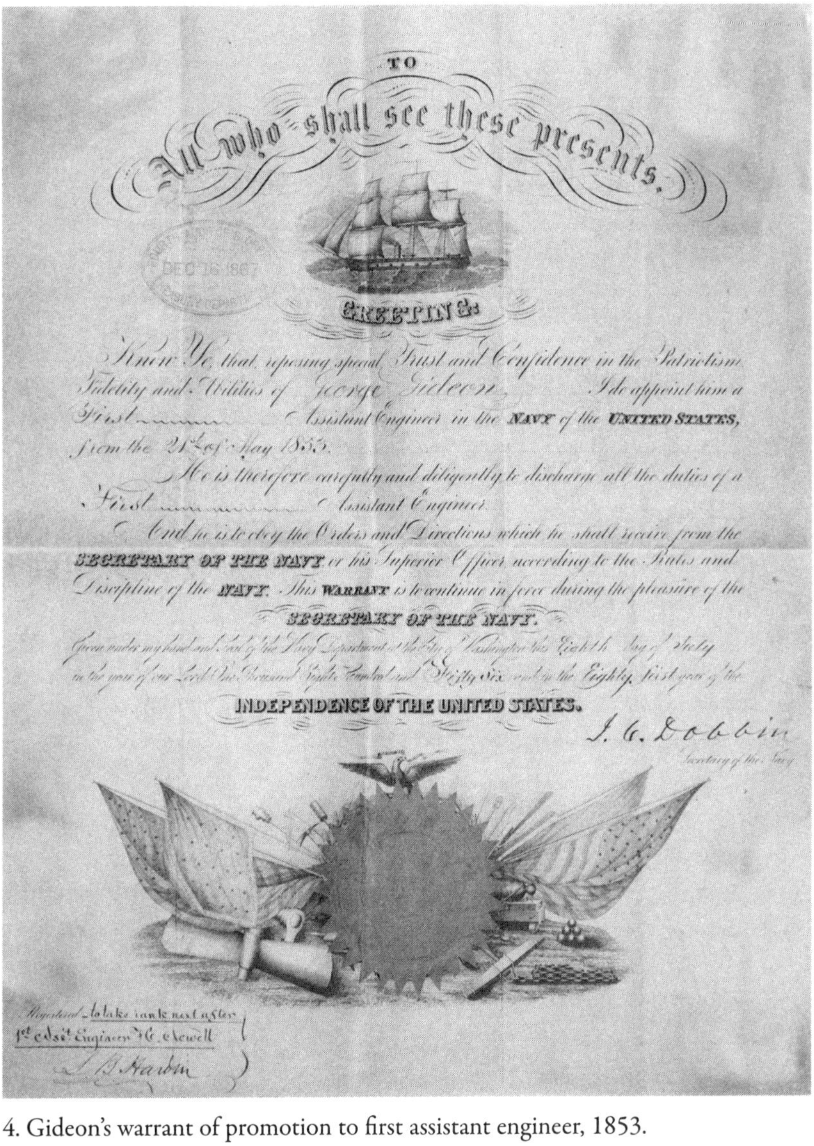
TO

All who shall see these presents,

GREETING:

Know Ye, that, reposing special Trust and Confidence in the Patriotism, Fidelity and Abilities of George Gideon, I do appoint him a First Assistant Engineer in the NAVY of the UNITED STATES, from the 21st of May 1853.

He is therefore carefully and diligently to discharge all the duties of a First Assistant Engineer.

And he is to obey the Orders and Directions which he shall receive from the SECRETARY OF THE NAVY, or his Superior Officer, according to the Rules and Discipline of the NAVY. This WARRANT is to continue in force during the pleasure of the SECRETARY OF THE NAVY.

Given under my hand and Seal of the Navy Department at the City of Washington this Eighth day of July in the year of our Lord One Thousand Eight Hundred and Fifty Six and in the Eighty First year of the INDEPENDENCE OF THE UNITED STATES.

J. C. Dobbin
Secretary of the Navy

DEC 18 1867

Registered — to take rank next after 1st Ass't Engineer

4. Gideon's warrant of promotion to first assistant engineer, 1853.

leak. We have to this but one exception, and he is a Mr. Haggerty,[44] one of the Lieutenants. A man too of superior intellect and sound understanding. A "gentleman and a scholar." Now Mr. Haggerty holds that when the ship struck on the Bar at Pensacola he saw the decks undulate, and from that he argues that the ship leaks and should be docked. The nearest dock is in the United States! As we progress towards Japan the docks, and that a Mud one, that becomes nearer is at Bombay. I say that home is nearer but on consideration I conclude not, but the difference is not much, and then it is questionable whether the docks at Bombay are large enough, and it is the very hot bed of disease and sickness. This is all speculation and moonshine. No fear either of our going to the United States or to Bombay to dock the ship. Those who talk so much about it will after we get a little further from home say that it's no unusual thing! And neither is it. All the water that the ship makes in 24 hours can be pumped out when we are steaming in 5 minutes.

From here we go to Mauritius. Start as soon as we finish coaling which will probably take a week yet. We have no later news from home although vessels arrive almost daily. Yesterday one arrived from New York, bound for Australia with a large number of passengers on board. She was 80 days from New York! The *Mississippi* was just 60 days from Norfolk here, and we were also just 60. An English Mail Steamer arrived yesterday from the East Indies. She brings news to the effect that the Steamer *Susquehanna*[45] is at Manilla[46] broken down! I could not learn what was broken, but she went from Macao[47] to Manilla with one engine. She also had much sickness on board, and Commodore Aulick[48] is lying very low with dysentery.

Chapter Two
August 30–December 29, 1853

Hong Kong, Aug. 30th, 1853

My Dearest Lide,

We left here as I wrote you was our purpose on the 5th of this month, and after a run of 4 days we arrived in the harbor of Nappa Kiang Loo Choo,[1] where we found The Sloop of War *Plymouth*,[2] Store Ship *Supply*[3] and "tender" *Caprice*. Commodore Perry had been there with The *Susquehanna* and *Mississippi* and left orders for us to return immediately to Hong Kong, but our piston became loose on the passage and we had to remain there and fix it. This took us about 10 days when returned here expecting to find either The *Mississippi* or *Susquehanna*, but neither were here. The *Mississippi* being at Whampoa[4] and The *Susquehanna* at Cumsingmoon.[5]

Perry has been to Jeddo with The Sloops of War *Plymouth* and *Saratoga*,[6] and the Steamers *Mississippi* and *Susquehanna*. He was received well and had a large house built for his reception. He landed over 200 men with two bands of music, and gave the Emperor some presents, among them a gold watch. He received some in return. He had a pair of handsome revolvers which he offered, but The Emperor would not take them because he could not by their custom give any weapons of theirs in return. They received whatever they wanted and remained in the harbor of Jeddo about two weeks, arrangements having been made between The Commodore and The Emperor to enter in conversation as to a commercial relations between The United States and Japan. Commodore Perry had allowed The Emperor until next May to make up his mind when the whole Squadron will proceed to Jeddo. At the Loo Choo Islands, where we were, there is a coal depot which Com. Perry made the Loo Chooians build for him.

The people at Nappa Kiang are strong and hearty looking set of people. In color they resemble the Chinese, but their features, manners and customs are entirely different. They shave their heads like the Chinese, but do not wear the long "tails." They comb their hair, which is invariably a glossy beautiful black, upwards and gather it in a bunch much like a knot on the top and through which they wear pins about the thickness of a large nail and about 6 or 9 inches long. The Mandarins (spies) and upper class dress with silver pins and the lower classes wear brass ones. 'Tis hard in many cases to distinguish man from woman for I could detect no mark except the hair, which in the woman is not shaved off and is brought around the back of the neck in a kind of fold, and then gathered on the top of the head and pinned the same as the mans.

The women do not appear to be very modest, for every one almost of the lower classes wore their dresses so loosely in front with nothing to fasten them except the girdle around the waist that they exposed their natural breasts! And yet when any of us would make an appearance in the streets, men women and boys would gather themselves up and run from us as though we were wild beasts. The 1st time I landed I was astonished at seeing so many people together. I suppose some 2 or 3 hundred. As I approached the crowd of strange looking beings I noticed quite a commotion amongst them, and as I got up to them they had bundled up their things which they had for sale (it was a market place) and were off on a full run, many left their things behind, and some few remained. Those that remained were old women, perhaps too feeble to run, having the most horrible fear pictured on their countenances. They would not sell us anything, though we saw nothing but potatoes and rice, with lots of rough looking cushions were on the ground.

We left the market place and took a look through the City of "Nappa Kiang," which for build and styles is the most unique ever I have seen. 'Tis nothing but immensely thick stone walls from 5 to 11 or 12 ft high, behind which their houses are built. Some of stone, some of bamboo and some of wood. On our approach the girls, boys and women would run like deers, and in the neighborhood of shops (streets appropriated for shops solely) a bustle in front of the door was all we could see for on getting in front of it 'twas closed—shut up and the owners out of sight! We afterwards took the large roads, most perfectly paved with stone, and we made our way for the Emperor Princes Palace, about 3 miles from Nappa Kiang and in the City of Lowzee (I spell as pronounced). This large road is most perfect, the thick walls left behind the most beautiful country opened to our view. Large fields of rice, sugar cane &c. We passed through or under a kind of bridge some 30 feet high and extending across the road, their [*sic*] commenced the city. The road and streets if possible were perfectly paved and the immense walls built with more neatness and much higher than those of Nappa Kiang. We walked until we reached the Emperors Palace, the walls of which are enormous. To take the whole thing together, that is the people, their manners, buildings, habits &c. I must say that they were the most strange that ever I have seen. Commodore Perry on his arrival sent word to the Loo Choo Prince[7] that he would dine with him. The Prince sent word back that he could very well excuse Commodore Perry, but Old Perry marched some men ashore and a band of music and *made* the Prince give him dinner.

There are no Chinese in Loo Choo, and Loo Choo has no trade with China, everything is Japanese. Don't mind what the geographers say about this. I have seen Chinese, and Chinese Junks, and I've seen Japanese and Japanese Junks (Junks you know are ships) and can tell the difference, so you can tell your friends that Loo Choo is Japanese.

Well we must have something to eat and the people would not sell it, we had to get a Dutchman, the only Europeans or other foreigners in the place and the Missionaries buy things for us and send them off. We bought chickens, eggs and sweet potatoes, all we could get, occasionally a piece of pork. Eggs were sold by the hundred and chickens by the doz. It was cool there to what we have had it and I got rid of the prickly heat, but since our return it has come back on some and it annoys me so much that I can hardly sleep.

Sunday, Sept. 4th 1853

Here we are at Cumsingmoon. Arrived this morning about 11 O'clock. The *Susquehanna*, *Vandalia*,[8] *Macedonian*[9] and *Southampton*[10] are here. [. . .] The Store ship *Supply* was at Hong Kong last week had orders to mount her battery and proceed to Canton[11] where she is now. She had been at Amoy[12] and while there the town was being besieged by the Emperors forces, some 40 junks. The town was held by the Rebels,[13] who are marching now on Pekin, and if they are successful there will be without a doubt a kick up at Canton and that I suspect is the reason of the *Supply* being moved there. Whampoa, where The *Mississippi* is, is but 15 miles from Canton. This Chinese War[14] may occupy as much if not more of our attention than Japan. I am anxious to see Japan now that we are here—at last here, and joined the Squadron.

A day or two before we arrived in Hong Kong a gang of Chinese stole on board an English vessel (an opium smuggler) in the harbor and murdered the Captain and all hands. No arrests have been made yet, and I guess will not be. Just after we got to Loo Choo news came there by a Junk that an English vessel with 200 Chinese and 40 Englishmen on board bound for California

5. Unknown Chinese artist, "Canton," Library of Congress.

had gone ashore on one of the islands not far distant and that some 200 out of the whole number perished. We sighted the island on our return to Hong Kong, but on account of the weather we could get no nearer than we were, and did not see anybody or we would have taken them off.

The boat is going, I must stop.

Truly Yours,

George

U.S Ste. *Powhatan*, Cumsingmoon, China, September 18th, 1853

My Dearest Lide,

A day or two after I mailed my last letter to you, and that from this place, I received one from you dated June 26th; it being the second letter from Lamar.[15] It is just two weeks to day since we dropped anchor in this harbor and since we have been here I have been just twice ashore. [. . .] My last letter too may not have reached Hong Kong in time for the Mail, and would remain there 2 weeks in the office, but it was a short one, and if the two come together they will make for a nice long letter. I would like to just drop into your room some nights about 12 O'Clock and take you by surprise!

I want you to work for me, and if you really want to make shirts, make them for me, for I am pretty certain that my stuff will be rather dilapidated when we get home. We pay 3 cents apiece for washing and you know that wash boards are unknown in the Celestial region and clothes are washed with stones to the great sacrifice of buttons and material. It is a very easy matter to poke a finger through a shirt tail or the top of a sock.

I have learned much about fitting one's self out for a cruise at sea. I had aplenty of everything. My cloth clothes are getting moldy. I cannot wear them because of the heat. We have had almost a perpetual summer since we left Madeira to be sure we had a little cool weather at Cape Town, but from Mauritius we have been in an atmosphere of *Fire*, and at Pulo Penang[16] I broke out all over with prickly heat, and said prickly heat has never left me but for a few days at Loo Choo. My entire body is now so perfectly covered with it that it would be almost impossible to stick the point of a pin between the pimples. My hair is coming out again. Though it is much thicker than when I left you in Portsmouth. I am getting very fat too. Much more so than I would like, I know [*sic*] doubt have become acclimated, for we see many fat and very large Chinamen.

We have visited the *Susquehanna* and they have visited us. They are extremely anxious to start for home, for they have been out here their full time, but as I will show in my news, I entertain the opinion that they will not [be] much earlier than us. Their Air Pump Beam shafts are broken and temporarily fixed, so that when they do start home they will have to go very easy. I may as well state here that the *Powhatan* is the *Fastest* as well as the best and most sea worthy sea Steamer afloat.

We are now overhauling the Engines and have 5 weeks to do it in, and every Engineer on board is on duty every day. I go in the Engine room at 9 O'Clock in the morning and remain until half past 5 and I assure you I am glad when Saturday night comes for I work Hard! Harder than I ever did at a Machine Shop, and Sundays I have to myself.

There is talk of ordering one of the *Mississippi*'s 1st Assts. Here. I would like Danby[17] if I remained, but Mr. Gay[18] will not on any account part with Danby and the probability is that Mr. Holland[19] will be ordered. Now as I mentioned a little something in my last about Whip[ple']s difficulties or hinted at them I will just relate somethings that have occurred. Whipple you know has done little of any duty since we left Cape Town, and therefore I have been playing 1st Asst.

Now to understand matters you must know that we have but three "watches" or as the are properly called Divisions, and by a written order in the order book the 1st Division *starts the fires* if the ship has been at anchor 24 hours or over and as we are nine hundred and ninety nine cases out of thousand *over* 24 hours at anchor we can safely say that such is the case as a whole: well as the 1st Division starts the fires the 2nd Division in as many cases starts the Engines.

We remained at Loo Choo Island about 2 weeks, and when we got ready to start Mr. Faron was called about 2 O'clock in the morning to start the fires which he did. I relieved him at 4 O'clock—Mr. Arnold on with me. Mr. Faron passed an order to keep 12 inches of steam and on no account allow it to rise. I immediately looked at the gauge and saw twelve inches and a half; then turned to Faron and said "I'll relieve you sir" then said it to the Fireman and Assist. Engr. "Shut your ash pit doors! Sprinkle your fires!" Turning again to Faron he angrily said call Mr. Sewell at one bell "Very well sir I'll *relieve* you." And he left the Engine Room. At the bell (half pass [*sic*] four) I called Mr. Sewell—about 5 O'clock he came down. The steam by the gauge being 12 inches exactly! He walked up and down, passed a remark or two and then asked if my side injections and out board deliveries were open. I said "I don't know sir, but will look" — "what" said Sewell, "didn't Mr. Faron pass the word to you whether he opened them or not." "No Sir." "Send for Mr. Faron." I sent for Mr. Faron and he came down. Sewell pitched into him for neglect of duty, and Faron to get out of it said that he told before leaving that they were not open, I said mildly, "that I didn't hear him, and there must be a mistake about it." "Well," said he. "I don't know anything about that" I then got some little angry and turned towards Mr. Faron one of those looks of mine and said, "Mr. Faron, you are in the habit of saying "I don't know *anything* about *that*" and in this case it implies his full meaning of being too cowardly to acknowledge his wrongs. He flew up and said "it is false"! I ordered him to leave the Engine Room. He said he would not do it. I then turned to Sewell and requested to be relieved. Faron made a reply that he would relieve me! I said then "I will hold you personally responsible for what you have said, and I immediately consulted Whipple, but he said that the best way to treat such a man was by contempt. We did not speak to one another for some time, and I was determined to have the matter settled as soon as we joined the squadron, but on getting here we were visited by the *Susquehannah*'s Engineers almost every day and in the intercourse Mr. Faron several times spoke to me and we now converse whenever occasion requires: but I have also understood that Mr. Faron is very much dis-satisfied on board the *Mississippi* and that he does not speak to either Danby, Hollands or yours.

On learning this I spoke to Mr. Sewell and told him that I intended to offer an exchange with Logan,[20] that I was well satisfied with the *Powhatan* and was pleased with him. He told me that I could not leave. I said that I had the right and could demand it because I was entitled to be the Senior 2nd Asst. Engnr. on board one of the three ships. This he could not get over and came down a little; said that he didn't want to part with me. I told him that one of the others no doubt would have to leave, as Roby[21] of The *Mississippi* has consumption and was condemned. Well said Sewell, Mr. King shall leave then. To end this matter which must be anything but interesting, I got him to promise that he would not interfere in my efforts to make an exchange with Logan, and when I see Logan I will make him the offer, although there is but little chance of its being effected. Sewell no doubt *will* interfere and prevent my going and from what I have heard I know that he would rather have me with him, and therefore I am good to remain on board on her the whole cruise. Sewell will no doubt endeavors to have King ordered to some other vessel. The exchange I think will be King to The *Mississippi* and Holland to the *Powhatan*, as it moves the unjust to evade any of The *Susquehanna*s Engineers to a ship whose prospects for going home were not as good as here.

I have met and been with all The *Susquehanna*s Engineers, and Mr. Hebard[22] Senior 1st Asst. takes particular care of me when I go there, and the others have scarcely a chance to say a word to me. He is from Buffalo and I first met him on board The *Michigan*. Then there is Harry Stewart[23] the other 1st Asst, who is from Philada., and we have become quite warm friends. His wife is in Philada. and he told me where she lives, but I've forgotten. Their first hand is a good fellow and Lawrence[24] who I didn't know before has told me all his troubles; he imagines the Chief Engineer is "down on him." The Third Assist. Are all pretty good fellows. One I don't like and that is a Shock,[25] a brother to the Chief Engineer of the same name.[26]

I rather think that Danby has acted a little mean towards me because he has not spoken to me a single word and although I sent him his things as soon as I possibly could, and that some 3 weeks or more ago. I don't yet know whether he has got them or not, but I will no doubt see him in a few days and all will be known.

I said I went on board The *Susquehanna* on Monday night. The men on board of her have rigged up a complete theatre, have a curtain, scenes, foot lights and everything. They rig it up on the Fore-Castle, and seats are rigged for the men, and the officers. Lake stood on the Hurricane deck. Some of the performers are very good indeed: in fact they played "Poor Pillacody" as well as it could be played. The messenger boy and drummer boy take the woman's characters and they really look well dressed with taste and stuffed to perfection. There were several English Ladies there as visitors, these ladies being the wives of the Captains of the Opium Fleet, and dressed gorgeously. This opium fleet is a fleet of ships anchored here and receive the opium from vessels allowed to deal in it. The opium is then sent by them in Chinese Junks into the interior to sell. I have been on board one of them, and saw some of the poison. It is a prohibited article in China, but I suppose the sale of opium for one year must amount to millions of dollars!

Wednesday, September 21st

I believe I quit you last night saying something about the Opium Fleet here at anchor. This is their Head Quarters, and their ships are housed over, well manned and armed. This "Fleet" never leaves here, but remains and receives the prohibited article from the vessels that bring it into these waters. They then watch their opportunity and send a cargo of it away up the rivers and into the interior by Chinese junk, if these junks get caught by the Mandarins or Police its cargo is confiscated and goes to the Chinese government. The Mandarins are afraid to attack the "Fleet" and they therefore remain here in perfect security. The Captains of them are getting very good pay, and in many cases have their families on board with them.

Cumsingmoon is a most miserable hole indeed. As bad as Labuan,[27] having but a few miserable huts ashore in which the poorer class of Chinese live; the Boat population that is. The people who live in the boats, altogether no doubt are as large as the Shore population if not larger; whole families live in what at home we would call a small sail boat—in some cases a boat family will consist of 10 and 12 persons, old, middle aged and young. The mother may be seen tugging away at an oar, or hauling bravely on a sail with her child lashed on her back and the young one bobbed first one way and then the other sleeps as soundly as does a baby prince in a couch of down.

We have had what we would call caterers at home amass with us since our arrival here and while we are here called a Compradore.[28] This Compradore of ours is an agent of the great Azouke who is worth they tell me a millions of dollars or more. Azouke is the principal compradore for the Squadron, but his agents are one on each ship. The name of ours is Aloo. The manner in which they do the business for us is as follows. Each agent is furnished with a large boat and crew by Azouke. His boat arrives here from Macao (nothing but fish, clams, crabs and oysters can be bought in Cumsingmoon) every morning about 6 O'clock. He then has delivered to the different ships what they ordered the day previous. He then finds the caterer, which is an easy matter and hands him the box. Caterer writes down what he wants, and the next morning it is furnished. The messses pay but once a moon that is once a month. This man furnishes everything as I said. All you have to do is order it. Beef, geese, eggs vegetables, fruits, liquors, cigars, books, shoes, hats—everything that can be bought in China.

Commodore Perry is living in Macao, has the Band of the *Susquehanna* there to enliven him and is living in state. He paid us an official visit a few days after our arrival here and returned same day to Macao. Since then he paid us 1 or not us but The *Susquehanna* a visit. I believe for the purpose of dining with the Captains of the squadron. At any rate he was there and so were all the Captains of the different ships. Capt. McCluney was there of course, and the next day after the dinner we received some "bricks," as follows, that we were to go home via Cape Horn and to touch at Oregon and California. That The *Susquehanna* to start in April and go home via Cape Town, Cape of Good Hope. This may or may not be so, but as the chances are rather in favor of The *Powhatan*s going that way I will remain I think, however, much as I want to remain with the *Powhatan*, if an exchange can be effected with Logan I will do it. Though there is but little hope of its consummation.

The *Powhatan* is the best Sea Steamer, and fastest war steamer afloat. When The *Mississippi* arrives the matter will soon be settled. The story that we were to go home *via* the Horn was accompanied with one that we were to leave Japan in April for the Bonin Islands,[29] where Commodore Perry has established a Coal depot, from there to Sandwich Islands, then to Oregon and California; from thence to Valpariso &c. The Bonin Islands are about 800 miles to the eastward of Loo Choo, and the run from there to the Sandwich Islands can be made by taking a deck load of coal. Now everybody says that Commodore Perry made arrangements with the Japanese to return there in May and how we can sail from there in April and not get there until May I don't see into. My opinion is that of the precise arrangements made by Commodore Perry none know. Some think that our ships were received with hearty good welcome and others think that the reception was very cold—of all that was said and done I about informed you in my last letter. I believe I also informed you of Commodore Perry's very decided manner of disagreeing with the Prince of Loo Choo. The report now is that the Prince was *banished* in consequence. This means that he has committed *Hari Kari*. By the Japanese Law or custom which is the same thing, any one in power who allows himself to be insulted, defeated, or in any way dishonored, he must rip open his bowels with his own hand, or commit suicide in that way. This is called Hari Kari, and the Prince of Loo Choo has done so on Commodore Perry's account on the Sunday after we arrived here and became attached to the squadron.

The orders were read to us on the quarter deck as follows: that no one attached to any ship in the squadron would be allowed to write home to any Public Press, or to his friends or family anything connected with the squadron or more particularly its movements. That no one should keep a private journal, or if so kept it should be handed to the Captain of the Fleet (Commander Adams)[30] and from him sent to the department at Washington sealed, and that the owner could have them after the return of the expedition. That all officers were *requested* to take up some subject, Mineralogy, Botany, Marine Algae, Ichthyology, Conchology, Mechanics, or some science connected with the many things they might see and in the work to be published after the expedition credit would be given to all who would thus contribute. Any and all curiosities that might be found or collected were to be delivered to the Commander in chief of the squadron who would have the receipt of them acknowledged by the government &c. &c. &c.

Its getting towards ten o'clock and I must again leave you. [. . .] Good night again. The lights must be put out. I'll think of you in my dreams tonight I know.

Friday Morning, Sept 23rd.

The *Susquehanna* I am told is to sail for Macaou [*sic*] today. Sewell I believe will not go. I was on board The *Susquehanna* a few moments yesterday evening and I had some private conversation with Stewart and Lawrence. Stewart told me that from what Archibald[31] told him, I was the Engineer of The *Powhatan*. That Sewell looks upon me as his right hand man. Now I knew this was the case, but I didn't know that Sewell would give me credit for it, or that he would speak about it to anyone, and I guess that I will gain no good from it. [. . .] We have a report here that a man was stabbed on The *Macedonian* last night by one of his shipmates. It is so early that I can't learn the truth of it yet.

We will receive The *Susquehanna* at Whampoa about the middle of November. That will give us a chance to go [to] Canton and see more of China, from there I suppose we will go to Manilla. [. . .] You may think it strange that I write in one letter one thing and in another letter another thing, but always take into consideration that in the time that must elapse there is much chance for the Rajah to change his mind. I always give you the latest rumors. The *Susquehanna* is firing up. I expect that The *Mississippi* will not be here now until Monday.

Mr. Schriver[32] has been detached temporarily from our ship and ordered to The *Susquehanna*. Mr. Bibby the Capts. Clerk that came out with Capt. McCluney first received the appointment from Capt. Buchannan,[33] and Capt. B[uchannan] wants to take him from McCluney on that account because the former Clerk of The *Susque.* has gone home. Bibby didn't want to go, and has several times asked me for advice because he says *I'm* a thinking man. I told him to consult his own wishes and act accordingly. So last night he told me that he would not go with Buchannan. The *Vandalia*, *Macedonian* and *Southampton* are still here. [. . .] What has become of the *Allegheny*[34] none seem to know whether she is finished or not is unknown to us.

As we came from Loo Choo we were very near running on the South end of Formosa.[35] The City that I spoke in my last as being the residence of the Prince and containing the Palace is called Shudee. I believe I called it Zouzee in my last, but 'tis 9 o'clock and I must stop again just as I get well started. [. . .] The *Powhatan* will remain here until about the middle or first of November. Then go to Whampoa, from there we will probably go to Manilla, and if we *do* go to Manilla, as it is a Spanish possession I will probably go to see another Bull Fight—*May I?* I didn't like the manner of the *Susquehannas* getting under way this morning, she is not the ship The *Powhatan* is.

The great hew [*sic*] and cry about this China War is in my opinion about all there is of it. So far as we or *I* am able to learn the rebels have possession of Shanghai, and are close to Peking. A part of their force have taken the outside of the Bogatagris[36] fort, an immense building between here and Whampoa. Here the rebels took from the government party about 30,000 dollars. No doubt the rebels will have full possession of China in about 2 years, then all China will be open to foreigners. Probably in my next letter I will be able to say something of Canton. The rebels are inching along towards Canton now. [. . .] That's all. Good by[e]! And God bless you. Truly and affectionately your devoted husband. In life, in thoughts, awake, in dreams, always do I think of you. Always Lovingly, George

US Steamer *Powhatan*, Cumsingmoon, China Oct. 17th

My Dearest Lide,

The population divided about equally between the boat and most miserable sorts ashore. The class of people in the rank of about one hundred to one the most abject poor miserable half-starved and rather wretched that ever I beheld. Everyday our ship is surrounded by small boats generally managed by the wife, mother and small children of a large family. The male children being absolutely naked and the females but partially clothed. The cry from the poor [. . .] with uplifted hands, or else lascivious countenances [. . .] for inflaming passions to a generous purpose is "chow chow" "chow chow." The sick, the lame, the hungry. the half-starved, the naked, [. . .] the wretched. The fascinating, the boisterous, the good, bad, honest and indifferent all beg aloud for "chow chow." Chow chow means something to eat. In nineteen cases out of twenty these floating beggars are families, the males being at work on shore as "coolies" or away in fishing boats, or as a hand in "fast boats." By "coolies" is understood laborers. By "Fast boats" boats that carry passengers from shore to ship, vice versa, and carry belongings as messengers to go from place to place. Then there are "Tanka boats" pulled by good looking china girls that do nothing else but carry passengers to and from the ships.

All in all I would judge the population of Cumsingmoon to be about 3 thousands. Ashore there are no places to visit. Nothing to be seen but barren hills, shave headed long tailed Chinamen disgusting though voluptuous looking women and a place to bathe. This bathing place was built by the clerks on board the opium vessels and by them an invitation was extended to our officers to use it. I have been there three times, generally go on Saturday afternoons. None of our officers go ashore for any other purpose except those who risk health, vision and honesty for a few moments gratification. As I have thus written. I may add that all who so far have made beasts of themselves have paid dearly for their whistling, and could mention amongst the numbers some of my own mess mates but this is both disgusting improper and uninteresting.

The *Powhatan* is now the only man of war in the harbor, the *Vandalia* being at Macao. The *Mississippi* and *Southampton*, the *Susquehanna* and *Supply* at Blenheims Reach[37] or Whampoa. The *Macedonian* at Hong Kong, and the *Plymouth* at Loo Choo, and the *Saratoga* at Shanghai. These vessels compose our Squadron. Commodore Perry is at Macao living in a large house, having the "grand bands" and all the Artists such as Daguerreotypes, telegraphers, draught men &c. were with him, but of all this I'll mention afterwards.

A few days after I mailed my last letter the *Mississippi* arrived here and the same evening I went on board of her. Saw Logan, Danby, Rutherford,[38] Alexander[39] and Capt. Slack.[40] Danby and Holland made me remain on board the *Mississippi* all night and I did not get on board the *Powhatan* until 10 o'clock the next morning.

The next day Logan came on board here and dined with us. I was with him almost all day and I offered him the exchange; having learned from his own lips that he did not speak either to Danby, Holland, or Alexander. He is worse off there than I am here and I told him so. I also told him that I had no inducements to offer him to join the *Powhatan* that my troubles were altogether of a personal nature and that on the whole I would regret leaving her. Logan tells me that he had heard of my intended proposals through some of the *Susquehanna*'s Engineers and had thought so much [of it] that he could not say which was best. He thought that if I could not agree it would be impossible for him to do [. . .] that he would give me an answer the next day.

The next day I dined on board the *Mississippi* and was treated handsomely by all hands, and it took some pains on my part to get some private talk with Logan. However, I obtained an opportunity and Logan told me that he would make the Exchange! I then told that as I made the offer to please him it was his place to make the arrangements which he refused to do, and I then told him that as he did not seem to care about the matters I would prefer remaining on board the *Powhatan*. So the chances are that I will return if spared in the *Powhatan*. All the Engineers and the Officers of *Mississippi* have bought their curiosities &c. They dined at Whampoa which is about 12 or 15 miles from Canton and Canton is the place to buy everything. Every vessel but the *Mississippi* and us had left here for other parts about the 1st of this month.

On the 4th Lieut. Jos. Adams[41] died on board our ship after about two weeks sickness. He was told only on the morning of the 4th by the Doctors that [he] could not live, and Dr. Wheelwright and Lieut. Pegram[42] commenced and finished his will. But Adams was too weak to sign it and it was only witnessed. He died on the quarter deck, where he had laid about a week during his sickness. Everything was kept as quiet as possible, no music, no whistling, and even the ships bell was not struck. On the morning of the 6th I witnessed a most solemn scene that of taking the body of Mr. Adams from our ship to the *Miss[iss]ippi*. The *Mississippi* got underway and took us to Macaou. About an hour and a half run from here. As many officers as could be spared from the ship went to Macao to attend the funeral. I went down on the *Mississippi*. We anchored off Macao and waited for orders from the Commodore. In about two hours the orders came and in effect they were to keep the body on board until the next morning. Faron and myself, and in fact all the officers from our ship and as many as could be spared from the *Mississippi* immediately went ashore. As soon as we landed a grand wish was made for the Hotel which are very large looking houses with thick walls and but little room inside. Danby succeeded in getting possession of a part of a room positioned off from the pantry as big as the room by a Calico curtain.

The next morning the corpse was buried in military styling. The Portuguese soldiers, (Macao you know is a Portuguese place) the Marines from the *Mississippi*, some sailors from our ship and about 40 officers. He was buried in a vault. Built on a beautiful burying grounds, and immediately joining the Camoes Garden, a place containing some of the most romantically seductive spots and beautiful retreats with natural curiosities imaginable. Here you see an overhanging rock far above your head weig[h]ing many tons apparently without support. There are long narrow walks with beautiful flower beds on either side arched by the naked long legged bamboo. Beautiful retreats on the very tops of huge trees ascended by steps and perched on adjoining rocks. This is Camoes Garden.

Then there is what is called the "cave" which is but two immense rocks touching each other at the top and spreading so as to leave a kind of archway between them at the base. Here 'tis said the Great Camoe[43] sat when he wrote his great poems and now much care is taken of it and a bust of the author adorns the cave with a monument containing inscriptions on each side in Portuguese and French, but enough of this.

In my last I said something about a difficulty that I had with Faron. That has all been settled. He understands me perfectly and thinks no more trouble will come from that quarter. Arnold has been detached from this ship and Holland ordered in his place. Arnold goes to the *Mississippi* and Holland or Old Dad [as he] is familiarly called is with us. They say it is but temporarily, but if Whipple doesn't get well and rejoin this ship Mr. Holland is good for the balance of the cruise on her. I am now on good terms, that is speaking terms with all the officers except Kellogg, and he is such a perfect hog and so much deception that I cannot put up with him. So the other day I made a request of him to have nothing whatever to say to me except connected with and concerning duty, as then there could be no possible mistake. He agreed and although there is no ill feelings we have nothing whatever to say to each other. Mr. Holland and myself are chums. Danby told me that Jessie Gay told

6. Unknown Chinese artist, "Macao," Library of Congress.

him that Sewell reports me to be his right hand man. Hebbard told me the same thing, so I am satisfied that Sewell would not part with me on any account, and that he will do all he can to make it pleasant and agreeable for me.

October 22nd

The *Mississippi* has just arrived here.

You have now answered my Cape Town letter. The letter about my sickness no doubt distressed you some little. You must go about so carelessly. You must dress up and look splendid. Why if you should only see me. I use a bottle of cologne water every week. Shave every day, scrub and clean myself both night and morning, dress up in white pants, white watered silk jacket, pumps of patent leather. Manilla straw hat and immense regulation whiskers. I am surprised that some of the Chinese Ladies of rank about fall in love with me. One feels so comfortable when clean all over. You feel satisfied with yourself and also a little proud.

We will no doubt leave for Whampoa sometime next week, probably Thursday. The Commodore sends the vessels around in this way to give the officers an opportunity to visit the different places ashore and make their purchases. As for purchasing china ware or dinner sets and tea sets I cannot think of it for I have seen much better at home than I have seen here. [. . .] I had a long talk with Jimmy Shirk[44] the other day and he gave me lots of Erie news! All of which I suppose you have heard of. When I get home and if I pass I will make a strong effort to get the *Michigan* as Chief Engineer. Old Rutherford has had enough of easy duty and he is just as able to go to sea as I. I really think that if I don't get there I will resign unless I am ordered to the Mediterranean and even then if I can get into other business I will resign. I have had enough of the Service.

Mr. Bibby wishes to be remembered. My very particular friend Mr. James Monroe Bibby our Captains Clerk wishes in due time to make your acquaintance and you may anticipate that we'll have a little "Chow Chow" together on the farm.

> As my particular friend Geo. Has kindly sent my regards to you although personally unacquainted I cannot refrain having of course rec'd permission to express in a very small space my appreciation of his goodness. Hoping I may at some future time have the pleasure of an introduction to his far better half & trust she will not believe one half that this very condensed epistle contains & with many many wishes for her future contentment & peace of mind in this "sea of troubles" I would with the kindest feelings after forgiving me for this necessary encroachment in expression but afraid of what I would say designates myself her particular friend.
>
> J. Monroe Bibby

Old Bibby is a foo! foo! Old Dad Holland say's so and his words is "Gospel." Truly George.

Love, Regards &c. to all as usual and to you as usual if not more so.

George

Sunday Morning [October 23, 1853]

Capt. McCluney who has been on a visit to Macao returned yesterday in the *Mississippi*, and as he of course has been with the Commodore we get the benefit of it in "bricks" relative to our ostensible visit to these waters. The reports are that a Russian Fleet consisting of one Frigate a Steamer, Sloop of War and a "tender" have been at Loo Choo and Nagasaka[45] and have sailed for the Bay of Jeddo. Commodore Perry first intended to rendezvous his squadron at Loo Choo in February but 'tis said that in consequence of the movements of the Russians he will collect them there in about 6 weeks from the present time. This is all rumor, and I can't vouch for its accuracy. This much I do know, that the *Powhatan* will sail for Whampoa this week, about

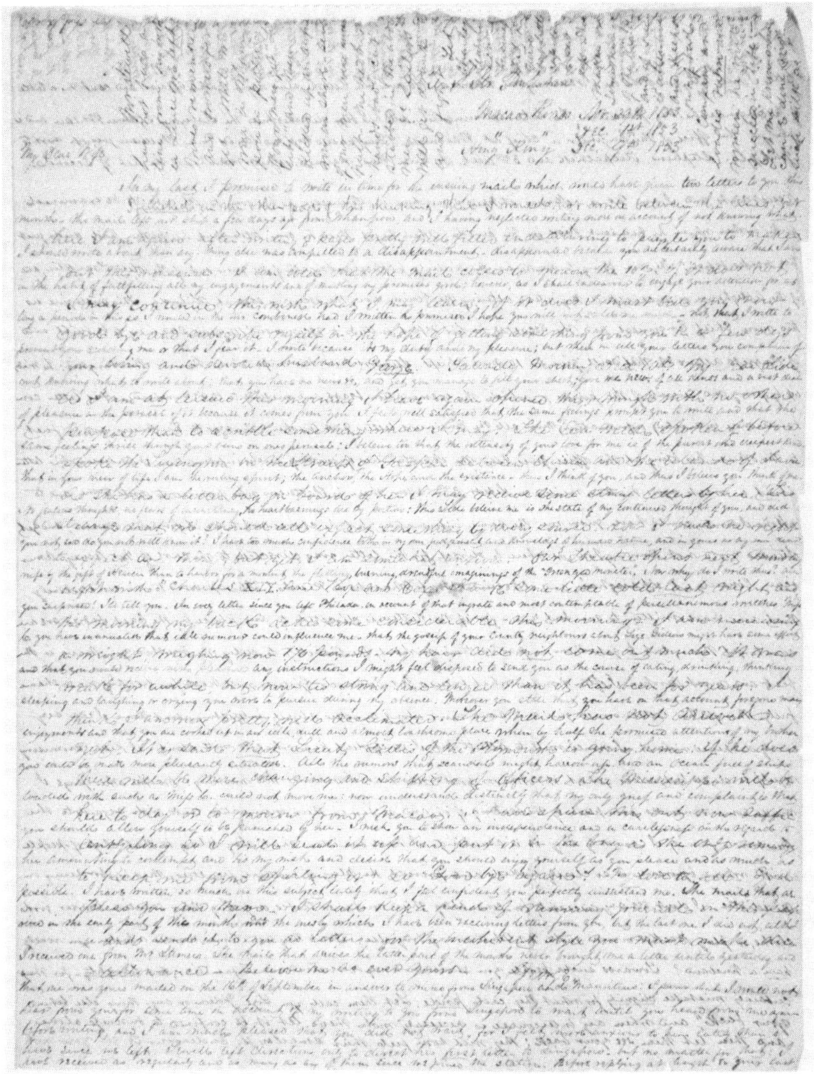

7. Example of Gideon's letters to his wife Lide, showing where he wrote in the margin and between the lines of existing sentences.

Thursday, as the Flag Ship of the Squadron. Commodore Perry intends to go there with us. I hope he will not like the [motion] of the ship, or I don't want to be humbugging on board a Flag Ship. All Officers, in fact every one, acknowledges that the *Powhatan* is the prettiest and fastest ship in this part of the world, and my only opinion is that as a Steam ship she can't be beat in the world.

In some of my former letters I believe I wrote something about the peculiar sickness of some of the Engineers. All were well a week ago. Now Mr. Kellogg is again caught and several others in the other steerage. In the Ward Room I know of but one case. The Purser! From one of the other ships I forget which, a Lieut. has been sent home as incurable! And he is married too! But I ought not write about such stuff 'tis uninteresting to say the least of it, if not disgusting. I suppose ere this you have informed my brother[46] that I have not yet received a line from him since we left the United States now over 8 months! Two thirds of a year.

There is nothing certain about our movements after the Japan affair is settled. We may be the lucky ship to take the Commodore from Jeddo to the Bonin Islands and from thence to the Sandwich Islands and California, but everyone seems to think it will be the *Mississippi*. The matter is between the *Mississippi* and the *Powhatan* for Perry has freely asserted that his [*sic*] intends taking one of the three steamers that way, and it is very well known that it will not be the *Susquehanna* for he is afraid of her.

Mr. Logan was on board yesterday and occupied me nearly 3 hours recounting his troubles on board the *Mississippi*. I am afraid that Logan is lost. He drinks very hard, and his mind must be affected by it for he is a very different man now. He tells me that Arnold is well satisfied, but that Arnold has been tight 3 times already on board there. Now when Arnold gets tight he soon becomes perfectly crazy. He will in the end be dismissed if he is not more careful. He is no Officer anyhow and I must admit that the service and the Engineer Corps could very well if not beneficially spare his services. Mr. Kellogg too [. . .] most deceiving man that I ever know. He is no Engineer and all I can say of him is that he is an Artificial Gentleman. As far as I am able to judge, and I may be so, for I have much indirect evidence of my ability in my profession. I judge that Mr. Fauth will make the best Engineer now in our mess.

U.S. Str. *Powhatan*, Cumsingmoon, China, October 29th 1853

My Dearest Lide,

The Court Martials of Mr. Wilson concluded its labours today after sitting the whole of this week. I gave in my evidence on Thursday morning and because I didn't swear just as the Ward Room officers who preferred the charges wanted me to. That is to condemn Wilson they are what is called "down on me." Now they took offence at this. One of the specifications charges Wilson with scandalous and outrageous conduct unbecoming a gentleman and an officer and tending to the destruction of good morals. On having the specification read to me before the Court I neglected to say whether my opinion was to this charge yes or no. I commenced to relate the circumstances as they took place but was stopped by the President of the Court who said that they had heard all about that and to just tell the court what Mr. Wilsons conduct and manner was. I replied that his manner was excited and spirited and decided. To all the specifications my answers were very brief and such a nature as to give the court an opportunity to cross question and to prevent Wilsons doing so, but no cross examination took place except of the accused himself. When I came out I said to Sewell that the Court was all one sided. That there was no prosecution whatever.

About an hour after this Sewell sent for me and said that the Ward Room Officers were very angry about the evidence I gave in and that he would advise me to alter it. He said that he went in the second time and corrected his and that I had now the opportunity to do so. I told Mr. Sewell that when the Court sent for me I would go. Not before. That I had given my testimony and that the Court had the power to examine me as it pleased. I admitted that I had neglected to say as much on that point as I should have said but that I would not ask for an alteration. I was a witness not a prosecutor or a defendant. He then said that he advised me to go at once and change it, as they were talking in the Ward Room of charging me with perjury!! I immediately and abruptly left his room and waited my chance to see him in the Engine Room. This happened in about an hour. I then asked him if he would be kind enough to inform me who the gentlemen were that talked of charging me with perjury, that such talk as that could not be allowed and that I wanted either to make a journal or official matter of it. He avoided telling me and attempted to agree the point relative to my remarks in the testimony. I then said once for all that I would not allow my name to be used in connection with such a crime as that and asked him what objective I could have in view to perjure myself in Mr. Wilsons favor or in any ones favor.

Mr. Wilson and myself have never been friends to any extent. I rather dislike the man and always have. That all who know me knows full well that I am one of the most unprejudiced men in the world. This thing has angered me considerably but on mature reflection 'tis very easy to be seen that the attempt was made by Sewell as the representation of the clique to scare me into it. Sewell's made an ass of himself before the Court and perhaps he derived to have a purpose but 'tis not as easy to rattle some as 'tis others. Wilson said his defense today. I did not go in the Court Room, but I am told that he made a very able defense. The Court being moved to tears.

November 1st

Mr. Wilson read his defense before the Court on Saturday and I am told that it was a most able production. John is a very smart fellow and I would not be surprised if he got off with nothing but a reprimand. We will learn in a few days what it is. He takes things very coolly. The Court is in session now trying a Marine for desertion. I saw Captain Slack on board here yesterday. He looks well, but he doesn't appear to dress so tidy and so nice as he did out Wash.

Well, Well. I'll quit now and take a smoke of a cigar. Goodbye for a while. Now I say good bye and really I don't believe you are out of my mind any one whole hour in the whole twenty four.

Macao, November 2nd, 1853

My Dearest Lide,

This morning we left Cumsingmoon and in about two hours arrive here, that is Macao Roads. Our engines have had a complete overhauling, and I have complete charge of one of them. I feel somewhat anxious about their going off so when they moved off and what too better than ever I felt a little pride. I have not been in the Engine room being yet on the sick list. Mr. Faron and Mr. Stamm are on the sick list also and with the same fever which is a kind of remittance. Mr. Bibby has it also but he is nearly well. I have a bad cold with it. I have been blistered and was cupped this morning. I feel very well, and indeed have felt very much worse and done severe duty, but in this climate I am determined to take care of *myself* and let the duty take of itself. I will get just exactly the same amount of credit.

This afternoon the Chinamen who had our daguerreotypes from which he was to and did paint likenesses. They were very chaulky affairs and we sent them back. I am sorry I have not a better daguerreotype of yours so I could get one painted. I may yet take the one the fellow has painted. Faron says he could pick it out of fifty and take it for you. I think Farons looked well in fact we all thought that others looked better than our own. So three of us took them. We may do so when money is more plenty.

8. Unknown Chinese artist, "Whampoa Reach," Library of Congress.

We leave this afternoon for Whampoa with the Commodore on board. He is only going as a passenger. He does not intend on making this his flagship. [. . .] I am sorry for it because the flagship of Old Perry is always well supplied with whatever is needed on board. Here there is no effort made by the Captain to afford any comfort whatever in that respect. [We are] underway, but the ship shakes so that I cannot write.

I suppose if I have looked at that daguerreotype that I got from the Chinaman yesterday once I have 40 times. Almost every 10 minutes I take it out of my pocket. Where I carry it in my pocket 'tis a positive fact. I suppose when you get this letter, good riddens you'll say "a great letter that is" but I can't help it. Nothing to write about. A whizzing in my ears from the quinine that I have taken and other little inconveniences must make up for an excuse. Whampoa reached.

Canton River,[47] Sunday Afternoon, Nov 6th, 1853

By the above you will perceive that we are now really in China. We left Macao on Sunday afternoon and at dark we anchored in the Canton River, or Pearl River, about six nights below the "Boca Tigress" which is about 30 miles below this place, and is under enormous passage with a Chinese fort on each side. The English for "Bocca Tigress" is Tigers mouth. On Friday morning we left the "Boc" as it is called and in the afternoon anchored about two ship lengths ahead of the *Susquehanna*. The *Macedonian* is also here but for another "Reach" called "Blenheims Reach." There are numerous islands started around here, and Whampoa is one of them and is about 7 miles long. Ships of all nations are here taking in cargo of teas, silks, camphor &c. We [illegible text] nothing coming up of interest except the site of two large "Pagodas" but as they were some miles from us we could only see the outline of them. Then we ran aground and that produced a little commotion so Old Jock (Perry) also up on the hurricane deck and said to Capt. McCluney, "what's that fellow" meaning the Chinese Pilot of course. I must respect all that the great Rajah says and does. I wish I could repeat what he *knows* of our movements towards getting home.

The most beautiful Clipper Ship or ship of any kind which I have ever noticed lays at anchor and is about the length of our ship abreast of us. She is called the "*Flying Childers*"[48] And is from Boston. On Friday night as we were swinging to the tide our stubborn Quarter ran foul of her jib boom and carried away some of our awning stanchions, part of the barge and two boat davits. The Clipper Ship had her jib boom carried away. Her Capt. said he would not have cared but he was ready for sea, and time with these ships is money. However, we have done everything in our power to advance the progress of her repairs so she will be able to leave on Tuesday. We pay all damages. There is another American ship close by us called the Gin Ship, and she sails soon for the United States. The "*Flying Childers*" goes to Lou Chou.

I hear that the hospital at Macao is to be broken up and all the sick to be sent home on the *Corsair*. In that case Whipple will go home. Poor fellow.

Today I have taken but one dose of medicine. Yesterday was my worst day. I had a most tormenting headache all day long. This fever is remittent since—have chills with it. It is of a very mild form, but from it very few escape. Almost all of the *Susquehanna*'s officers have been down with it, and the way that quinine is administered is a caution. 30 dollars worth of it having been used on board our ship within two months. We have First Class Fireman by the name of McManus on board here and he is a very old man, pretty well read and uses very good language. This man has been sick for over two months [he] was off and on the "list" ever since we left home. I noticed him first as being unable to fire and succeeded in getting him to be one of the "oilers," the easiest billet a fireman can have. He often expressed his satisfaction to me—wished (and in fact all the men do) always to be on watch with me &c. This afternoon he saw me on deck and came up to me and said that the doctor told him yesterday that he was going to send him home in the *Corsair*, and that he never flattered anybody, but that he must say that he felt grateful and would always remember me. That I had gained his love and a lot of other stuff when his heart filled and the tears rolled down his cheeks, his eyes on me he couldn't say any more and I turned from him feeling sadly about him. He supports a large family [in] New York.

Today and yesterday our ship was crowded by Chinamen having all kinds of articles to sell. Yesterday I bought three flannel shirts and six pairs of drawers. The shirts were one dollar apiece and the drawers 50 cents. Today I bought a very neat writing desk of nut wood for four dollars.

I have missed some money out of my locker and a great many cigars, and other things have gone I suspect but I have missed nothing but pocket handkerchiefs and drawers. The writing desk contains secret drawers and a patent lock. There I keep my money and such other articles as might stick to boys fingers. I *know* who the thief is, but of course having never caught him at it, I can't accuse him of it, he is our boy, one that we got from the *Princeton*. I will catch him yet.

Macao Roads, Dec 1st, 1853

We left Whampoa in consequence of a protest sent in by the Doctor, at the time we had 64 cases on the Sick List of the fever. I had it twice. None of the Engineers escaped but Holland and King. Not one fatal case. In Macao, where we are now, the fever assumed the form of an epidemic, and Dr. Maxwell[49] who was here was taken and he had a hard time of it. We lie at anchor in the Roads about 6 miles from the city of Macao and as the weather is bad being rainy damp and blustering but few go ashore, in fact there is no security either in getting ashore or when ashore in getting off. For my part I am content to remain on board having seen enough of Macao in October.

The Commodore has chartered the Steamer *Queen*[50] and about 10 days ago she passed Whampoa while we were there. She stopped awhile and the Commodore who was [on] her on his way to Canton came on board to "make a look see" as the Chinamen say. Mr. Whipple who is Chief Engineer of the "*Queen*" came on board to see me. He looks well, better than he has since arriving in China. He is very anxious to go to Japan with us, but I fear he will not be able to do so, because it is the intention to keep the "*Queen*" at anchor off Canton to protect the "American interests" there, and as it may be necessary for her to leave there she requires an Engineer and I know of no other than Mr. Whipple to remain by her.

About two weeks ago Mr. Holland and myself took a "sand pan" a kind of small boat we have here, the nature of which I believe I explained to you in a former letter, having taken a couple of muskets, revolvers &c., with us and with a family of Chinamen started for and arrived at Canton. The reason of our taking the implements of war along with us was that an order to do so had been issued by the Captain, and that the whole river between Whampoa and Canton was infested by Pirates. Several boats had been attacked and robbed. We never saw the shadow of one either going or coming and I hold that the Pirate affair is a humbug.

Mr. Follins[51] the Boatswain of The *Susquehanna* having resigned secured for himself a situation on board the ship *Corsair*. This Mr. Follins is a particular friend of Mr. Fauth, and Mr. Fauth sent home by him a box containing some of his purchases, and in this box I put a piece of the black silk as a specimen. I don't know how much is in the piece I sent, but I thought it would do for an apron. I paid 87 ½ cents for it as it is. I put the silk in loose. Mr. Fauth's brother will send it to you.

We will leave for Hong Kong tomorrow. The *Mississippi* lies abreast of us here. The *Susquehanna* is at Hong Kong. We will, it is supposed, remain in Hong Kong until about the 1st January when we will either go to Shanghai or Loo Choo. The Commodore has broken up the Hospital and the sick sent home in The *Corsair*. All the arrangements here have been broken up and everybody attached to the "scientific corps" ordered aboard their respective ship. This looks like going to Japan. The weather is getting quite cold now and I am glad of it.

While we were in Whampoa a portion of our men got "liberty" and they kicked up an awful row on shore. Six of our men were injured. One had his hands badly cut, one stabbed in the abdomen. Sailors will get drunk and fight.

I'll ask some questions by way of variety. [. . .] What do people generally think of the Japan Expedition? My opinion is that it will never be of any service to the United States than trade [and] from all I can learn about it consists principally in the export of Copper and of that we can spare them some from Lake Superior.

I learn the Second Asst. Engineer Stephens[52] has resigned and that 3rd Asst. Engr. Gorton[53] died in Pensacola with the yellow fever. The leader of the Commodores Band died lately at this place with consumption. Amongst the sick that went home from our ship was a fireman named McManus and a coal heaver named Ward. I have lots of fun to tell you about China women we meet.

I was at a "Sing Sing" or concert the other night and while there, had a smoke of opium. The pipe being filled and lighted while I smoked by a small footed china woman. Of course the room was full of Officers and others. These small feet are disgusting. They stink when uncovered.

All who see me write wonder how on earth such letters can be read. Some say they would not attempt it for dollars. I tell them I would not like to be compelled to read them myself but that I know a person some distance from here who would have to be paid some dollars not to read them. Am I right? I know they are difficult to manage, but then so am I. There it goes. The light I mean. Good night.

Dec. 2nd

We left Macao this morning at about nine o'clock and arrived here (Hong Kong) about half past one this afternoon. I took the watch at 12 o'clock and brought the ship to anchor; therefore had the balance of the days duty. The days duties now are comparatively easy for we have everything in good order and all of us Officers and men feel proud of our ship. She is the best looking and fastest Naval Steamer afloat. This is acknowledged by all hands and everybody.

Lieut. Taylor[54] of the *Mississippi* has command of the Steamer *Queen*. It is reported that Commissioner Marshall[55] has applied to the Commodore for a Steamer to take him to Shanghai, and that the Commodore, instead of giving him a Steamer, had chartered a small Brig called the *Brenda*[56] for the purpose and as Mr. Glisson our First Lieut. is the oldest one they have without a command he is to have command. Now this [is] rumor, but I hope it may be true although I would like to have the Commodore order the *Powhatan* there. I would like to have Glisson leave the ship and indeed no one that I can mention would regret it. If he and Purser Eldredge[57] were to leave the *Powhatan* would be a happy ship. They are the two evil spirits amongst us.

We are now in a place where we need not fear to take a full breath. 'Tis healthy here, but both in Whampoa and Macao the Foreigner was and is to some extent yet in fear of the fever. This fever is the "Remittent Fever of China" and appears in the full always. I believe the Rice harvest is the cause. It is very seldom fatal but it wrecks ones constitution. Produces in its worst stages congestion and inflammation of lungs and bowels. The severest cases in the Squadron were Dr. Maxwell of our ship and Mr. Draper,[58] Manager of the Telegraphic arrangements and attached to the *Susquehanna*. Maxwell is entirely well, but Draper is yet too sick to be moved. He will be about in a week, entirely out of danger.

Yesterday we had lots of visitors on board and the same thing has occurred today. I have promised to dine on board the *Susquehanna* tomorrow. The weather has become settled and today we had sunshine. The first for 3 or 4 weeks. Residents here say that we will have good weather now for a long time. On Friday evening the ship *Jamestown*[59] at anchor in this harbour took fire from "spontaneous combustion" which was put out by the assistance of our men. She has on board 600 tons of Labuan Coal which is liable to ignite spontaneously above any kind of coal known. The *Jamestown* being the 6th ship out here that has taken fire from it. The *Susquehanna* has some of it in her bunkers which has been there two years. We have over 200 tons of it in our bunkers and it is supposed that when the Commodore hears of the *Jamestown's* taking fire that he will order ours taken out, to do which will be an awful job and take us 6 weeks to do it. I would rather he send us on a cruise to Manilla and Shanghai so as to burn it up, but for my part I don't entertain any fears about it and would sign a protest against taking it out if it would do any good. We have every facility for putting the coal out in case they do take fire.

Monday Morning, Dec. 5th

I have no additional news this morning except that there is a report current that the Emperor of Japan is dead. This news came from Shanghai. Now if the Emperor is dead by a custom of their country, they are not allowed to transact any business for the space of three years and this would interfere greatly with our Japan Expedition. For my part I don't believe one word of it for we have no reliable source of information, and I feel satisfied that it is nothing more than what we call a "galley yarn." Someone probably who has read about Japan and aware of the custom that I first spoke of had started for the purpose of exciting either the hopes or fears of us forming the expedition. Some will say "good" we will go right home now for no business can be contracted. Others will say "no" the Commodore will wait 3 years and keep us out here. Then some will say we are going home immediately for our presence is needed in the Mediterranean. Such is the manner in which we all talk. Some are anxious to get home immediately others want to see Japan first and some wish to go around the world. Of the latter part I am one and would willingly hail the news as welcome tomorrow that we were to proceed home via Cape Horn, and I would feel satisfied at not seeing Japan. We expect the Store Ship *Lexington*[60] every day. She sailed from Philade. nearly 6 months ago, and as soon as she arrived I think we will all start for Japan.

Dec. 6th

Yesterday I was ashore awhile and enjoyed myself a little by playing 2 or 3 games of my favorite game. You see I will enjoy myself. [. . .] My favorite game you know is Billiards. 'Tis the only amusement I take. We have ten pin alleys here and the use of the English Club rooms, but I never indulge. Only in one game; you know that is what I used to "go out" so much for when I was home. You don't blame me do you?

Last night there was a performance on board the *Susquehanna* by the theatrical troupe. Our troupe will be about in a week or 10 days. Amongst them is an old scene painter and for the act or drop curtain, he has made a painting from an original design of Pocahontas saving the life of Capt. Smith in which Old King Powhatan stands out in bold relief.

The "whisker" order has been rescinded and all the Officers are splurging. Moustaches &c. Sewell has a perfect brush or bristle heap over his mouth. Faron has about 10 hairs on his upper lip. Stamm don't shave at all and Kellogg only his upper lip. I have the same old Erie goatee under my chin, but I think of letting all grow for vanities sake.

I don't know when I have been so hard pushed to fill a sheet as I am this. I see something perhaps every day chinesely that would be novel to you at home but being here amongst them and seeing so much filth and degradation one is filled with disgust and dislike to mention anything connected with them. The deplorable state of morals here would astound you. Girls at the age of 10, 12 and 14 years being [s]old in sin. In the streets you come across the most horrid cases of disease. Girls are often worn out and thrown aside to die at the early age of 16 and 17 years. The families that live in boats are often unable to procure sufficient employment to feed themselves. On all the boats where there are children, the boys have a kind of buoy made fast by a girdle around the waist which floats them in case they fall overboard. The girl children are not provided with anything of this kind and if they fall overboard they drown. Nothing is thought of it.

Dec. 7th

Our weather for the past two days has been the most miserable. Nothing but rain and wind, and the transit to and from the shore the most disagreeable. A day or two ago we received information through a doubtful source that one of the Slope [Sloop] of War *Plymouth*'s boats had been sent ashore. She being then at anchor at the Bonin Islands to fish and hunt and that a short time after the boat left the ship a breeze sprang up which soon increased to a Typhoon. All were anxious on board about the return of the boat. Night came on. The next morning and the next, yet no boat returned. The gale decreased and another boat manned and sent in search of the 1st one. The search was kept up for twelve days. They having scoured the whole neighboring coast and islands without success, and the sad tale ends by stating that in the missing boat there were 13 men and an Officer.

Yesterday, Mr. Fryer a merchant here, and Mr. Pegram of our ship received letters from Officers on the *Plymouth* which verified the above statement with very little deviation except that the first report stated the Officer in charge of the boat to be Lieut. Balch[61] which was a mistake, the unfortunate and much regretted loss being that in the person of Lieut. Matthews[62] and thirteen men! It has cast a gloom over all hands of us. I knew Matthews slightly, having met him at Lou Choo.

The *Plymouth* arrived and anchored in this harbour this afternoon. Mr. Glisson our first Lieut. has gone on board of her. When he returns we will learn all the particulars of the most sad affair. Matthews was an unmarried man, but probably more than probable some of the poor unfortunate sailors who were thus hurried to their Eternal Homes and summoned to appear before the Holy Shrine with "all their imperfections" and "with no recovering" left behind them wives and children, mothers, sisters. Oh! 'tis sad, sad, sad. 'Tis now near nine o'clock and Mr. Glisson has not returned. I can well imagine how few in the Navy will regret these losses of Lieutenants. I mean amongst the Passed Midshipman particularly. Their first impulse will be to get the Register and scratch off their names. The names of Adams and Matthews. Adams died as I have written you on the 4th of October. The boat that left the *Plymouth* on the 25th of October occasioned the other loss. I have but little else if anything to write about tonight.

I learn that a row had occurred on board the *Susquehanna* (she lies close by our ship) this morning between Lieut. Randolph[63] and the Master Mr. Bennett.[64] They came to blows and Randolph has preferred charges against Bennett so that we will have another Court Martial, and probably another Officer will be sent home. The force of Officers in the Squadron is becoming very weak and 'tis said that the Commodore has written every mail to have Officers sent out here to fill vacancies. We are now short two Passed Midshipmen and one Engineer less than what we started with. Gray[65] who was ordered to the *Southampton* and Wilson who was sent home, and Whipple who has been ordered to the *Queen*. The vacancy occasioned by the death of

Adams has been filled by Nicholson[66] our former Master, and his place filled by Lowry ordered from the *Susquehanna*.

Today has been my "day's duty" and as I will be my own free agent to-morrow I will have plenty of ti[m]e to fill up this much drawn and windy letter. So for the night, I will stop, trusting that you are well, in good spirits, thinking occasionally of the one who is penning this to you in the strong hope of a speedy return to you and then Lide one of the most endearing and confiding embraces. It makes me glow to think of it, but good night. I'll have my sheet filled with nonsense as you will perhaps think it and give you the pain of reading it. Again good night and may God Bless you.

Dec. 8th

I finished last night when I was in a humour to continue all night. Mr. Glisson returned from the *Plymouth* and the statement of the sad affair in which poor Matthews perished beyond a doubt is alas too true. Capt. Kelly[67] the Commander of the *Plymouth* was on board today and he states that he was going in the boat with Matthews, but that recollected just before the boat shoved off that he had engaged himself to meet a gentlemen that after-noon. So he didn't go. He says that Matthews was the best Officer he had and that the men who were lost were the best men he had on the ship, and that Matthews went on the boat reluctantly. That he had been in ill spirits for 3 or 4 days, having had for several nights previous had most horrid dreams of which he had spoken to his messmates. A vessel named the *Koohinor* has ar-rived here, and report having spoken to the boat in which they were on the same day they left the ship, and advised them to remain as it would certainly blow a gale of wind before the night. This is the last we know of them. Not a doubt but that in this terrible gale the little boat swamped and all were lost.

A Russian vessel arrived here some days ago and reported that the Zio-goon or Emperor of Japan was dead. There I mentioned this before I know.

I have been Caterer of our mess now nearly 6 months and during that time we have lived well and at a moderate price. Yesterday there was some discus-sion about my buying some furniture for the mess deck room and I strenu-ously objected. This morning it was moved by Mr. Faron that I be broken and a new caterer elected. Kellogg and Stamm against me. There being an equal division I at once threw up the books and the money for some voted against me. So we were unable to get a caterer when at last Fauth was elected. [. . .] I have just discovered that some pusillanimous wretch has taken the whole inside of my portfolios out and so help me if I can find out who. [. . .] There are some confounded scoundrels lurking about the mess. Whether one of my mess mates or not I can't tell but I am inclined to suspect, and I have my eyes on him.

Saturday Morning, Dec. 10th

My Dear Lide,

Our Theatre opens next Monday night with "Charles XII and Box and Cox." I took some little cold last night and this morning my back aches some considerable this morning. I am increasing in weight, weighing now 170 pounds, my hair did not come out much, it felt weak for a while but now 'tis strong and longer than it has been for years. I think I am now pretty well acclimated. The mail has not arrived yet. It is said that Lieut. Gillis[68] of The *Plymouth* is going home if he does there will be more changing and shifting of officers. The *Mississippi* will be here today or tomorrow from Macao.

U.S.S. *Powhatan*, Hong Kong, China, Dec. 16th, 1853

My Dearest Wife,

In my last letter to you I mentioned my intention of journalizing my future correspondence and this morning I find myself seated, as Dan Ward[69] would invariably write in commencing an epistle, to carry my intentions into effect. As a preface or an excuse I have only to say that I claim you're most patient indulgence and beg that you will suspend any hasty judgment upon remarks that may be introduced tending to create uneasiness or disquietude. My idea is to write not only of subjects that may be interesting, instructive, or amusing connected directly or indirectly with the "Expedition" but to unfold *myself* to write in fact as I feel and think, without reserve. In such a correspondence there must necessarily be a constant mutability of style and subject, and this in unison with inability will make the arrangement, I fear, tedious to you. I would make it in form a diary but for my variable and uncertain duties but hoping that by it I may improve myself and afford you some pleasant moments. I thus commence.

Yesterday I went ashore with Mr. Lawrence of the *Susquehanna*, and Mr. Faron. We landed on the main road, or as it is called [Q—n?] Road about a half mile below the town and immediately in front of the English Barracks where Red Coats and crowns were drilling. This road extends around the entire island of Hong Kong and is beautiful, level, hard cut tracks of pleasing and ample width, the entire length being about 25 miles. After reaching town by this road we stopped by the City Hotel kept by an Englishman named Shaw who bought it a few days ago from a man by the name of Brooks and in the occasion of the transfer Mr. Brooks gave a splendid "Tiffin" after which there was music and dancing. At his place we remained awhile, played a couple of games of billiards and started for an establishment unknown to Faron and myself but according to Lawrence well known by him for the purpose of getting some sausages. Now we have heard no doubt that in China, Dogs and Cats are considered delicacies, though I must say that amongst my Celestial acquaintances and they number about a hundred, cats not dogs are eaten. Never the less the idea of going to an unknown place in China to eat sausages was rather revolting. I imagined all sorts of things on our way, but suddenly we brought up and was ushered into a well-furnished room in which we seated around a "groaning table" I met some 3 or 4 Captains of Merchant vessels with whom I was acquainted and Mr. Schaeffer, our former Masters Mate who deserted at Whampoa. He was now the most polite man in the world—done the "Gentleman" to perfection insisted upon our taking something to eat and drink which we done, excused ourselves and left. Lawrence inquired for sausages but they had been eaten save one link which I was fortunate enough to get. From here we returned to Shaw's where L[awrence] and I played another game and returned on board at 9.

Since this morning I have done but little else than read *Steam* awhile, and Shakespeare awhile. Our Theatrical corps made their debut last Monday night and surpassed everything in China. They performed well and the scenery and dresses cannot be surpassed. A goodly quantity of liquor was drank by the officers and their guests. The Hurricane deck being the "Boxes" was graced by the appearance of some 8 or 9 English and American ladies. Several of them "good looking" too. Last night a similar entertainment was given on board the English Frigate *Winchester*[70] for "Admiral Somebody"[71] I forget names. I am told the "chow—chow" arrangements were excellent but the theatrical arrangements were not mediocre.

I feel dull tonight my hand feels bloated. Mind wanders. I'll go and smoke. So good night. This ends the first day or rather the "commence" of this style

Dec. 17th

Awoke this morning feeling very well, and during the entire day until this have felt well, but I now have a very slight headache. Last night had most singular dreams, awoke during the night several times and my thought would revert to home and Lide and once muttered "God grant that we shall meet again." This dreaming is periodical with me and whole weeks will pass and not a dream. Then for a succession of nights there will be a constant dream. Nothing of any note has happened today. We finished coal about 12 O'clock. The day brought clear and warm, tonight 'tis cloudy. The *Mississippi* arrived about 5 O'clock this afternoon, none of her officers have been on board yet, but as she comes from Head Quarters we may learn something when they all come up. I much detest this ship visiting, nothing follows from it but drinking. Now there is no use denying that I drink, but little as it now is I intend lessening it on the first of next month. I intend taking a most solemn vow to drink nothing intoxicating in the space of one year. We have now in the Harbor of Hong Kong the *Mississippi*, The *Macedonian*, The *Plymouth*, *Susquehanna* and the Great *Powhatan*. Now we are the fastest, best looking Steamer of a naval kind in the world, and we have the best corps of "Thespians" and best band of Negro Minstrels[72] afloat. The Minstrels are making preparations to give a grand concert next Tuesday evening.

Sunday Evening, Dec. 18th

One week from Christmas! One year ago we were apart but living in the hope that would not be long ere we met—how is it now? What are our hopes? When will we embrace each other again? There are questions that I am unable to answer, and I look forward with anxiety for the arrival of the mail from home and devour the news from there with avidity in the hope to find something promising to the intense desire of getting home from this Japan Expedition. I know little else that when we first arrived at Loo Choo, and since the *Mississippi* arrived with the Commodore last evening with his entire suite of scientific gentlemen we have had our fill of rumors out of which after putting them in sieve and collecting the most sensible and likely of the lot I conclude that all is glorious humbug.

The Commodore transferred his flag from the *Mississippi* to the *Susquehanna* this morning after which the *Mississippi* got underway and left for Macao where she takes on board the Hon. Humphrey Marshall and then proceeds to Canton with him after which she returns here. One of the rumors likely to have a foundation is the following: that the Ringgold Squadron is at Manilla and that Commo. Ringgold is remaining there to avoid reporting to Commodore Perry which he has orders from the Department to do. So the Rajah (Com. P.) intends sending one of the Steamers over there, and that Steamer is the *Powhatan*. The run from here to Manilla is only about

3 days and for my part would like to go. These rumors, or as they are called on board ships "Galley Bricks" state that the *Lexington* is there. These reports you are aware must give rise to a great deal of conversation—such has been the case today. And all the talk and excitement resolves itself into these facts. That the Hospital at Macao and the Residence ashore of the Commodore and the gentlemen composing the scientific corps have been broken up. That the *Mississippi* has arrived and left as above stated. That the Commodore has changed his flag to the *Susquehanna*. That the *Southampton* has arrived at Macao from Loo Choo and that we are going to have a great entertainment on board this ship next Tuesday evening! I did not see any of the *Mississippi*'s officers.

I went ashore this morning and remained about two hours at "Shaws" reading California Newspapers. The latest dates of which are October 25th. On my return on board I found Messrs. Draper and Williams[73] of the Lithographic corps and from them gathered the "say so's" as they are always near the Commodore. Draper looks bad yet he is quite well though. The reason of the change of the "Broad Pendant" is that the *Susquehanna* affords better accommodations for entertaining and better quarters for the "Artists." I think that we will make a move to the Northward inside of a month. "We shall see, what we shall see." There has been a difficulty on board the *Susquehanna* between Lieut. Randolph and Passed Mid. Bennett. It appears that B[ennet] met R[andolph] on shore and because R[andolph] would not settle a former difficulty with pistols which Bennett had with him. Bennett slapped the others face. R[andolph] has preferred charges and we may have another Court Martial. Everybody wants to go home. I don't know one officer in the Squadron that would not prefer starting for home than for Japan.

Monday Evening, Dec 19th

This morning took a walk ashore with the Chief Engr. for the purpose of hunting up Thermometers, Hydrometers, Steel, &c. we found all the articles in want and at One P.M. returned on board ship. Weather good during the day, save a pain in the back! All persons in this climate get a kind of Muscular Rheumatism or Neuralgia and that is what ails me. I either have it [in] my head, back or sides. I learned today of Mr. Parkers[74] sickness. He is a man 56 years of age and a grandfather. He is our Sailmaker. There is no use mentioning the matter. You can guess. Very few of those who have indulged in such luxuries have escaped. How men can make such perfect *animals* of themselves; I can't for the life of me imagine. What horror depicted on the countenances of those who have been attacked by this most dreadful disease. Thank God that I have you too think of whose soul unites with mine in this, whose very being I feel installed in mine and if she could see me, see my heart and all my actions she could do but little else than thank her maker for uniting two such spirits. This is strong language Lide, but 'tis my thoughts, my feelings, my heart that dictates it.

This morning I went in a store, kept by an Englishman named Lane, to buy some points for pencils. I took a box and when I was about paying for it I stopped and asked how much it was? 75 cents said he! I paid it. That is 6 cents for one point to a pencil! I only mention this to show how things sell here. That Chinamen do not make.

This evening I passed our front [illegible text] room listening to a rehearsal of the Serenaders [illegible text] grand affair spoken of last evening does not come off until Thursday now. This is in consequence of the Commodores sickness. He is confined to his room with the "Gout." I hear that the *Plymouth* and *Macedonian* have orders to get ready for Sea. At our last performance the Boatswain Mr. Whiting[75] invited some friends, and when they came alongside they were ordered to shove off. On hearing this the next day Mr. W[hiting] made some noise about it, and Mr. Glisson the 1st Lieut. and the biggest ass that ever lived said Mr. W[hiting] had no right to invite anyone! Mr. W[hiting] said he had, and so he had as much right as any officer in the ship. In consequence of this Whiting is doing his best to get exchanged to some other ship. I hope he will not get away for he is one of the best sailors in the Navy and we would miss his services very much. No more tonight.

Dec. 20th

Today I had the duty, and the manner in which scrubbing brushes and white washing. Disposed of themselves. Everything of minor importance being thrown aside to the cleaning and brightening of things. The great affair has changed so often that I am now almost afraid to say when it will be, but as the invitations have all been given out for tomorrow evening we may then expect it.

For some time, and in fact until within a few days past Mr. Sewell has appeared estranged and addressed himself to his assistants only in an official capacity. Sewell and myself, used to have lengthy conversations and often I would go to his room but this stopped suddenly after Mr. Holland joined the ship. No fault of Holland at all. But as I said above, within a few days past Mr. S has been very sociable. I can account for it only in the light that

Sewell has learned the fact that because an Engr. is a 1st Asst. he has not the largest amount of "savi" as the Chinamen say in French. Again I am about to close for the night, and if I keep up writing a good night every time I put this aside 'twill be filled with "Good Nights" so here ends those.

Dec. 23rd

Last night the Great Entertainment and concert came off on board this ship. Though announced for Thursday, for some reason they changed it and a most magnificent affair it was. The Quarter Deck was enclosed with a splendid array of Flags of all Nations, and the Captain was dressed in Chandelier Style with bayonets, muskets, flags, evergreens and bouquets. The Gangway and ladders were dressed in fine style, bouquets suspended over each Hatchway and all illuminated by some 300 candles. The Engine Room was illuminated and on the Port Side of the Quarter Deck a stage erected for the men. The Capt. gave a splendid supper, so did the Ward Room, and both steerages. The Concert passed off admirably and everyone appeared and were truly highly gratified. Supper commenced about 10 P.M. and 'twas Midnight ere the guests had all left the ship. The attendance of ladies was rather small, but we had the Governor of Hong Kong[76] and The Great Sir Admiral Fleetwood Pellow K.C.B. M.G.K. &c. &c. &c. The Englishmen have an idea that the performance of the Serenaders was a facsimile of our Negroes at home. It being in [. . .] perfectly [. . .] to them. You may imagine that some considerable liquor was drank and that in consequence several individuals more or less got pretty tight. I enclose you by way of variety one of our "bills" of course I could not do anything in the way of writing last night as our steerage was crowded all the time and the table spread with the "chow chow." The *Powhatan* has again "taken them all down." They give an affair of the Theatrical Kind and a supper to follow on board the *Susquehanna* sometime next week. I received an invitation to dine on Christmas by Mr. Stewart and I have promised to attend. This is the season you know for festivities and everyone here seems determined to participate and talk much of their friends at home. The toast most frequently drank amongst us here is "the old folks at home." I am in hopes that my friends with whom I may drink a toast on Christmas will be careful not to mix it with anything like a Lola Montes[77] arrangement for I had sufficient of that last Christmas at Geo. Bourdettes.

The *Macedonian* sailed today. It is said for Loo Choo. An order was issued by the Commodore yesterday for the several American Men of War in the harbor to take turns as guard ship. That is to send from the ship what has [. . .] duty sends a [. . .] to any ship with American Colors that may [. . .] and to gather any kind of information that they may be possessed of, ascertain whether they have any provisions for sale. I can't imagine the reason of the issue of the order. Only one thing occurred last night to mar the harmony of the whole affair. One of our Coal heavers got drunk and commenced yelling. It lasted but for a moment when he was soon cared for by the way of a gag and double irons. Our officers and men are very proud of the entertainment. My head aches again tonight and in consequence must stop tonight. Many sore heads no doubt were felt this morning, too much punch.

Friday Evening, Dec. 23rd.

This morning got up with some headache which has continued unremittingly all day. Took a dose of Rheubarb and Magnesium about 1 O'clock and am to take some quinines tonight. The trouble is a severe cold in the head. The Store Ship *Supply* arrived here this afternoon from Macao. This morning we rec'd orders to paint our Water Wheels black. They have allways [*sic*] been red. [. . .] We have a Bom[b] Boatman by the name of Sally who furnishes the men with extra provisions, fruit, &c. and is a good natured inoffensive Chinaman. Some cowardly rascals got him Below Decks this morning and beat him shamefully. All hands were called to muster and their ring leader picked out by Sally and the Jack ass of a 1st Lieut. let the rascals go unpunished because the man said he didn't do it and then issued an order that the bom[b] Boat should not come along side anymore and that all the bounty and ration money should be stopped. Thus punishing all hands innocent and guilty. This is injustice and tends to make them sulky and almost insolent. I wish Congress would repeal the law doing away with flogging.[78] Indeed 'twould do some of our "civies" a "powerful good" to feel occasionally the "stripes."

Immediately after that event one of the Engineers of the *Susquehanna*, Mr. Henderson,[79] was ordered the other night to go in a boat as Officer of the Boat, a duty which belongs to a Passed or other Midshipman, and he refused. He was then ordered by the Capt. after refusing the 1st Lieut. and he would not go. He was suspended and 'tis said he will be tried by Court Martial for disobedience of orders, and if he is, he will get the best of it. I would like it to be my case, and then I would like them to send me home for it. I am heartily disgusted with all China and all Japan Expedition. It really seems to me that doing laboring work for 50 Cents a day at home is preferable to one's situation out here. However we have got our feet in it and there is no getting them out.

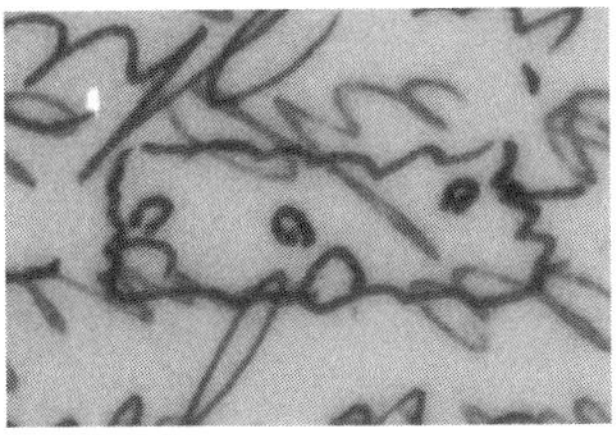

9. A small drawing of a pool table.

Christmas Eve! [December 24th], 1853

The most dull and "poorest" one I have ever spent. Indeed 'tis a most miserable one, to be sure. In the last one we were absent from one another but then the distance was not so great. (Just this very moment an invitation came in from the Ward Room to take a glass of Punch with them and I have done so and returned.) The toast drank was "Sweethearts and Wives" although I had just taken a dose of quinine I drank a large glass of the Punch. [. . .] They are now laughing and talking in the Ward Room making the best of it. One thing was said by Sewell which struck me. It was "I hope Gentlemen to spend the next Christmas Eve in California." Now I want you to tell me why this expression struck me. Was on shore this afternoon and played a game of billiards with Mr. Rogers. I only mention this because I wish to refer to it some future time. I will mention one thing which you will not understand by its brevity my space not permitting a lengthy uninteresting explanation to you. (Thought the white held instead of the red. Followed ensuing game by wrong stroke for a six.) [*sketch of a pool table with several balls on it*]

King, Faron, Holland and Kellogg are ashore as it is Christmas Eve of course. Chinamen know nothing of that. The English and Americans wish other European residents ashore are making the best of it as we do at home. Our Ward Room is festooned and draped with evergreens and bouquets. Our Commodore made the different messes a "Cumshaw" today. (Cumshaw in Chinese means present.) We received a quarter of Mutton, a ham, 2 jars of preserved ginger and several baskets of oranges. Among the oranges was a lot of the "Simon pure Mandarin Oranges." They are the best I have ever tasted and require no knife to cut them. The inside being free from the skin and the skin is loose so that it has only to be taken off by the fingers in the process of which there is no danger of coming in contact with the juice. Now hams cost out here from 25 to 75 cents per pound and mutton from 30 to 40 cents, and the Mandarin Oranges cannot be purchased so you can imagine the value of the "Cumshaw." I forgot to mention two chickens, very large ones. The Captains received a Turkey, Turkies out here are very dear, bringing 3 to 5 dollars apiece. Our mess has purchased one for tomorrow and if the *Susquehanna*'s have not I will have to do without turkey.

Yesterday I mentioned the affair of beating a Chinaman by the name of Sally and the fact of his selecting the man that done it. This morning the same man was arranged before the Captain at the instigation of the Chinaman who was anxious more to have the bom[b] boat come alongside so that he could make the "pigeon" than to have the man punished, and the Captain talked to the man in such a manner as to make him reword it. He really said up and down that he done it. He was immediately trussed up to a stanchion in double irons and the restrictions taken off the other men. The man whose name is Moreley christianized Martin, performed the character of Ulica in Charles the twelfth. This you know is a ladies character and the lady therefore has painful aides in this. During the muster yesterday and before all the names had been called for the purpose of giving the Chinaman an opportunity to "claim the man" the Governor of Hong Kong was announced and the people "piped down." This Governor is the Gerovis or Jarvis that was taken prisoner at Lundys Lane. He was saluted with 17 guns.

Christmas Night, [December 25th], 1853

This morning I brewed a batch of Egg Nog for the Mess—hot, never drank hot Egg Nog before. Afterwards joined in a bowl in the other Steerages. At ½ past 11 started from the ship and went onboard the *Susquehanna* where I was received most cordially by the Engineers and took dinner with them. Had roast pig, roast mutton, capins [capons] &c. &c. A very fine dinner. While onboard there the British Steamer *Hermes*[80] arrived in port and the *Mississippi*. The *Hermes* is the Steamer that has been successful in arresting Chinese pirates out here. I would mention some of these cases of piracy but it is so common an occasion and so little thought of here and decidedly uninteresting to me that I forbear they answer to our petty larcenies at home. Seldom is any life lost except on the side of the Chinese and they have plenty to spare. They are like mosquitos.

About half past 3 I went onboard the *Mississippi* and saw everybody enjoying themselves in wine and "chow chow" to keep hearts content. Danby I never saw so tight before. Perfectly happy, but he would not drink or listen to anything like "old folks at home." Corp. Slack looks slovenly compared to his appearance when in Erie. Jimmy Shirk has been transferred to the *Vandalia* now at Loo Choo.

'Tis now near 8 o'clock and things are comparatively quiet. Our men today smuggled liquor onboard and a considerable quantity of them are tight. All around they have made it as merry a Christmas as possible, and my earnest hope and prayer is that the next Christmas may be spent by me with you. We have spent but two together since our marriage and they were in Erie. One at Browns, the other at the little house on Sassafras Street. Hoping that you have a special and most happy Christmas and that you may spend a merry New Year. I will close tonight as the noise has again commenced. For tomorrow 'tis my day of duty but I think I will be able to fill up this sheet.

The *Mississippi* brings the news that the *Lexington* has arrived at Macao. She will probably be down here in a few days. There has been considerable talk amongst the Engineers here as to the Examinations should one take place out here. They all seem to think in that case that I would pass No. 1 of the Seconds. Nothing I cannot deny for it is even palpable to myself and that is by the Chief Engineers in the Squadron. Messrs. Gay, Archibold, and Sewell. I am well thought of.

Of this Chinese war, we know but very little, as we do not feel in any way interested. We never examine any of the papers published here. I understand however that Peking is the hands of the Rebels. Shanghai and Amoy have been for some time. I saw the Commodore on the *Mississippi* and he was wrapped up in a blanket, said that he did not receive a letter in the last mail and although he had a bad cold he thought because he did not receive a letter was as much the matter with him as anything.

All conviviality has ended in the Ward Room, ended by one of their officers being suspended. The Officer being Dr. Wheelwright. It appears that it occurred in consequence of the Doctors guest asking for a Violin and as Mr. Boudinot owns one, and at the time Officer of the Deck. Dr. Wheelwright sent one of the boys on deck to ask for the loan of it. The boy returned and said before all hands that Mr. B[oudinot] said No he would not loan it, where Dr. W[heelwright] said he was no gentleman. What occurred afterwards except the suspension of Wheelwright, I have not yet learned. Mr. Chief Engineer Jesse Gay has been appointed "Fleet Engineer" by the Commodore. So Mr. Danby is Chief of the *Mississippi* and is now and has been acting in that capacity for some time.

I am now at a loss for something to write about and must really close. So good night my Dearest and first love. May God Bless and Protect you and may you live in easy quietude and patience for the return of your most devoted and attached husband. And when the tidings from him may happen to be gloomy and the dark clouds of despair look threateningly at the hope of a speedy return, think then that his heart is ever with you. His hopes your hopes, his life your life. George

This prayer is my only Christmas Gift.

U.S Ste. *Powhatan*, Hong Kong, China, December 29th, 1853

Today all of the ships in the harbor or at "half mast" and the American Man O' War fired and it guns at noon, on account of official information having been rec'd of the death of Vice President King.[81] The information came by the *Lexington*. Of course we were before aware of it.

Chapter Three
January 1–June 23, 1854

Sunday Night, January 1st, 1854

Another year gone! And perhaps there will be another till we meet! Yesterday the Store Ship *Southampton* came in from Macao. All the squadron are now here except those on their way to or at Loo Choo and Shanghai. Our Boatswain, Sailmaker and Carpenter with gangs of men from our ship and other ships have been on board the *Lexington* every day since her arrival making repairs and getting her ready for sea—'tis expected that she will ready by next Saturday. Comm. Perry made a signal yesterday inviting the officers to "call" on him today, and many of them availed themselves the privileges and they tell me that he had a most sumptuous table set out with brandy too. The mail is not in yet. 'Tis reported that we all sail for Loo Choo next Monday and that we are to take the *Lexington* tow. The Officers of the *Lexington* are the seediest looking crowd extant head cases.

Jan 2nd

This morning rec'd an invitation from Mr. Alexander to dine with him as it was his birthday. [. . .] It was without a doubt the most "stylish" and best cooked dinner I have eaten since I've been in China. The other guest was Mr. Fithian.[1] [. . .] At sundown I went ashore and met greatly serious drinking parties. I found Logan and Al Rutherford very "tight." I heard a boat and took them aboard the *Mississippi*. I took a pledge on New Year's day to not drink any at all, and although sorely tempted with wine &c. at dinner, and afterwards ashore. I remained firm and intend to keep so. This is no vain or idle promise. I intend to keep it. [. . .] All the different departments and the messes are making preparations for leaving next week. A rumor is afloat that we are all to be in Japan by the 15th February.

I feel better than I have for a long while, and feel dearly more disgusted with the United States Navy.

Jan 3rd

I learn that a Court of Inquiry is assembled on board the Flag Ship this morning for the purpose of investigating the conduct of some of the Officers. I opine that the *Lexington* crew will be handled without gloves. We shall see. Refusing emphatically to even drink wine I was asked if I didn't fear being Court Martialed as the cause! No! for 1st I never have been that drunk that I was unable to do my duty or present myself before any one. You know that, for I have been as much under the influence of liquor in your presence as ever I was in my life, too much makes *me* sick, not a *beast*. 2ndly I quit because it suits me. The reasons I tell them are my own. They are as follows: Rum costs money, it affects the mind as well as the body, its influence in action is a false energy and an impure irrational excitement. I have been using the accused poison now some nine years. It has never benefited me. At the end of every year I was not better off than at the commencement. So I eschew it. I sign no pledge. I take no oath but simply promise myself the *balm*. So here I am not an advocate but an actor of Temperance.

I learn that Mid Shipman Stockton[2] of the *Susquehanna* took "french" the other day as has been his habit for some time but until then escaped—is to be Court Martialed. This Squadron ever it gets home will present a series of Court Martials in extent unheard of in the Annuals of Naval Service if they continue as they have been going on for the short space of time that we have been here.

Alexander is sick yet, with inflammation of the bladder which arose from a disease of another nature. He told me himself yesterday. It was as I expected. Lost man! I saw daguerreotypes of his "Kitt," his Mother, his Wife, a madam somebody, the French woman he had in New York and one of a very pretty woman, the wife of an Army officer with whom he got acquainted at East Port, and used to his own purpose!! He is called a "*Fast Man.*" He does a little of everything but drinks to excess. He is a most polished rascal in a gentlemanly way. Some time ago he was cured of a something. This is very indelicate and although [it is] my journals and your letter. I have the face to write it and then ask to be excused! I am writing now of things anything but interesting to you I know.

This evening an order was passed that a Passed Midshipman should go with the working gang. This I suppose is to keep the men from getting drunk. Now we only have two Passed Midshipman and they keep watch on deck. Thus they are thrown into extra duty and that too of a kind the most disagreeable. Then we have to tow the "tub" to Japan. The ship is as bad as her officers. To be sure there are some of her officer's good fellows. Minor[3] and Harris[4] are the only two of that kind though. We will no doubt sail for Loo Choo early next week.

On Thursday night an Ethiopic and Dramatic entertainment is to be given on board The *Mississippi* and I have promised to be there. [. . .] I expect by this time you are in Philada. where I will continue to direct all my letters until further orders from you. By having my letters sent there as I do they cost me 50 cents. Rawle Drinker & Co[5] charge twenty-five cents for every letter they receive and that your letters to me cost us 75 cents altogether. Rather than not yet getting them I would allow any charge that I could possibly pay. Through Drinker & Co. they are safe so keep on directing as usual. R.D. & Co. have "busted" and the business is carried on by Drinker & Co. now. Rawle was the sufferer as I learn, and that to such an extent that a subscription had to be raised for the support of Rawles family. They are all Philadelphians.

There is poor Charley Gray a Passed Midshipman who came out on our ship and was transferred to The *Southampton*, I fear a goner, he is eternally drunken. I am afraid he will be "hauled up" if he doesn't soon "hold up." He is one of the best souls living, has a heart full of goodness, and his only enemy is Rum and none ask him to make friends with the "destroyer" but himself.

Jan 4th

This morning Sewell,[6] Bibby and myself went ashore and ascended the mountain on the island called "Victoria Peak"[7] a height of about 3500 feet. We were an hour and a half getting up and only 25 minutes coming down. On the peak we found two Chinamen asleep alongside a basket of sweet potatoes a bamboo reed with a flag on it and a little fire. We roused them up and learned that they were "look outs" for the Mail Steamer and that the flag and stick was the signal. We just got at the foot of the hill on our return when the gun fired announcing the arrival of the Steamer. The two Chinamen made the Signal to The Peninsular and Oriental Steam Navigation Companies office. Where the gun was fired as we were pulling off to the Ship, we saw The Steamer coming. It will be 4 or 5 hrs yet before the letters come on board.

This morning Passed Midshipman Robb Selden was detached from our ship and ordered to The *Lexington*! Now Bob is one of the best old fellows alive, quiet, reserved and obliging. We are all very sorry that Bob is to leave us, but then the story says that Wager[8] and Stockton are to be ordered here! Mercy on us—worse and worse—one a drunken Passed Midshipman and the other a noisy troublesome boy. I hope the story may be untrue. I believe the

10. Unknown Chinese artist, "Victoria," Library of Congress.

Commodore feels some delicacy about trying that *Lexington* crew on acct. of their being so short a time in the Squadron.

I do really hope that an end will soon meet this most magnificent humbug. The humbug of the 19th Century. This Japan Bubble.

Jan. 4th (continued)

I have learned since my former sitting this morning that the Commodore said that all vessels should be ready for Sea by Wednesday and that 'tis not his intention to have them sail until after the arrival of the mail which will be due, or in fact is now due but which will arrive about the 12th after which we proceed at once to Loo Choo where we remain for a while and then go to Japan. I may make an hypothesis thus. We go to Japan, the emperor says that he will kindly treat all Americans who may be thrown accidentally on his shores, but that he will not conclude or enter into any Commercial Treaty. There remains for us to "dig out" with our tails between our legs and await instructions from home or endeavor to force a treaty by cannon balls and bomb shells. This would keep us out here our full time.

Another case: The Emperor says that he will enter into and make a Commercial Treaty. All the hopes of the projectors of this scheme and its present friends (if it has any) fulfilled to a letter. This would elate Commo. Perry to such an extent that he would send some vessels to California at once on her way home to make known the joyfull tydings. In the latter case the *Powhatan* being the fastest and most to be relied on Steamer he would send her. I think this is a fair description of the future at any rate 'tis all I know about Japan.

Monday Afternoon Jan. 9th 1853 [1854]

Mr. Arnold has been suspended on the *Mississippi*. I can't learn exactly for what but I presume for being drunk and raising some kind of row.

Eight o'clock. [. . .] I have heard all about Arnold's case which is kept a little secret. It appears that Alexander seeing that Arnold was in sober earnest with the sword, requested him to wait until he got a heavier sword and left Arnold in between the boilers waiting for him. Of course Alexander did not attend [*sic*] to go back, and while Arnold was waiting for him one of the Fireman who had just returned from "liberty" saw him with the sword and noticed that he was drunk. He went up to Arnold and wanted to take the sword from him. The man being drunk also and Arnold ordered the man to the mast. Ordering a man to the mast is sending him to the Main Mast where he remains until his case is investigated by the Executive Officer. When Arnold went up to make his report the 1st Lieut. could not tell which was the "drunkest" Arnold or the man, and he sent for Gay the Chief Engineer. Gay ordered the man away and told Arnold to go below. The next morning Gay sent for Arnold and was about giving him a lecture when Arnold broke out on him and with a curse said he would do no more duty on the ship. They might Court Martial him and be d[amne]d. This of course Mr. Gay had to report to the Captain, and the Captain at once suspended him. This is the extent of the case at present. The next step will be to report it to the Commodore and the result will follow. Arnold still swears that he will not do any more duty. How it will end I can't say, but likely Arnold will be dismissed.

US Steamer *Powhatan*, Hong Kong, Jan 10th, 1854

My Dearest Lide,

Every ship in the Squadron is to be placed under what is called "Sailing Orders" tomorrow, and the word has been passed that after tonight no officers or man shall leave any ship. Some appear to think that some of the ships will sail tomorrow, and as we are to tow the *Lexington* and she not being ready it is presumed that we will wait until she is ready and bring up the rear with the mail. However it is all surmise and speculation, not only as to starting but much more so as to returning. For my part I don't believe that Perry knows himself when we will return. The general impression, however, is that we will be back here next June. We will all be at Loo Choo before this month is out, and I suppose we will be in Loo Choo about another month before making the final start for Japan.

Morning, January 11th

Everything and everybody are ready for sea except the *Lexington* but I see no move towards starting. Tonight several men attempted to run off but were arrested. Six escaped from the *Susquehanna* last night and have [not] been arrested yet. Charges have been preferred against Arnold, but I think he will not be tried for the Commodore will know that he can't spare any Engineers, though some of the Engineers seem to think that half the number out here would be sufficient. These poor creatures think that because a machine works well for a while it will always do so. They may someday discover their mistake and alter their tone. I have dreamed two nights in succession of fire. Can't account for it.

The weather here is quite mild, like the month of May at home. [. . .] This morning they hoisted three Bulls on board and the decks are filled with bags and baskets of Potatoes, Fruit and Vegetables. The coops are full of Geese, Chickens and Ducks, and things look as if we didn't intend starving at any rate.

Evening of Jan 13th

The *Susquehanna* leads off, the *Powhatan* with the *Lexington* in tow on starboard quarter, and the *Mississippi* with the *Southampton* in tow on her port quarter. Here is the position. [*sketch of boats tied together*] How they will be arranged from Lou Chou to Japan I can't say. This is only half the number of vessels. The others being now at Lou Chou or on their way there. They are as follows: *Susquehanna*, *Powhatan*, *Mississippi*, *Macedonian*, *Saratoga*, *Plymouth*, *Vandalia*, *Supply*, *Southampton* and *Lexington*. Quite an army, and if I mistake not will make the Japanese look some astonished.

Good Night! Good bye again. Faithfully yours
George

Jan. 28th

Dr. Wheelwright told me this afternoon that the Commodore did not intend coming on board here until we get to Jeddo in consequence of a letter that he received from Capt. McCluney and that the Commodore had said

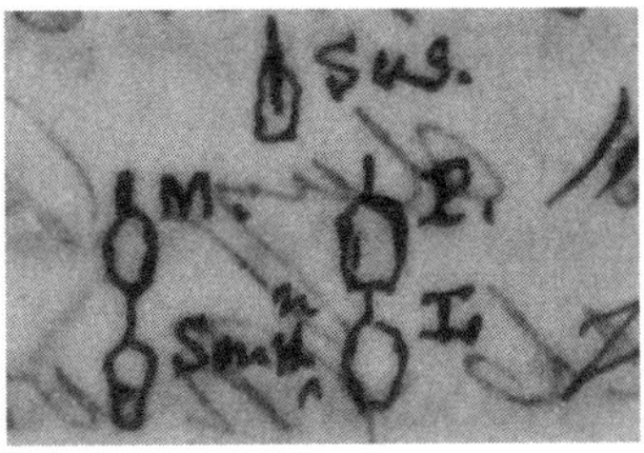

11. A small drawing of the alignment of the ships.

that if he had received the letter of McCluney's in time he would have sent the "house" on board. We can believe as much of this as we like. No doubt McCluney is terribly agonized about Perry's coming, but he can't prevent it or postpone it and if he has the sense he gets credit for he will make easy of the whole affair.

Mr. Bettleheim[9] the missionary resident at this place is of opinion (and it must be acknowledged that he has sources of information through his intercourse with the natives here) that the Japanese authorities will receive Perry kindly and give him a letter in answer to that of the President of the United States. The contents of which will translate that the Japanese are now as happy as they wish to be. That they will treat kindly all Americans that may be thrown accidentally on their shores and that they have now sufficient commerce with foreigners, and appreciating the kindness and goodness of the American people, nevertheless they find it impossible to engage in any acts of commerce or intercourse with them. He also says that the people here seem more and more reluctant to furnish us with provisions. (Through him everything of the kind is obtained) where he sends or orders six pigs, they send him one. Should anyone be desirous to learn anything of the Japan prospects give them the above information.

We leave here on the 5th proximo. The weather here moderate and we are coaling ship again. The Cabin for the Fleet Captains and the Captain of the *Powhatan* is nearly finished, and the house on our poop deck for the use of the Artists and sleeping apartments for the interpreter (Mr. Williams)[10] will be finished tomorrow.

Jan. 29th

At about 10 o'clock this morning I went ashore in company with Dr. Wheelwright, Messrs. Lowry, Sewell, McCauley, Bibby and Fauth. We tramped up to Shoudy[11] the great city and mounted the walls and entered the temples in spite of the resistance of the Loo Chooan Priests. We however satisfied them in one of their whims which we were made to understand in pantomime. That of taking off our shoes before entering the great temple, which is nothing more than a great barn of a place containing three joshes, and a quantity of filigree nonsense. Saw in the enclosure of the massive walls two enormous bells which we took the liberty of ringing. Leaving this place we made an ineffectual attempt to enter the gates of the palace, but the gates were too strongly barred and the walls too high for us.

We met one fellow, a Mandarin who spoke a few words in English and at first we tried to coax him to get us an entrance into the palace and then we threatened him, but to no purpose, as he said the Prince Regent was but a boy and that his mother was sick. From this fellow I learned that polygamy is not practiced here. We left him and continued our walk through the city and around the palace walls, when all of a sudden this fellow with a couple of others came up to us and offered us a kind of gingerbread, but as tough as leather, which out of compliment we partook of and darned stuff gave me a pain in the belly.

From here we continued our walk until we arrived in front of another temple where we met Messrs. Ochiltree[12] and March[13] from the *Mississippi* and Mr. Adams from the *Susquehanna*, our officers from the Ward Room and those from the *Mississippi* had provided themselves with the necessary eatables and drinkables and we all joined in and had a "tiffin." The quality of which was superb. After "tiffin" Dr. Wheelwright made a speech followed by Mr. Ochetree, then Mr. Lowry. Then we hung bottles on the trees and fired pistols and stones at them for amusement. Some of the party kept up drinking and by the time we got started for town a couple of them "felt their oats" good and the balance with the exception of the Engineers a little "so so." We formed in soldier order, two abreast, Lowry Captain and started for Nappa Ki[a]ng at the tune of Ben Bolt quick step, sung by all hands. On our way we charged on several parties of Loo Chooans and whooping like Indians. They must really have taken us for barbarians and the way they scampered was a caution to wild deer. It was indeed amusing. We made several halts and those who was of the drinking party (all but Mr. Fauth and myself) liquored up, and before we reached the harbor they were a pretty decently served up party. Wheelwright fell into a paddy field and covered himself from head to toe nails with mud. Fauth and I becoming impatient left the party and proceeded onward, where on arriving at the landing we met a large number of officers from the different ships. Amongst them was Nicholson from our ship who had been gunning and killed several ducks and snipe and Danby and Jimmy Shirk. Jimmy came on board with Fauth, Bibby and myself leaving the balance of the party ashore.

Jan. 30th

I have learned the particulars of Arnold's case. By his story, him and Alexander were in fun and although he was suspended and things occurred as I related them with the above exception, he is now restored to duty. Moreover he had a very narrow escape the other night from drowning. It appear[s] that he was asleep on the guard in the mid watch and the rolling of the ship rolled him overboard in a heavy sea. They heard him in the water, lowered away a boat and picked him up! This is miraculous, but nevertheless a fact.

The Engineers of the *Mississippi* under the disagreeable Chief Engineer Jesse Gay have been keeping night watches in Port ever since that ship has been in commission this last time, and upon her arrival out here. The *Susquehanna* under the Irish Chief Engineer Archbold instructed the same regulation. Upon our arrival it was boldly asserted by the Assistant Engineer of the *Susquehanna* and *Mississippi* and bets freely offered that the Engineers of the *Powhatan* would be ordered to do the same thing. (Keep night watches in port) I had some conversation with Sewell on this point at that time and he said that such thing would not occur on this ship and that he was opposed to it. So up to this time we have been exempt.

Now a few days ago, at the eleventh hour, the Engineers of the *Mississippi* entered a protest to Capt. Lee[14] against this duty without consulting their Chief Engineer, and had the obnoxious regulation removed. Mr. Gay took offense at this and spoke to Capt. Lee about it. Capt. Lee referred the matter to Commodore Perry and he sent for Mr. Gay and Sewell. Gay dictated and Sewell was silent, and the results are an edict issued by Perry for the Assistant Engineers of all the Steamers to keep night watches in Port. Of course we have to obey the order, and I have seen it, but it has not been passed yet. Alexander and Robie of the *Mississippi* and Fithian of the *Susquehanna* were on board at the time we heard of this most unjust order. We had some heated conversation about it and it was proposed to write a joint letter of protest against it but no conclusion was arrived at about it. Mr. Holland was consulted this evening and he thinks that it will do no good. My opinion is that he is afraid. Sewell and I had some talk and he says that keeping these watches is unnecessary and nothing alter it.

Jan. 31st

Today the Assistant Engineers talked over the new order and deputized me to write a protest to the Commodore which I done. 'Tis not finished yet as it may be necessary to make some alterations. Then Sewell has the order but he says he has no instructions to carry them in force and that he will not do it until he is ordered. So we shall remain quiet until the order is attempted to be enforced when come what will we shall do our best to frustrate such outrageous imposition, and without boasting. We are the boys "solitary and alone, amongst the fear and taunts of my opponents, I set this ball in motion." We may be "weathered" but not without an attempt to get to "windind."

All the sailing vessels except the *Supply* left for the Bay of Jeddo today. I wish this confounded humbug would end, this Japan Bubble must or soon burst. It has voll[ey]ed long enough and gathered in its course sufficient of Uncle Sam's [sake] to satisfy the go aheaditiveness of young America and I can now see in our ship humorous caricatures of Perry and his Host!

We will now soon be off for Jeddo. The stopping point of our glorious squadron with its noble, great, immense tub of rum and victuals Commodore Perry. Oh what a great man he is to be sure. What a glorious conqueror. What a vast deal of importance and wealth he has, has been and is to the United States. I want to see the time when men of sense will be chosen by our government to take charge of important affairs. God forbid that, he should remain on board this ship. I'm afraid now of his keeping the *Powhatan* to go home in and if he can find a trough made by a seal he will no doubt take a roll in it. His glory will soon be over, and when his name will be mentioned people will say, "Oh! Yes! He lead the Japan Humbug, and came back with his tail between his legs." Why the poor miserable, half clad, bare foot, timid, God forsaken wretches with whom we are to deal with will look upon a plough with as much savvy as a hog would. And when they are shown a Locomotive with steam up, unless the Locomotive is a very fast one she will be unable to catch them. They are the best runners I have ever seen. Anyone of them can beat Gildersleeve.

Feb. 3rd

Today the Commodore and a party of Marines with Officers called on the Prince. That is they went to the Palace but the Lou Chooans begged hard that he did not insist on seeing the boy. I don't believe there is any Prince here but that the Mandarins make the people believe it. Though I have heard it reported he has been seen.

Feb 4th

Today I finished the coal account and mighty glad of it I am. After I finished I went ashore and took a seat on Capstain Rock a most beautiful and romantic spot. I was really enchanted and thought I could make my home there had I you with me. The Commodore has purchased some land here and a flag staff is erected upon which is to float the American Flag. A Mr. Randall who came out on one of the ships as a Masters Mate is to be left here as Governor. A party of Officers who have been on a tour through the island have just returned and say they have discovered a coal mine! If this proves true somebody will get rich. I would like to speculate if I had the money.

All the Artists came on board with their baggage this afternoon. The Commodore it is said don't come on board until we get to Jeddo, as the new cabin is not dry from paint yet. Everybody is "down on" the cabin which ruins the appearance of our quarter deck. We sail for Jeddo on Monday (day after tomorrow) and will be there in about a week. Jeddo being about 900 miles from here. The *Supply* will sail for Shanghai on Monday. Another man was buried from the *Susquehanna* this afternoon. He died from the effects of self-pollution! We have been extremely fortunate—not lost a single man since we have been in commission. [. . .] We are all ready for a six month siege. Plenty of provisions and water. [. . .] So I now bid you a good bye again and [. . .] by my usual regret. For I love to be writing to you. But speak has me say God Bless you my dearest and beloved wife.

U.S Steamer *Powhatan*, Napa Harbor, Great Lew Chew, Feb. 7th 1854

My Dearest Lide,

We left the harbor of Napa, Great Lew Chew, this morning about seven o'clock and sailed in the same order as we did arriving from Hong Kong. At ten o'clock we made a sail which proved to be the *Saratoga*. We stopped and communicated with her and she went to Loo Choo and we continued our way. The weather is moderate. The ship pretty sturdy. We have been put in an allowance of water of one gallon per day, and as this amount is allowed to all. Officers and Engineers have 10 times the amount of washing that the others have. We complained about it and tonight we received 2 gallons extra, and Capt. says he will telegraph to the Commodore tomorrow that one gallon is insufficient for us and we may be allowed more.

I had the watch from 12 to 3 and go on at 9 this evening. We are running along slowly. The Commodore comes on board our ship as soon as we arrive in Japan. All his crowd are on board now except his clerk[15] and secretary[16] and the Fighting Captain Adams. We will probably be in Japan in a week. Shortly after the tale will be told. We may be assaulted by them, and then we will have to fight. I'm in for a fight. To be sure some blood will be spilled, but our business is to fight, because we are a Navy Man O War! There don't appear to be much anxiety about the affair anyhow. All look upon it as humbug, and the general feeling amongst all is to get through with it as speedy as possible.

Feb. 11th

I have just come off watch, now almost 10 o'clock. We made the land to-day. Passed some very ugly looking rocks which no doubt have been the cause of many an unheard of shipwreck. The wind is blowing a gale. We are lying to under trysails and steam. The engines working out 4 or 5 revolutions. We have stopped several times. The night is clear and cold. The coldest I have known since leaving home.

Last night had quite a "war talk" with Sewell. He had spoken to Stamm who is on watch with me about leaving bad fires and as I am the responsible agent I made it known, and Sewell left in bad temper. Ten o'clock. Good Night.

Feb. 13th

One year today since we left. Now on the Southern Coast of Nyphon. Last night we [had] a clear, serene, cold, beautiful moonlight night. The volcano of "Foosi"[17] looms up in magnificent grandeur. Its peaks extending into the clouds gave it the appearance of the [frustum] of a cone, and covered with snow. It looked like an immense pearl. This silvery streak of moonlight playing at bo peep on its slant sides perfectly enraptured me. How grand! How beautiful! Heine[18] the artist sketched it.

This morning an active volcano is in sight. The first I have ever seen. I can't picture it. A mixture of cloud, smoke, hills, and sunshine in systematic chaos if you can understand that. At six o'clock we raised steam and made fast to the *Vandalia*. The *Susquehanna* to the *Lexington*, and since then we have been "humbugging" in stopping and starting, waiting on the *Mississippi*. She trying to make fast to the *Macedonian*. 'Tis now near 11 o'clock and they are not underway yet. The active volcano spoken of I have heard called "Orizeema." Said by some to be 17,000 feet high! I guess this is a little stretched. This morning is beautiful. Somewhat colder than a year ago. I slept well last night.

The volcanos spoken of above were both one (awful bull that). That is I saw Mount Orizeema this morning and Fusi [Fuji] last night. Fusi [Fuji] is the active volcano. We continued our way up the bay passing by the City of Uragua[19] or government of that name, and kept along the boldest most rugged and picturesque shore I have ever beheld.

At about 3 o'clock this afternoon we came to anchor in the Bay of Jeddo about 20 miles from the city. This bay is truly magnificent, large to float and anchor all the navies in the world! Some Japanese headed by the Governor of Uragua[20] wanted to see the Commodore, but he would not see anybody but the number 1 man of the Country, as he says he is the number 2 man of the United States. This is the right way to deal with them. He sent Capt. Adams on board our ship to receive them, and they came on board. They are more intelligent than the Chinese, and some of them had "two swords" and "Petticoat trousers" of silk. They were all dressed very well, and at the prow of the boat in which they came hung and [*sic*] immense silken tassel and astern two flags. One white with a blue stripe in the center, and one white one with two red stripes. Tomorrow a conference is to be held. These fellows looked good natured and seemed to be pleased at our presence here. Two of the Royal Blood are coming down from Jeddo soon to call on the Commodore.

Coming up the Bay we were at Quarters. Everything cleared for action. The guns shotted "and all ready for the fight." I opine there will be no blood spilled. The *Southampton* got in here some days ago. Old Junius the Pioneer! Thems'um! as old Boyle[21] always says. This cold air has astonishingly revived my spirits. I feel young hearty—like a look! I am well satisfied that we will be better treated here than we were at Lou Chou. The people there were frightened. But "We shall see what we shall see." My opinion is that we will remain here 4 or 5 months! I feel it in my bones. But is it not remarkable that we should get here today! Just one year from home. I feel good tonight!

Feb. 14th

Today a kind of conference was held between Capt. Adams and the Prince Governor of Uragua. The Japanese wanted us to remove from here and anchor at Uragua and to await there the Ziogoons reply to the Presidents letter, but this we would not agree to, and insisted on remaining here. So in a few days another "palabre" is to be had.

The Japanese are in color a light brown, some of them are very light but have a chalky look. The boats that brought the "Blood Royals" to our ship came alongside and we kept up with those in the boats all kinds of motions and spontaneous. We threw them tobacco and they threw us some in return. Then they ate some hard tack that we threw them. The "Royals" that were on board all wore two swords, silken gowns and trousers, straw shoes, no hats,

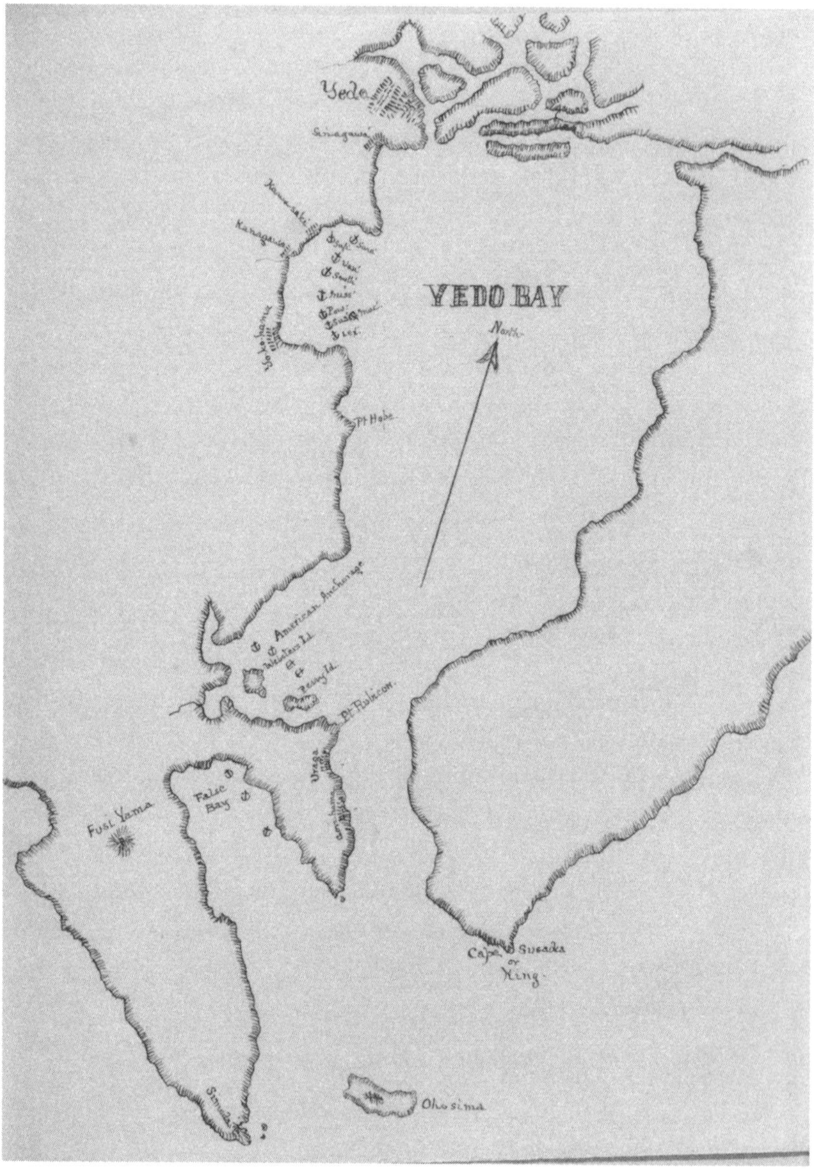

12. William Speiden Jr., "Sketch Map of Yedo Bay," Library of Congress.

but a kind of scarf which they wrapped around their faces and heads. Altogether they were a fine looking set of men. The conference last a long time. We looked at the swords of those on board and they looked indeed like fine ones. They are as sharp as a razor and in shape like them except the end being turned like a carving knife. The handles of them being long so as to be used with both hands. They appeared to be very inquisitive and one of them took a musket and went through the manual with it! The Engines surprised them very much. No doubt we will do something as already we have done more than any other people in the world.

No boats are allowed to come near us except those on official visits which are very few. We being the Flag Ship of course see it all. Those on other ships have not seen these fellows today. We are not yet the flag ship either, but will be in a few days, but we receive all the visits and the flag officers come on board at the time. Perry is sick with gout. He will be on board in a day or two.

Our marines on post have their muskets loaded and everything is in warlike order. Huzza for Japan humbug. If Perry don't go up to Jeddo he is no "punkins." We are now about 30 miles of Jeddo. But for beauty this place is sufficient. There is no town or village on the shore and unless for the advantages of the harbor, I can't see what we anchored here for. However, time will tell.

Feb. 18th

This morning at nine o'clock the Broad Pendant of Com. Perry was hoisted on board the *Powhatan* and during the day baggage and boxes, bundles and baskets kept coming continually. Some dozen men constituting the "Big Mandarin Train" have been transferred. At two o'clock the Rajah came himself. He was not received with any show. He declined. Another "palabre" was held to day in the Cabin, and the Japanese insisted upon our withdrawing to Uragua. When they were told that according to the laws of Nations the Capital of a country was the place to treaty and that if they do not point out a harbor between this and Jeddo he would go to Jeddo. He gave them until next Tuesday.

I feel very well. I shaved my moustache off yesterday. They are disgusting things. Mouth full of hair all the time. I have had quite a conversation with Draper the daguerreotypist who was in the Erie office in '48. He has told me some rich things.

I have heard that the *Susquehanna* had been ordered to Philada. when she returns. They expect to get home next October! I even had hopes that the *Powhatan* would not be much longer than that, and yet think that it won't be a great while longer. Unless something turns up I will have to quit this kind of writing for it does really seem to me dry stuff and must be laborious to you. Would you like to see me in a moustache? If so let me know and I will raise one again by the time I get home. Good Night. Saturday Night.

Feb.19th

I went on board the *Mississippi* today and dined there. I was astonished at their knowing so little about the Japanese. The same way on all the ships. Nothing relative to the Japan Affair has taken place on any ship but ours and we thus see all "big guns" and hear the most of what is said. I came on board before sundown and I found the ship crowded with officers from the other ships and great many Japanese.

Another interview was held today and I hear that everything is progressing finely, and that we have reason to suppose that we will get all we ask for. They bought with them a quantity of chickens, vegetables, and oranges. The plumage of the chickens is the prettiest I have ever seen. A dozen of these chickens in the United States would be a great thing. They would really pay to exhibit.

I am hoping that in two months we will have everything as we would wish it out here. When people talk of Gold and Silver in Japan, tell 'em it's a humbug. I have seen but very little and that was in the shape of very small ornaments on the swords of the Nobility.

The day has been very pleasant. We made the first signal from our ship this morning. It was to the *Lexington*. The *Southampton* got underway yesterday and went up the bay towards Jeddo about 3 miles where she is now at anchor. We send surveying boats out every day and she is up there to protect them.

Feb. 21st

Yesterday I worked all day in the Engine Room packing the slip joints of the Steam Pipes and did not get through until after Midnight. Having the mid watch I turned in at one o'clock. The way which the watches will be kept always. This morning I got up and felt a little stiff having taken some cold last night. At present feel very well. Stewart and Fithian are on board, and it's blowing and raining so hard that they will be unable to return to night.

The *Vandalia* got underway this morning with a party of Japanese on board and ere this is anchored off Uragua. The Commodore thus satisfying the Nobility of Japan by sending one ship to their spot. Sewell was sent for this morning and he had to give a lengthy detail of causes why the *Powhatan* could not run slower, blaming it principally on the throttles. Perry said he would have new ones cast and put on! (Nonsense) He has ordered that all the ships shall make as much condensed water as possible and save it in casks, for he says we may run out of water and may have to fight these people first, and doesn't want to do that. (more nonsense) He is sick with the piles and is going to "play the devil" when he gets well! McCluney is sick yet.

The telegraphers by order of the Commodore occupy in conjunction with us the office of the Guard. The printing press is being got ready, so likewise the daguerreotype apparatus. These things are to be exhibited to the Emperors [lucques?] and explained by them to him. Then I suppose he will consider the propriety of taking them. Things are working.

Yesterday I saw the first Japanese woman. She was rather pretty, but too dark for my taste. She was in a boat passing the ship. They have had the *Mississippi* careened over to get a chance to stop her leaks, but it has done no good. No doubt she will have to go home direct and give us the chance or the better chance of returning via Cape Horn. One more year and I think we will be home. I don't know what will keep us long.

Feb. 22nd

At 12 o'clock today we fired a salute of 21 guns in honor of the day. The other ships followed in regular order. A party of Japanese were on board to see the firing. At about one o'clock the Com. ordered the fires started and we made signals to the other ships to do the same and in 10 minutes after the order was countermanded, Sewell and he had a row today about condensed water pipes. He suggested a plan to Sewell and sent to know if he had done it. Sewell told him that he did not order him to do it. Com. said a suggestion of his was as good as an order and he replied that he could not obey suggestions. Perry then intimated that he would have to get someone else in his place. He is the greatest humbug extant. He can't bluff Sewell though! We will have some fun yet.

Feb 23rd

Yet at anchor in the old place. I know no anchorage name for it except Jeddo Bay. Some call it the American anchorage.[22] [. . .] An order was issued today by the Commodore that all officers must wear their swords and Belts at Quarters. What a world of war, and humbug and nonsense and ignorance we live in! God speed the time when this trial will be over.

Bay of Jeddo about 10 miles from the
City of the same name, Feb. 24th

This morning we raised steam and slowly moved from our former anchorage about 3 o'clock. The fires being yet banked and a regular "Sea Watch" kept up. I earnestly believe that 'tis Perry's intention to go to Jeddo, for the boats were sent out this afternoon surveying, and in a few they will have surveyed up far enough for us to go ahead again. Old P[erry] was on deck and directed all the movements. About 2 miles ahead of us there is a beacon, indicting something, either shoals or rocks.

The oysters that are found in the Bay are said by those who have been tasted them to be delicious, we are having tongs made so that we can get some. The City of Jeddo, or Yeddo, can be seen from our topmast head. The *Macedonian* was left to wait for the *Saratoga*. I feel extremely well this morning, but tonight I am somewhat feverish, slight cold probably. Will keep quiet and eat some liquerice. Go on watch at 9 PM.

Feb. 26th

The *Vandalia* arrived from Uragua this morning and the result of the interview was that the Japanese are willing to come to terms! They say that for 200 years they have had no intercourse with other people than the Dutch, but the Imperial Council had abrogated that law with respect to the Americans and they were prepared to enter into arrangements for concluding a commercial treaty, and that as soon as the treaty was concluded we could go anywhere and purchase what we pleased.

Today a party of the "Big Uno" came on board and suggested this place as the one to make the treaty at. So Capts. Adams and Buchannan with Messrs. Pegram and Portman (the interpreter) went ashore to select a place. One has been selected and a house is to be built next Friday when the interview is to be held. They had a tiny house built at Uragua and fitted up in fine style, but Perry would not go back. They made presents of silk and lacquered ware to some of those who were at Uragua on the *Vandalia*. This place is called Kenagarwar [Kanagawa].[23] I spell as pronounced. So you will tell of the "Treaty of Kenagarwar [Kanagawa]."

They weathered us no doubt for our surveying boats went up within 2 miles of Jeddo today and found 5 fathoms of water all the way. This they knew very well and seeing that we were determined to go to Jeddo they suggested this place to prevent us. They say that they have counted one hundred and sixty American Vessels passing through the straits in the last year. There are government boats hovering around us all day. They arrest all boats that come alongside. Some do and are anxious to get our hard bread which they seem to be fond of. We will go to Jeddo undoubtedly, and have a chance to buy some curios.

Some of the poor miserable devils stand up in the boat naked. A small bandage only securing that which Adam and Eve first put the fig leaf on. The women are very pretty and dark complexioned. The married ones shave or pluck their eyebrows and blacken their teeth. I have only seen them in the boats from the ship. I am anxious to get ashore to see what the single ones are made of. Been over a year now, and I'm afraid I will forget how if I don't go soon. 'Twould be doing a kindness, for a mixture I think would improve the race.

Feb. 27th

Four years ago tonight we joined our hands and our hearts and fates, and though we have been at times reduced in health, reduced in worldly goods and darkness, brooded o'er us we have no cause to regret that event. We have been happy in our misfortunes. The love which had hardly knocked before it unwrapped us on all that love can yield has gradually cemented itself so unalterably in our natures and being, that nothing seems possible to shake it. I feel happy and ingratiate myself that I possess one who loves me as dearly as I know you do. There, you will not talk or write love to me so I do it myself. May there be many returns of our anniversary, but none like this. All that are in store for us I hope to pass with you. I feel very well tonight.

This afternoon raised steam and came some 3 miles nearer the shore. We can see the houses very plainly from the ship. I saw some pictures today that were sent off to the Commodore. They were indecent and extremely vulgar and obscene! I have heard that the Japanese said that their ladies on hearing that we have large whiskers and wishes us to shave them off. All such nonsense is talked of. Some of the officers are almost angry to get ashore, thinking to get all they want, &c. I fear they will get more than they bargain for, if not very careful. We shall soon see now.

March 1st

Sewell had another row with the Commodore. He sent for Sewell and Sewell went in the Cabin and stood up with his arms folded and the Commodore said, "Don't stand in that independent attitude sir! Sit Down!" So Sewell sat down! 'Tis laughable. Everyone on board seems disgust. The Commodore has created a moroseness and disquietude all over. He is like an evil genius. Whenever he makes his appearance everybody leaves as if scared to death. "There's Old Perry" one will exclaim and in an instant the decks will be deserted.

In the first place he ran against the Captain, then against the 1st Lieut., then the Chief Engineer. He says (so I have heard) that if he had known there was so much dissatisfaction he would not have come on board, and intends to leave as soon as possible. We are all glad of this. He is a mighty big humbug and we are all sick of him. He can go willingly.

March 2nd

Yesterday Sewell said to me that Hassin (the man's name) had commenced his journal, but that he wrote so slow he had got tired of him, and that he was some weeks behind and requested that I would bring his journals up. Today I went in his room for that purpose, and instead of finding it some weeks behind, I find it is a month behind! I commenced and got through about two weeks. It is very rich. Some of the most original spelling to say nothing of the idea and quotations deserve to be exhibited as specimens to the literature. However, I do my best towards the corrections, to preserve the style. I have again taken up the study of Pambour[24] and my head is full of "Relative Volumes" temperatures, maximum densities &c. &c. A party of the Japan Nobility dined with Capt. Buchannan on the *Susquehanna*.

March 4th

I understand that the first landing takes place on Monday and that on a return visit by the Japanese the Commodore intends giving a large dinner to them. McCluney has not spoken a word to the Commodore since he has been on board. I do really feel a little for the Commodore. He has not a soul to speak to except officially. No wonder he is scared and peevish, but he played the tyrant too soon on board here. How things will end between McCluney and him I am unable to opine.

March 7th

Everything is ready for the landing tomorrow. Sewell, the Purser and Doctor Maxwell are the part of the sailors represented from this ship. The Lieuts. and others that go have charge of boats, and of course have to remain in them and not be present at the "reception." The purpose of the landing tomorrow is to receive the Emperors answer to the President letter. We all feel satisfied that it will be favorable to the treaty.

One of the Marines on the *Mississippi* died yesterday.[25] Whether they will have to throw him overboard or bury him ashore remains only to be seen. The *Mississippi* had been "keeled" over for a day or two for the purpose of ascertaining where the leak is now. This is the second attempt.

March 8th

The landing was accomplished today in most beautiful style, and negotiations entered into. The Commodore left our ship at twelve O'clock and received a salute of 17 guns from the *Macedonian*, as acting Minister Plenipotentiary. The boats numbered 27 and the launches had the brass field pieces in the bows from them a salute of 21 guns was fired in honor of the Japanese Flag and followed by one of 17 guns in honor of the Japanese Commissioner. It was a beautiful sight. I nor any of the Engineers but Sewell went.

At the "Reception House" an entertainment was given. The "chow chow" arrangements composed of cold soup and candy. Sewell brought off some of the candy and gave me some. It was red with white streaks on it and just like any mint stick at home. What was effected I don't exactly know but from all I can learn the negotiations are to continue from day to day. Something was said about the Coal produced by the island and the selection of a Port to trade in. Arrangements were concluded about burying the Marine on the *Mississippi*. The Japanese wanted the body taken to Uragua and from there they would take it to Nangasaki and bury him in the cemetery there, but Perry told them there was no use in that and they concluded to bury him tomorrow morning at 10 on a point just below this place.

Commissioners are to be appointed to approve the products of Japan so that we can buy what we want. It is hoped that in two or three days we will get ashore. Mr. Gay was sent for this afternoon by the Commodore to settle the railroad "pigeon." He goes ashore tomorrow to put it up. The Emperor is only 25 years of age, and the Commodore wanted to send him a present of some mead wine but the Commodore said better send him some books as he was too young to drink! Several kegs of Sake and some boxes of oranges came off for the men this afternoon. Japan is brought to terms! The Expedition successful!

March 9th

Today Mr. Brown[26] the daguerreotypist took a group of the Japanese, nothing further took place on board here today with regard to them. Hereafter, as I learn all the interviews are to be held on board the *Mississippi*.

This morning the dear Marine was buried. Old Jones[27] the Chaplain (Episcopalian) done the honors, or as he expressed it "had the melancholy pleasure of burying the first American in Japan"! After Jones, one of the Japanese priests officiated. For his services they paid 80 cents, the first purchase in Japan. Thus the first article purchased was a priests services. Some say the money was for the ground. Conflicting statements are made as to the method of ceremony performed by the Japan Priest, but from them all (I was not there) I judge there is a similarity to the Catholic ceremony.

March 10th

This morning I commenced Sewell's journal again, but from the multiplicity of mistakes and there being no punctuation I made but little headway. I saw some were casted up yesterday and directed to the Emperor different Councilmen, Commissioners &c. as presents from the Commodore. I believe some of the presents sent out by the government are to be delivered on Monday, but there is no knowing what is to be done or when. An order for chickens and eggs with some vegetables was sent off today and we may soon get some fresh provisions. I am sick of salt grub. I have a constant heart burn, and I feel satisfied that it arises from the use of said food.

The Marine that was buried the other day had three volleys fired over his grave, as has always been the custom. The Commodore sent for the Marine Officers and ordered that no more of it should be done hereafter. That is if any more should die. There may be something done about it when we arrive home [. . .] I have finished "Tom Burk[e]" and I am sure that reading novels make me feel as I do, that is a kind of hankering to be with you, to hear from you. Now when I read "Steam" it is different. Just take up some novel and read it, see if you don't feel more anxious about me afterwards. Not supposing for a moment that you do not always feel so, but the feeling will be more apparent.

No news today. Weather cold and windy.

March 11th

Danby was on board today about some Yankee Clocks. He is requesting some that are to be presented to the Japanese. The presents in the shape of stoves, cavalry swords, self-priming muskets, Francis Metullie Life Boats (3), perfumery, tea, flour, cotton goods, clocks, miniature railroad and engine, and some agricultural instruments are boxed up in parcels to go on ship on Monday. What else may go I don't know, but the above I saw on deck today except the railroad and Locomotive.

This morning the Japanese brought off some fish, chickens, and oysters. *Miss.* got some of the fish. They are great big ones and we got a half one. They tasted good of course. The oysters and chickens went further aft. My day's duty today, nothing doing.

A subscription has been started headed "Japanese Expedition Subscription to The Washington Monument." I give $2.00. The same as all the rest. I subscribed once before while I was at the "Brick Ship" *United States*[28] on Lexington Street.

March 13th

The day has been rainy and disagreeable. This morning all the presents intended for the Japanese were taken ashore and steps taken to introduce the mysterious workings of the Locomotive, Telegraph, &c., &c. I suppose there will be more or less going ashore now every day. Today Messrs, Holland and Kellogg from our mess went. It appears that the Japanese, notwithstanding their apparent proveness in favor of commerce have taken the right steps to scare a Yankee off, for being charged for the fish, we had the other day one dollar and sixty cents apiece. I can't vouch for the truth of this, but it is common report. Now nothing will drive a Yankee wild quicker than extortion. It would be useless in me to recite the quality and quantity of the presents. The locomotive is a miniature concern only. I am decidedly sick of Japan, and I must say I would much rather be in China.

March 14th

Messrs. Gay and Danby with some men went ashore this morning, to put up the locomotive and railroad. Messrs. Williams and Draper went and commenced putting up the telegraph poles. Some others went who are connected with the scientific corps and Mr. Bittenger, priest of the *Susquehanna.* About noon some Japanese came off and reported that an American officer was going towards Jeddo and would not return although they had requested him to do so. The Commodore ordered the Cornet[29] to be hoisted and a gun fired, which was done. This is a signal for all officers and men to report on board. After some time all got on board but Mr. Bittenger,[30] and he has not got back yet to my knowledge.

Mr. B[ittenger] is the man and he knows very well that to stroll off in the manner he has done is against orders, and he may expect to get "Jesse" when he does come, if he is a Minister. Quite an excitement has existed all day about it, and the Commodore has been as mad as a bull.

Major Zeilin[31] was surveyed on board our ship this morning by the Doctor. He had the asthma very bad and has been doing his best to be sent home ever since he has been out here. He came out on the *Mississippi*. He will probably [be] condemned and sent home on the *Saratoga*, but in a few days we will know all about these things.

Day before yesterday one of the Messenger boys of the *Mississippi* fell down the Engine room hatch and remained insensible until this morning. Doubts are entertained of his recovery. All the officers are very sorry for the boy was liked by all. Mr. Roby is able to be about with a cane. He had the greater part of his large toe amputated. He is all safe.

We have yet received no fresh provisions from shore except those fish that I spoke of the other day. I am getting sick of the "Salt" and my appetite is failing. The Commodore has geese, and chickens left so he don't care, and us poor devils suffer. But it can't last much longer or the men will be very unpleasant. The members of the other steerage, midshipman, clerks &c. have instituted a secret society called the "Red Revengers" and have meetings every Tuesday and Saturday night, when they drink punch and sing a song and make speeches. Of course none but the members no [*sic*] anything about their transactions, but it must be very funny for they do considerable laughing. They ought to get three cornered paper hats, stick rooster feathers in them and make a parade. I know they would look pretty!

March 15th

Mr. Bittenger the gentleman who strayed away yesterday returned last night in a Japanese boat about ten o'clock. The boat was filled with lanterns and looked like an "official messenger." This morning he was sent for by the Commodore and report says that he got a "pitching into," but for my part I believe that the whole affair was understood between him and the Commodore. I saw him first after he came out of the cabin and he didn't look or act like a man that had been very severely reprimanded. He gave a glowing description of what he had seen. Temples, fire proof houses, magnificent processions &c. He went within a few miles of Jeddo. He has seen more than any white man alive so far, and although he has spoiled the "fun" for great many others. I think he has done well, for his ship leaves soon and therefore his chance for seeing "wild" Japan. We expected him to be brought back in a cage. The Mandarins ashore would not allow any more.

Telegraph poles to be put up today, and operations have been somewhat suspended. I suppose on account of Bittenger's jaunt yesterday. There is a report in circulation to me that in the [interview] on board the *Mississippi* today the Treaty was returned by the Japanese signed, but that there was some alterations, of but little importance. Something has been done about the treaty certainly but whatever is exactly I can't find. I would like to get ashore before I send this so I could, or you could say I had been ashore in Japan.

Today there was a boat alongside the ship with some Mandarins in, and they handed up some filthy vulgar pictures. They represent monstrosities. Some are exceedingly obscene, and I think indicative of the character of the people.

Today I finished putting the smoke pipe damper in order. It has been out of order ever since we left Madeira, and for some days back I have been engaged on it. I saw Capt. McCluney on deck today. His last attack of Neuralgia was a very severe one, and I would not be surprised if he went home before long overland.

I have learned since commencing this that the Japanese have conceded to everything mentioned in the treaty. But some few matters which is not perfectly understood they want talked about, and tomorrow a party headed by the Commodore go ashore to conclude the matter. Japan stock is up, and some aspiring men go so far as to talk already of getting extra for our service out here! Perry will no doubt be made a liar of when he reaches home. When the Russians were here they had nothing to do with them. This was told to Captain Adams by one of the Japanese officials. I am glad things took so favorable, for I think it will hasten our progress towards home. If it is possible I will get something and send by the *Saratoga*, but I fear she will leave before I get the chance.

I have learned that the presents that remain on board the ship are for the Emperor of Siam,[32] where one of the Ships, most likely us, will call on our way home. If this is true our prospects for going around the world are gone, but I will not give up yet, for so long as things are so unsettled, and even Perry himself in ignorance. I will hope.

March 16th

Today has been the most unpleasant day we have had hard, heavy rain all day, and tonight the wind is blowing strong and cold. I suppose we are in the Equinoxes. In consequence of the rain a delegation of Japanese came off this morning in order to ascertain whether the Commodore intended going ashore on the business I mentioned last evening, and they were told that it rained to[o] hard so they left.

Last night expectations ran high, Japan stock was up clear above par. Tonight 'tis down! Down in consequence of the report that instead of conceding all the points in the treaty the Japanese have only offered one port to trade in. The trade to commence in one year from now, and to last five years! This is the report, and although I can't find the authority there is reason to believe there is something in it, for everyone seems affected by it. You see how fluctuating and uncertain are these conditions, but it is not for us to know, and we can only watch the movements and reason on the many rumors that float around and sum up the whole for an approximations.

March 17th

This afternoon the Commodore and suite went ashore to make progress in the Japan negotiations, and they have returned, but what has been done I know not, only that during the interview the Commodore was heard to say that he wished to know whether he was to go to Jeddo as a friend or as an enemy, and this was said in a loud tone. Report says that permission will be granted for the officers to go ashore tomorrow. None of our mess will go off. Mr. Glisson has the authority to allow it, for he thinks Engineers ought do nothing else but work, but he is occasionally "taken down." I am determined to get ashore. Between this and Monday, for report says that the *Susquehanna* will sail Monday.

From the Commodore's remarks as mentioned above it is pretty certain that he is going to Jeddo. I will endeavor to gain what information I can and sum up the whole on Sunday. The day has been cloudy.

Last night after I closed I went on deck and had a long talk with Mr. Haggerty.[33] Mr. H[aggerty] is one of our Lieutenants and is in himself a perfect Encyclopedia. He has the most astonishing memory that I have ever met with. He has often talked to me before on different subjects. But last night I happened to mention that I was attached to the *Michigan* under McDougal[34] as First Lieut. and remarked that I thought him a tyrant in which he perfectly coincided and then he commenced telling me about the affair of Mac opening a letter of Capt. Slaughters[35] while attached to the Brig. *Bainbridge*[36] with some more of his acts on the Coast of Africa. He gave McDougal the most unenviable character and repeated acts of his to support him in his assertions.

Young Adams[37] told me tonight that he was going on board the *Saratoga* in a few days. From this we judge that Capt. Adams is going home in her as bearer of dispatches on the Japan question, and I heartily wish it was over.

March 18th

Some time ago I mentioned the fact of a man coming off in his canoe from Lew Chew,[38] and asked the protection of the American Flag and was taken on board the *Susquehanna*. This man has been transferred to our ship, and is now the Engineers Mess Boy. He learns very fast, and says "Lew Chew" no good, me go to America.

This afternoon some Japanese officials were on board and this boy was in our mess room and seeing the Japanese he became frightened and crept under the table! Holland and myself hustled him out of that and made him stand up which he could scarcely do for trembling. I never saw a man frightened worse in my life. The people here are no doubt the most abject slaves in the world, and it would create no great effort to attempt a revolution amongst them! Even those who wear one sword are but poorly clad, while the two sworded gentry are dressed in all silk. Some of them (the commoners, or no sworded crowd) even in this cold weather I have seen in a state of nudity. Their "thingumabobs" enclosed in a little bag tied around the waist by a string. 'Twas my day's duty today, nothing doing. Good Night.

March 19th

This morning I got "sky larking" with some of my mess mates and knocked the knuckles of my right hand against Faron's nose and "stunned them."

March 20th

You speak of receiving papers from Buffalo, New York and Philada. containing an account of the Japan Expedition. The one from Buffalo must have been sent by Stimers.[39] I have seen some of the accounts. B. Taylors[40] are pretty correct, but that of Contees[41] first published in a Washington paper and stating that "the cry is still they come" is a poor weak effort for popularity. Taylor was a Masters Mate, pay $25.00 per month. He has gone home, left before we arrived. He is well spoken of by those who know him and worked with him.

We have a report here that the Russians succeeded in forming a treaty with these fellows, but I don't credit it. Today we took in water, and this morning the *Vandalia* and *Southampton* sailed for a port some 50 miles from here called "Ohisima or Ohoysima."[42] They have gone there to survey the harbour, and I understand it the Port offered by the Japanese for us to trade in. Whether they have offered only one or two I don't know, but report says five. You may depend upon the information I give regarding the Japanese progress, and as much as has been published I will take off the restrictions I urged to keep secrecy with regard to what I write and if any one desires information you can give it if you see proper.

Flag Ship: Japan Expedition, Jeddo Bay abreast of place called
Kenegawa and within 10 miles of Jeddo, March 23rd

On Monday we are to have a grand feast on board, get up steam and make an excursion around the harbour with some Japanese aboard. The *Susquehanna* leaves early in the morning and the mail bag closes this afternoon, so I must hurry up. Dr. Wheelwright goes in her and joins the *Plymouth*. Dr. Gambrill[43] is dead, he died at Hong Kong and therefore Wheelwright goes in his place.

The day is cloudy and cool. Nothing doing in Japanese affairs but making preparations for the landing again tomorrow. The telegraph and locomotive are in operation ashore. They have about a mile of wire up. The locomotive runs. 'Tis said that after tomorrow we will all get ashore certain.

So now Good Bye! And may God bless and protect you, keep you in health and happy hours for you in my absence. Truly and devoted I remain yours. George.

U.S Ste. *Powhatan*, Bay of Jeddo near the city
(Kenegawa [Kanagawa]), March 24th, 1854

My Dearest Lide,

This morning I awoke on hearing our band playing "Sweet Home" and on getting on deck I saw the *Susquehanna* underway. Although they all fondly hope to be soon on their way home I fear that their hopes will linger for some time yet. They will be in Hong Kong in about 10 days from now. All kinds of preparations are now being made to land again, and the boats from other ships are congregating previous to the departure for shore. Mr. Faron goes from our mess. My turn comes next, which I hope will be in a few days.

I will give you an account of the landing today as far as I can learn. The boats are getting ready to start and I will go on deck and see them off. The boat with the Commodore and suite have been ashore and returned. An immense amount of presents were received from the Japanese for the Government consisting of silks, crapes and lacquered ware, all of which have

13. A small drawing of a Japanese copper coin.

been stored away on one of the Store ships. Presents were also received from the Emperor by the Commodore, his Secretary, the two interpreters, Capt. Adams, Messrs. Gay, Danby, Draper, and Williams. Gay and Danby only because they ran the locomotive and Draper and Williams because they put up the telegraph, but they will not be allowed to receive them because our Government prohibits Naval Officers from receiving presents from Foreign Powers and as the silks and crapes are perishable articles I can't imagine what will be done with them. The other things will of course be put in the Patent Office. And the officers who have had presents made them may be allowed them. We shall only see.

What transpired with regard to the "Treaty" I nor any like me know, and all that has been said about it is that two Ports have been granted for us to trade in being Mutsmay[44] and another to the Southward of this.

I had a glimpse of some women today in a boat. I noticed the black teeth and the shave eyebrows. They gave an exhibition ashore for the edification of the Commodore and our party generally. It consisted in gymnastic exercises by the largest men in Japan. A body of immense fellows numbering over fifty and averaging in weight over two hundred pounds! They were naked all but the bag containing their "dusenberries." They wrestled and but[t] each other on the shoulder and the shocks are so violent as to split the skin on the forehead in many instances. On the whole the day was the most interesting one that we had since our arrival in Japanese waters.

Our band of Negro Minstrels are rehearsing tonight preparatory to giving a performance to the Japanese next Monday afternoon on which occasion a grand feast is coming off. Turkey's, Geese, Fowls, Sheep &c. have been killed today and prepared. Of course all this "livestock" belongs to the Commodore. I saw a piece of Japanese Copper Coin for the first time today. It was in shape an el[l]ipse with a square hole in the center with Japanese characters on both sides. [*sketch of the Japanese copper coin*] The crapes and silks that were presented are very beautiful and fine, of all colours.

Tonight 'tis raining and during the whole day it has been cloudy and I have a headache so I'll bid you Good Night!

Sunday March 26th

Yesterday Mr. Sewell sent for me and asked if I would accept an invitation to the feast, or Commodores dinner tomorrow. Only one from each Steerage being invited. I accepted although I do not consider it proper for the Chief Engineer to pick out the one who should go for the invitation should be sent to the mess, and the members decide by ballot who should go such occasions, but as Messrs. Holland and Faron were thus invited to go ashore and the mess not consulted I considered it but doing what they would have done under the same circumstance. So I dine tomorrow with the Commodore and the "biggest bugs" in Japan. After accepting I informed the mess of it at the Supper table and said I would decline on anyone's favor that was desirous to go, but none would say "me" through modesty (?) although I saw the picture of jealousy and envy on every countenance.

The most unfair thing I have ever seen was the distribution of the provisions that have brought off every day. The Ward room taking exactly 20 eggs for our one! This morning it rained and in consequence we had no muster. The wind is now blowing very strong and cold. The presents were all packed up yesterday and I saw some of them. They are very pretty. The crapes being the most perfect imaginable. We get up steam tomorrow to show the "Bloods" the working of the Engine.

I mentioned in my last letters that we had a Loo Choo man for Mess Boy who became very much frightened at the appearance of Japanese on board the ship. Now this fellow is a confounded rascal, for he is not really frightened but 'tis a trick of his to evade work and today he attempted to leave the Mess Room and I prevented him. Afterwards our Stewart told him to put down some knives that he held in his hand and he would not do it. I then ordered him to do it and he refused, so I struck him on the hand and he dropped that handful but he held on to the other when I made another lick at him and he dropped the others. I then made him go to work. He went to the 1st Lieut. and we were requested to get another boy in his place. The Master at Arms has him in charge now. He is the most perfect scoundrel and if he ever makes his appearance in the Mess Room again I'll kick him out. I mention this because I want to refer to it in case the man remains with us long enough to understand our language properly. The day towards evening became clear.

March 27th

Today was the "grand day." This morning it blew very strong, and continued to do so all day and [...] the ship was dressed in flags and awnings spread and canvas bulkheads put up yet it was feared that the Japanese would not come off, but about noon a party came off and stated that it was the intention of the Prince and Suite with Commissioners to come off, and with the message they brought a quantity of flowers which were festooned and placed around the deck in such a manner combined with the various flags and "groaning table" as to make the scene really beautiful.

Just before three o'clock the Prince Suite and Commissioners with some fifty of the highest officers of Japan were discerned coming to the ship, on which the National [Ensign] of Japan flew from our Fore Top gallant head and the Princes particular flag from the Mizzen, which were saluted by the *Mississippi.* Shortly after they came on board, but as there had already been two watches in the Engine Room I went down and took the watch at three o'clock.

About four the Commodore, Prince and Commissioners with other American Officers and Japanese Officers came to the Engine Room and I started the engine ahead for them. Thus having the honor of being the 1st person who started a Marine Engine in the presence of such a crowd. I had scarcely room to turn around, the engine room was so crowded. After this, which lasted about 20 minutes they went on deck and as nothing further was wanted with the engines I was relieved and having washed and put on a clean collar I made my appearance on the Quarter deck amongst the "chow chow" and drinkable arrangements. The solids I partook of very tasty and drank a couple of glasses of champagne, just to show the Japanese that it was not poison. After dinner the minstrels gave a serenade, and the whole affair pleased or appear to please them very much and under a salute from the *Saratoga* they left about sundown. Hardly a sober Japanese in the party. They are the most playful set of people I have ever met, like a party of boys, fond of whipping, and tricks &c.

I must close tonight as it has just struck 10.

March 28th

Sometime during the Mid Watch last night the Commodore's Orderly with a select company went into the Cabin and took from the table two immense pound cakes in shape of pyramids which had been presented to the Prince. (I could not begin to write the name, and there was three of them on board yesterday, and they were the 1st, 2nd, and 3rd in rank to the Emperor, the first ones name sounds like Highass-no-caque-der-marmie.[45] The others such jaw breakers that I am afraid to attempt sounding them.)[46] Besides the cakes they took a ham and a pitcher of punch. On discovering the robbery this morning the Commodore felt very much hurt, because he had promised to send the cake ashore today, and what to do he knew not and felt very bad. So after some study he ordered others to be made and told the Japanese that he had some fresh ones made for them which were soon done and sent off.

The Commodore and a party of Officers went ashore today and met the Princes and Commissioners and the articles of the treaty were discussed and on Thursday the affair is to be settled. Nothing remains to be done but the Commodore to sign it. We get three ports immediately and three more in a year.

Two of the Commodores Orderlies have been arrested and put in double irons for committing the larceny last night, and just now a boy named O'Neil was reported for having stolen a piece of silk from among the presents the other day. These things with the continued ill feelings between the Commodore and Captain McCluney will disgust the Commodore, and we now have reports that he intends to leave us and go to the *Mississippi* and that he goes to Jeddo in the *Mississippi* and also to the port of Matsmay, what is to be done with us report says not and my opinion is that this is all humbug and nothing is known until it is done. The Japanese intend giving a grand feast to us as soon as the treaty is signed.

Yesterday all kinds of toasts were drank, cheered and accompanied by the *Mississippi*'s band of music. That we have secured more than was anticipated is without a doubt.

Today one hundred and fifty ducks and a quantity of chickens were sent off as a present from the "Prince Dasenberry" to Commodore. The Japanese do not eat meat or fowl, and only keep fowls for their eggs, but say that any quantity can be raised and in a year they will have everything of that kind in abundance. "We are a great people."

March 29th

The *Vandalia* and *Southampton* arrived this morning from the Port of Shumuda[47] where they had been surveying. I have not learned yet how they report, and I have just learned the names of all the Ports offered to us. Matsmay, Shumuda and Nappa Kiang Loo Choo. I have also learned that all this report about signing the treaty tomorrow is speculation. Nobody knows as yet when it will be signed, and in consequence of this confounded humbugging and uncertainty I have been tempted to destroy this sheet, but as it shews the phases from day to day, on "sober second thought" I concluded that it might be interesting.

This afternoon and yet (now after dark) a body of Japanese are in the Cabin in Council with the Commodore about the treaty. The latest report is that we are to have the three ports above mentioned and in a year one more, and to be allowed any and every Port that may be granted to any other nations, but of all this you no doubt will be informed before I am because Capt. Adams will take with him the whole truth of the affair and it will be published in the newspapers. We may learn the particulars as soon as the treaty is signed.

Today has been very cold and we have all kept to our rooms. [. . .] One of the Captains report Shumuda a good harbour and the other is a bad one. I don't know which Commodore believes.

March 30th

Today there has been the greatest quantity of Japanese on board that there has been yet and this morning some of them came in our room and I endeavored to exchange some coins for theirs and to make some other little trades, but they wanted about a hundred times the value for any little article so I did not trade. One fellow was anxious to see inside our drawers and to gratify him I opened the drawer containing my shirts and the fellow spied your daguerreotype which was laying on them. He looked at and in a jiffy it was up his sleeve. A trick they have, their pockets are contained in their sleeves and I had to choke the fellow, and he had two swords on, before he gave it up. They are so accustomed to extortion from the poor miserable peasantry ashore that they forget themselves on board a ship. I fear that I will get but little from them because I will not be humbugged, but I will trade or buy at fair price anything for a curiosity.

This afternoon I was smoking my pipe on deck and Mr. Bibby my particular friend said that he would break the pipe. "You do" said I, "and I will break your head" so he up and took hold of the pipe and broke the stem, and I accordingly struck him a little harder than he has been accustomed to alongside the ear. He looked daggers and was about to get angry when I only said "be careful" and he turned it off in a laugh. So much for fun. No doubt the friendship is severed but I can bear it, and friends and foe must understand that I will not be humbugged or trifled with.

14. Anton L. C. Portman, "Conference Room at Yokohama Kanagawa, Japan. March 1854," Library of Congress.

March 31st

Today the treaty was signed by the Japanese officials! This morning everything was prepared for landing and at noon the boats shoved off from our ship and landed. Just after breakfast Mr. Sewell told me to stand by to go ashore and accordingly I put on my best "duds" and was ready at the appointed hour and landed with the party. My first footsteps in Japanese Soil, or on the Islands of Nippon being planted today. There was a manifestation of ill feeling in the Mess this morning about my being selected, but I paid no attention to it, although I consider it against to select in this way, and I firmly believe that Commodore Perry is not aware that there are officers on board who have not been ashore.

When I landed I met Danby who has been ashore every day for twenty five days taking care of the small locomotive. Shortly after we landed the Commodore landed and we assembled on the beach to receive him, and that done we followed in after him and marched into the building erected for the reception. The floors of the building are thickly covered with white straw mats and the sides are covered with wall paper and paintings of birds resembling cranes or storks. Running lengthwise with the building there are tables and benches alongside of which we seated ourselves. The Commodore, Interpreters &c. going to the extreme which was made private by the intervention of a silk curtain of dark purple colour bearing the Coat of Arms of the First Commissioner of Japan. Shortly after we became seated we were served with a small table or stool sitting on the larger table and containing lacquered ware cups some of them filled with tea and others with candy and cake. After partaking of this I took a walk outside with Danby and examined the small locomotive and miniature railroad car and railroad, and I found the whole affair one of the most perfect working miniatures I have ever seen.

I was not here long before I returned to the festive hall and partook of the second course which consisted in oysters of which I took only four plates and a variety of other dishes that would come by Japanese names, but in English I can't name them. They all appeared to be sweetened. Being different kinds of nuts, vegetables, omelets and a cup of muscle [*sic*] soup, one of something else with beans and onions in it and one fish soup with a dish of fish and snakes (I thought they were snakes) and as much sake, or rum, a kind of sweet sickening wine, as one could drink. After this came another course consisting of shrimp, lobster, fish, rice and a kind of paste on a board with red characters on it. I wrapped up some candy, some cake, a whole fish, a whole lobster and the paste on the board and took them on board where they were demolished.

About five o'clock we returned on board and were invited in the Cabin by the Commodore to see the treaty, and I have seen it signed and sealed! We get the Ports of Matsmay, Shumuda and all the Ports of the Lou Chou. But this is not a commercial treaty. The only things stipulated are that vessels can visit these and trade as they can at present. We are allowed to go ashore at them and go anywhere within a circuit of 14 miles. Perry appeared to be very much pleased with his success.

This is only an opening, now we may begin to calculate about our getting home. Capt. Adams will go in the *Saratoga* and probably return overland with the ratifications. This is only supposition. We will visit the Ports and return to China and from there probably here. And from here home.

It is said that the Commodore intends going to Jeddo to salute the Emperor, but that the Japanese object.

April 1st

The *Saratoga* sails next Tuesday or Wednesday. Then or shortly after we will begin to disperse. Some going to Matsmay or the Port that commands the entrance to it, called Kakadada, or Cacky daddy,[48] the Port which is stipulated in the Treaty and others to Shemuda.

I calculated that in about two months Capt. Adams will get home with the Treaty. In one month after the Department will have considered it and send Capt. A[dams] or someone else out bearer of dispatches. Then in two months after this messenger will arrive. This is 5 months, about the time I get the answer to this. Then orders will come to proceed to Jeddo or Japan and Ratify the Treaty which will take two more months. [. . .] Now allowing six months to humbug we ought certainly to be home in 18 months from this time. This is an outside calculation but better not disappoint ourselves for "hope deferred maketh the heart sick." I will constantly keep you advised of the prospects and I hope this may tend to shorten the time. We expect to move from here in about 10 days, but where I can't say. We have a thousand and one rumors about it, but it is all Gas!

I don't believe the Commodore has considered it yet. He is too busy about the treaty to think of anything else yet. We will know soon enough about it, and I think my next letter to you will be mailed in Hong Kong where we will certainly be in a couple of months. We may go to Shanghai first and I hope we may for I am anxious to see the place. We have had a very fine day, winding up with an April shower.

Sunday Evening, April 2nd

A Bazaar is to be opened at Shemuda and free permission granted to roam within a circuit of fourteen miles, or nearly so, the specification being seven Japanese miles.

Mr. Maury[49] who is now the First Lieut. of the *Mississippi* came out in the *Saratoga* and is therefore entitled to go home in her, but he has superintended all the Surveys of these Seas and he is anxious to remain to conduct the remainders of the Surveys, but again he don't wish to remain on account of interfering with the advancement of other Lieutenants. Mr. Pegram is anxious to go home in his place. The affair is not settled yet, but must be in a few days.

Commodore Perry and many other Officers have and do receive presents from the Japanese, or the Emperor. The Japanese have been made to understand that officers in the employ of our Government cannot receive presents from Foreign Powers, but their wives or sisters can, so the presents that have been made have been to Mrs. Commodore Perry, or Mrs. or Miss somebody else! So you see how many ways there are to avoid being scolded.

On Saturday I saw a beautiful writing case and a small dog in a cage for the Commodore, and today another dog came on board as a mate so the breed can be propagated in America.[50] [. . .] Today Mr. Portman the Commodores

Clerk was presented with the pen, or rather the brush that the Commodore signed the Treaty with. Yesterday I had a tin box made to contain this precious article of a Treaty.

April 3rd

We have taken the Port of Kakadada because of its affording a good and near harbor for our whalers. The coast off the northern point of Japan being the best whaling grounds in the world. The Japanese can furnish us coal in any quantity at the ports granted us. All the ports in Japan are open to vessels in distress and vessels so going into any Japanese port will be fitted out and repaired, provisioned and watered, the people in her well treated and everything done to relieve her and expedite her wellbeing. Everything has succeeded beyond the fondest hopes of all. We have done more than was expected could be done with such a people.

We had a great laugh the other day at our First Lieut. The man Cody who got drunk and was put in irons and stanchioned was asked where he got his liquor. "Made it" said Cody. "What out of?" said the 1st Lieut. "Dried Apples" "Where?" "In the ships Coppers" and the 1st Lieut. at once put off and pitched into the ships Cook for allowing the Coppers to be used for distilling liquor! He was completely sold. I never did see such an ass. He beats Billy Bleecker[51] all to pieces.

So again Good Bye. God Bless you. Truly and ever your affectionate husband.

George

U.S. Ste. *Powhatan*, Kenegawa, Bay of Jeddo, April 4th, 1854

My Dearest Lide,

This morning the weather was fine and has continued so during the day. About 9 o'clock signal was made to the *Saratoga* to get underway which she soon did in most beautiful style. Passing the *Mississippi* she was cheered and returned it, the *Mississippi* band playing "Sweet Home." Passing the *Vandalia* she was cheered, and also the *Macedonian*. At this time Capt. Adams left our ship and was cheered. As the *Saratoga* neared us she fired a Salute to the Commodore which was returned by us with 9 guns. We then cheered her and she moved handsomely out of the Bay. At two o'clock she had rounded the point at the "American Anchorage" and was out of sight. Her crew cheered heartily, but the crews of the other ships cheered rather meekly. The poor fellows on the *Saratoga* have been out four years and 'twill be six months hence ere they arrive home. Lieut. Bent[52] joined our ship this morning as Flag Lieut.

Commodore Perry has sent home a request to be relieved, and 'tis thought that he will be relieved and start for home sometime next summer or fall. Of course he will go home on the *Mississippi*. Capt. McCluney still keeps ill, and I am afraid he will not finish the cruise, but go home soon. Lieut. Maury did not go in the *Saratoga*, neither did anybody go in his place.

'Tis getting warm and the Japanese (common people) begin to appear naked. Capt. Adams had his son with him as clerk, and instead of his going home with his father, he goes as Capt. Abbotts[53] clerk on the *Macedonian*. Capt. Abbotts son going home to study medicine.[54] When the old man left the ship this morning young Adams looked very much like despair, his eyes filled and I know his heart ached. But 'twas his choice to remain. I wish I would get a chance to go home. I know how much I would refuse.

April 5th

Last night Mr. Draper had some conversation with the Commodore, and he was told by the Commodore that if he and Mr. Williams wanted to go home (as they had finished with the telegraph, and unless they were sent for from Jeddo no more use could be wanted of them) he would send them home in the Store Ship to sail next fall or he would take them with him in the *Mississippi*. Draper said that he would prefer going with him in the *Mississippi* if she was able to sail soon. The Commodore said that he would remain here 4 or 5 months longer, the[n] return to China and from there home. So we may expect to part company with two more ships within six months viz. the Store Ship *Supply* and the *Mississippi*, and our chance will be next. I hope 'twill not be many months after either.

More presents came off today for the Commodore and Suite, in the shape of Chinese or porcelain cups. When the Bazaar opens at Simoda we no doubt can buy a few "Shaws." No chance have we otherwise.

April 9th

Some Japanese were on board today and Euinoski the Chief Interpreter said in the most solemn manner that if we anchor off the city of Jeddo the four Commissioners and himself would commit Hari Keera, or "Happy Dispatch" that is they would commit suicide by ripping open their bowels. He was laughed at when he said it and looking very solemn and apparently laboring under tense excitement said "you may smile, but I will do my duty the moment an anchor dropped whether I am on your Quarter Deck or in the Commodores Cabin." How many more besides these 4 or 5 would thus destroy themselves we know not, but the Commodore is going to Jeddo, but he says he will not anchor. These people might make good their promise to themselves, but it is very much doubted, and the general impression is that they say this as a "clincher" in diplomacy or in other words it is a "bluff game."

They are a strange people and as my Yankee go aheaditivness and earthly rationality cannot do entirely away with a respect for the sanctity of even Buddhist rites or customs, I would not venture an opinion. Then my knowledge of the character of these people is very limited and I do not consider myself justified in advancing a common sense argument to refute the act of Hari Keera or call it as it appears maniacal. These fellows are taught to believe this an act of justice to themselves and probably their Gods. I would dislike to see anything done to provoke the act. Euinoski is a go[o]d looking fellow and a very intelligent man. He left the ship this afternoon under intense excitement. Some of our officers jest about it, and some go so far as to say they would like to see it! I would not turn my head away, but endeavor to prevent it. What a horrible thing to contemplate. There is considerable excitement on board about it, and much argument about it getting in fact to high words. We will go to Jeddo, but not anchor, and thus no Hari Keera will be committed.

Tomorrow we shall see, until then I will stop as I could fill this with argument pro or con.

April 10th

This morning we raised steam and in company with the *Mississippi*, the sail vessels followed. We proceeded slowly up the Bay until Jeddo was in sight, and could be seen quite distinctly with the glass, when we turned around and proceeded back and kept our way passing Kenegawa and Ukahamma[55] until we reached what is called the American Anchorage which is some 12 or 15 miles below Kenegawa, and here are now at anchor. The Commodore made good his word "to go to Jeddo" but we just got a glimpse of it, and as we did not anchor no Hara Keera was committed. The Interpreter (Euinoski) was on board and went up with us so did some 8 or 10 other Japanese. The "Sweet sight for Vulgar eyes" as the act of Hara Keera might be called therefore was not witnessed.

I had the watch from 12 to 3 and the continual stopping and starting made it a "hard watch," and part of the time the Commodore kept stopping and starting just to show the Japanese how quick the Engines could be stopped. He is a Savant in Steam Engineering (according to his own opinion).

April 11th

The *Macedonian* started this morning for a cruise on the coast of Japan to ascertain the nature of the currents and winds. The Squadron now together consists of the *Powhatan* (Flag ship), *Mississippi*, *Vandalia*, *Lexington*, *Supply* and *Southampton*. The *Plymouth* is at Shanghai, the *Saratoga* on her way home, the *Susquehanna* at Hong Kong and the *Macedonian* as above.

April 12th

The Mandurian Junk that was close by us when we were off Kenegawa has stationed herself here to avowedly watch our movements. To prevent the scurvy the Commodore has ordered the men to exercise the sails twice a day. I exercise with the "dumb bells" daily with a good effect, but I am getting weak for the want of animal foods, for I cannot eat "salt horse." I also drink lime juice. This morning I saw a dish on the table in the shape of balls which looked like potato balls but on examining it I find fried rice and fried rice constitute my foods now. How long this will last I know not, but we all seem satisfied. This results from the fact that what cannot be cured must be endured.

In my description of the people here I feel satisfied that I have not been as explicit as I might be, and I feel like writing tonight so I will take hair for my subject. The Chinese you know wear a tuft of hair growing from the crown of the head and which tuft is allowed to grow to its greatest length and placed in a braid and allowed to hang down over the back like a tail. The head is shaved all around except the circle in the crown from which sprouts the tuft.

The Lou Chouans shave just the crown and gather that which grows on the sides front and back in a tuft or knot in the top of the crown, thus hiding the shaved part. Through this not [*sic*] they stick 2 pins about six inches long, some of the pins being brass and some silver. The higher classes wear the silver pins and the plebeians the brass ones.

The Japanese shave the crown and the front part of the head allowing the hair to grow on the temple, sides and back of the head. This hair combed upwards from the back and sides and back from the temples. The whole thing gathered at the crown and there tied by a piece of thread, the ends being allowed to project from the tie about 4 inches. Their end lies in the shaved part of the head and is cut square off at the end thus resembling black pigtails about 3/4 of an inch in diameter cut short off. So much for hair. You can adopt the Lou Chou style when you pick sufficient from your crown. If you can't get the pins I will bring you a pair. Good night.

April 14th

This morning I brought up Sewell's journals to the present time and as he said that when that occurred he would continue it himself so I am done with it. I have been told that the *Southampton* and *Supply* have gone to Simoda, and that the *Macedonian* to Bonin Islands. The latter to get a quantity of Turtles and bring to the Squadron for food. The Islands of Bonin abounding in such animals.

A few days ago the purser paid out to the men, altogether amounting to twelve hundred dollars and since the men have been gambling in all the hiding places of the ship.

During the negotiations at Kenegawa the Japanese wished to insert a clause in the Treaty prohibiting American women from landing in Japan. This being a feature strictly carried out in their treaty with the Dutch. Upon hearing this Perry threw up his hands and exclaimed "My God, if I would make a treaty of that kind, when I get home the women would hang me!" This so pleased or astonished the Japanese that the Commissioners immediately agreed to strike it out. So if American Consuls or Ministers in embryo to Japan wish to bring their wives and families with them they can do so. Some of the former Dutch Presidents at Nagasaki, Heir [*sic*] Blomhoff[56] in particular, attempted to land his wife, child and nurse but as they were not actually necessary to the carrying on of trade they would not allow them to remain altho they did land. So that during the whole time a Dutch President is in Japan he is separated from his family. We have knicked that arrangement into chaos.

The *Mississippi* has been coaling for some days past. I learn from Capt. Tansill that the Commodore says he will be in Hong Kong about the middle of July and that we go to Simoda next Thursday, remain there sometime and then go to Kakadada

April 15th

This morning the Commodore and a party of Officers went on shore, and just after they left the ship a party of Japanese came on board, the first I have seen since we left the anchorage off Kenegawa. The Commodore and party returned about noon and the Bay inside of "Webster Island"[57] is said to be in connection with the Bay we lay in one of the prettiest and best in the world. I had some conversation with Capt. McCluneys Clerk and he told me that the Capt. said that he would have to be a very sick man before he would go home without finishing this cruise.

When men's times are out they receive one fourth more pay, and in the case of firemen their pay would be about $40 per month, and not only this the men get discontented and insubordinate [. . .] Capt. McC is getting better but he is seen very seldom. Keeps his room almost constantly. Old man City, our Gunner, has been taken sick today and the Doctors say it is a rupture. He is nearly 60 years of age.

April 18th

This morning at two o'clock the fires were started and at five o'clock we got underway. I went on watch at 8 o'clock and the port crank pin was reported warm to me. I ordered the oiler to attend to it and pull the journals and report their condition. Sewell stood by and said don't put any oil in the cups in the main journals for the run will be short and a little can be poured in occasionally through the tubes. So I said to the oiler to report immediately any indication of warmth. At 9 o'clock everything was cool. At 20 minutes past 9 the oiler came towards the store room where I was standing and said the Port inboard main pillow block journal was warm and he wanted piece of wire to clear the tubes. I told him to go and pour some oil on it and I would get the wire as soon as he reached the journal he sung out that it was getting much hotter. I ran up and felt it and ordered water to be poured on it, but before the water arrived the Babbitts metal commenced running out. I ran below and slowed the Engines and sent for Sewell. By this time the metal was running very fast and 'twould have been dangerous to put the water on so I had to stop which occurred at 9h 30 min.

At 10 the *Mississippi* caught up to us and also got some distance ahead when having slicked up the cup and cooled the journal we started ahead and soon overhauled and passed the *Mississippi*. In about two hours we were far ahead of her and she put on all her sails up to Top Gallant sails, and then could not catch us although we had not a stitch of canvas set. This must be very interesting to you, but I write this for my own benefit. Then again this is the first journal that I have ever heated, and it is one of those things that an Engineer most dreads. Gives no one to talk and has the appearance of neglect, but the fault this time was not the Engineers having the watch, but lays in the fact of not having the cups filled and prepared as is their purpose. So not a word was said to me. Sewell said that it mortified him very much.

Shortly after we started ahead I had a man stationed at this journal with the hose, and our Mr. Faron was standing alongside of him when the hose slipped out of his hands and caught between the eccentrich and pillow block tearing the hose, twisting the butt off and carrying away a drip pan and displacing not seriously the eccentric! I had to stop again and clear this wreck which took about a minute, when we started ahead again, and everything went smoothly. At twelve I was relieved, and indeed felt relieved.

We kept gaining on the *Mississippi* and at three o'clock we made the harbor of Simoda and anchored. Here we found the *Vandalia, Lexington, Supply* and *Southampton*. Shortly after we anchored the *Mississippi* came in and here we all are again, in a bay making in to the Northward for a distance of about 2 ½ miles and branching out into coves and smaller bays on either side. At the head of the bay lies the town of Cocksakie, and on the west side of the bay is Simoda. Near the head of the Bay a large rock rises out of the water to the height of nearly a hundred feet, its top covered with a kind of pine or cedar tree. At its base there is a large coffin shaped hole running East and West and completely through from one side to the other. The rock is in shape of a semi elliptic spindle and quite a prominent feature. The land on all sides of us is very high and presents every variety of hill and valley. The country looks barren on the hills but well cultivated in the valleys. We are very well protected except from the South and South West. This is a place at the Southern extremity of the Empire and the other, Hakadada is at the Northern. Some are growling about it and others in ec[s]tasies. We will be allowed to go ashore here and after I have so been I'll speak of the places.

April 19th

I learned today that the Treaty of Kenegawa was not taken to Jeddo until yesterday in consequence of our remaining there and as a result the people here or the authorities have no official information of the affair. We have received no provisions of any kind yet and I feel satisfied that what we do get will be in restricted quantities and course [*sic*] quality.

This place is indeed very picturesque and is to form the subject of Mr. H[e]ines fourth picture. I had a tussle in spirit with a Japanese this morning and the fellow was very strong and would have got the best of me but I tripped him up by a "turn of the foot" and he caved in perfect astonishment. They do everything by main strength.

April 21st

Today we have had it clear but very windy and the winds too direct from the open sea tailing us onto cliff of rocks not over a cables length from us, and we were to go on, good bye *Powhatan*!

At ten this morning the Commodore and party went ashore for some purpose or other that I am not aware of, but seemingly the Japanese consider women a necessary of life, for they had women of every grade paraded before him and they are spoken of as being very pretty. I guess he didn't do anything to them, but I wouldn't trust him, because he is known to love such luxuries and not extremely nice in his selections for a trial.

April 22nd

This morning I took the duty, but instead of putting the men to work about the engine &c. I received orders to send them all to the Captain [Bass] to assist in unmooring and mooring the ship our position being a little dangerous. As there was considerable excitement on deck I went up having no man to look after in the Engine rooms. Our first Lieut. was really crazy and made a great noise and fuss about some Coal heavers that were to go the *Lexington* to bag coal for the *Mississippi*, and said that he had sent to the Engineer of the Watch and he couldn't be found, and in the midst of this raving the men were all reported ready to him and in the boat! Our anchors became foul and the whole business of moving up to eleven o'clock was a complete failure.

I was on deck at the time and Commo. Perry seeing me, beckoned to me and told me to jump into the dingy and go on board the *Mississippi* and tell Capt. Lee to get a "kedge" out and lead a "stream" to us, which I did. The first boat duty I have ever done, and I done that knowing that Perry mistook me for Mr. Rodgers who is about my build. I was not ordered as an Engineer either, and I could have got out of it by simply saying I was on duty in the Engine room. But I done the best by going. It will perhaps be of benefit if I should ever want to turn it in that way. About six o'clock they got the ship moved "after a fashion" and to pay the men for working so hard the "Main brace" was "spliced." In other words all hands got an extra tot of grog.

April 23rd

The houses are built of wood and thatched. Built immediately adjoining one another and but one story high. The fronts are nothing more than a series of sliding doors, and windows. Semi-transparent paper doing the duty of glass. The women do not appear to be afraid, but rather disposed to sociability which is prevented by the confounded officials who follow and watch all who land from the Squadron.

The married women with their blackened teeth and red gums, and shaved eyebrows, are in looks the most disgusting beings I have ever seen. If this custom is a preservation of constancy in their opinions, I think it a good idea. For there would have to be a previous love to engage ones appetite for such a dish.

The young and unmarried women are in many instances very pretty. [. . .] Their teeth are white and clean as they can be made and very pretty. Their hair done up in a style too unique for me to do it justice in description. The hair jet black and fastened up with gilt strings and red ties. A portion of the crown of the head shaved.

Their dress similar to the mens. The dress crossing the breast low down so as to expose the bust, and the legs confined by a simple narrow wrapper passing a la frock around both. A large cotton or silken girdle around the waist confining all. The breasts of the women and girls are small in comparison to American women, as the Loo Choo women are large. The young and pretty women, brunettes occupied my attention and out of curiousity I felt their arms, and stood them up in front of me and examined their condition, just to see how they were developed, and I found that they were built about like other women from the girdle up. I of course was not rude, nor bashful, for wherever we would go at least thirty was around us and they understood that it was curiosity not lasciviousness.

We were unable to make any purchases, and being tired and disgusted, because as we approached the stores and houses the spies would order them shut, and in those that we did get in we opened the doors and took possessions. I saw nothing for sale in the store but common candy and cake, and straw shoes or sandals with some cotton goods, and I have that to go ashore in Simoda is to exercise my legs by scrambling over the hills. Otherwise I am sufficiently amused, and want to go home!

Mr. Bibby told me today the whole of an affair of honor that came off yesterday. Some time ago Passed Midshipman Houston,[58] and Acting Purser McLanahan, both of the Store Ship *Southampton*, had a quarrel and McLanahan challenged Houston, and he accepted and choose small swords as weapons. Yesterday being the first opportunity to settle the affair they went ashore with their seconds. Bibby acting for McLanahan and Dennisson[59] for Houston. But no blood was spilled. The affair being settled on the ground by

McL[anahan] saying that he did not intend to insult Houston, and H[ouston] withdrawing his language about McL[anahan]! Fools! They should have fought and both got stuck just enough to hurt them. Don't mention this affair to any one, because both have a wide circle of friends in the United States.

April 24th

The day clear and warm. This morning I received orders from the Chief to conduct several jobs about the boilers, and having them all underway after dinner I went ashore. I walked through the town and along the beach with Holland. We met a great many Officers from the other ships. In consequence of an order or demand from the Commodore we were not followed today by any of the Officials, but every house was shut up and we could perceive young girls a distance ahead standing by a house, but on our nearer approach they would run in and close doors and windows. We opened several of the doors and entered, but all we could see was the matted floors, and some sewing or other work lying on the mats deserted. Even the tea kettle which we found boiling, and the tea cups with the rice and other food left partially eaten. All deserted. An old hag probably would remain.

In the streets the married women would not run, but on our approaching them they or the men near them would point to the black teeth! Undoubtedly thinking our sole object in coming ashore was to go to bed with them. And then! What fools! The married women would excite a connoisseur like me about such things about as quick as would a cow. Their looks are emphatically disgusting. Even the beauties with unshaved eyebrows and pearly teeth can be but animals under such a government there can be no development of mind nor a recognition of sentiment. The very seasoning and essence of the thing itself, but nevertheless I dreamed last night and probably saved a candidate for the gallows. So far I remain immaculate, and seriously I think I shall remain so, and embrace you as just as you will me.

I joked before about this Japanese Stock in such a way as to lead you to think that I might do something, but "fun is fun," and I prefer dropping the subject. Perhaps you may say "sour grapes" under the circumstances. I noticed a great deal of blindness and some Herpes amongst the lower class.

We begin to get a little fresh grub occasionally. Eggs, sweet potatoes, and dandalines constitute all. I saw both McLanahan and Houston ashore this afternoon. Everybody says they have a quantum sufficient. I have another boil on my neck. The one I had on my cheek has left a scar there but I think it will go away.

April 25th

Last night very late two Japanese came on board and wanted to be retained and go to America, and did not leave the ship until three o'clock when they were taken ashore in one of our boats. They having let their own boats go adrift. About their intentions there is a diversity of opinion about it, some think that they came as spies, some that they were sent by the government to build an excuse which to break the treaty by managing in some way to find we thus interfered with their laws. And some think that they came from pure motives, being disgusted with their despotic rulers and having noticed our Republican Spirit men have allowed the spark of Liberty to kindle, and risked all for the consummation of its glories!

The Commodore has rented a suite of rooms ashore for himself and is making arrangements for engaging rooms for the Artists—Messrs. H[e]ine & Brown. The Com. went ashore this afternoon and went in his house where he found several of our Officers who had been playing cards, and altho he did not detect them they were somewhat frightened.

The boy Jack Canoe, from Loo Choo, and Sam Patch[60] the Japanese had a fight today on board the ship. We have been coaling ship today, and by Perry's plan we got the enormous amount of 16 tons on board! We have before received over two hundred in one day. Capt. McCluney keeps sick yet.

April 26th

We finished coaling from the *Lexington* today, heaving all that she had. The quantity falls short, and 'tis said that the Naval Store at Hong Kong from whom the coal was received is in the habit of giving short allowances. Whether anything will be done about it I can't say, but the matter should be investigated. The officers who were ashore today report that the stores were all open and anything could be purchased. Mr. Misch was on board our ship all day setting type by the manuscript. I see that he is setting the Presidents letter and the Emperors reply. He will no doubt be employed several days.

Mr. Dudley[61] purchased some things today and the Commodore heard of it and "pitched into" him for it. The bazaar opens the 16th of June when all the purchases can be made. As yet I have seen nothing in the shops that I would buy.

April 27th

Today the first copy of the Presidents letter to the Emperor of Japan was printed on this ship.

Mr. Misch has orders to join our ship of course to do the printing. The Rev. Mr. Williams supposes himself to be a printer, but knows but little more about it than I do.

I was standing alongside of Stamm today and Glisson came up to us and told us about the Commodore pitching into Mr. Dudl[e]y for buying things ashore and that less officers would have to go or else the Commodore would stop all going ashore. Now we do not understand whether we are allowed to buy or not. There has been no order issued about the matter one way or the other. While Glisson stood there I asked him if he had ever seen us two together before "Oh, Yea! I know you now." Stamm said, "Well what is my name?" "Stamm" said Glisson. I asked him how he told and he said by Stamm's big whiskers. Notwithstanding all this I would wager the very next time he speaks to me he will call me Stamm. I can't understand it, for we neither look alike, act alike and I am much the largest. We have been with Glisson two years next month. He says that Capt. McCluney is the same way in regards to us.

April 28th

This morning I went ashore in company with a party of Officers, and as we landed met Danby and Logan. Mr. Bibby and I concluded to take a walk quietly into the country and as [we] emerged from the town we met Bresse [Breese][62] and McCauley who joined us and we followed up the valley passing through two towns the names of which I forget, being such "jawbreakers," a distance of nearly five miles, where we halted and secured some stones for seats and a large "rock" for a table situated under the leaves of a thick wood and alongside a stream of cool fresh water we considered ourselves fixed. We played reversal games of whist[63] and then ate our luncheon. After which we smoked and played a few games of poker and returned just in time for the sundown boat and came on board much pleased with our own little "pic nic."

On the way I noticed a couple of rice mills driven by ten wheels about 5ft in diameter, and a kind of tilt hammer for pounding rice also driven by water. The water falling into a scoop fastened on the end of the tilt. When the scoop had caught sufficient water it would descend and emptying as it descended it would come back and strike.

15. Wilhelm Heine, "Public Bath at Simoda," Library of Congress.

The scenery throughout the valley is very picturesque and thoroughly cultivated. The people in the country manifested the most intense curiosity, and at one time I was hemmed in by some 15 or so women examining all parts of my clothes. They were the ugliest looking devils extant. I gave some children a few cash (there are 12 cash to a cent) and some navy buttons. On our way up we found a stream. Bresse [Breese] and myself took off our shoes and socks, rolled up our breeches and drawers and waded through. Bibby and McCauley were carried over on the backs of Japanese. The water was clear as crystals and cool, and 'twas decidedly refreshing.

On coming into Simoda we met Alexander and Roby who pointed out to us a bathing establishment and in we went, and Oh how did thy blush. Men and women, girls and boys as naked as the day they came into this world [. . .] and dabbing water over themselves from one common tub. I saw an old woman and she must have been 80 years of age. A girl probably 14 and one a little older with a very pretty face, and men with everything in sight. These people can have no idea of modesty and certainly none of refinement. The women made but a feint effort only to hide their "agility" which they, as it appeared to me, thought no more of than their feet. This scene took away all sentiment and romance as to the Japanese. In a word the whole people are animals. Leaving you to reflect upon this strange custom and to decide how under the circumstances virtue can remain immaculate. I quit it by asking as excuse for bringing a subject before you notice which disgusted me.

A general order has been issued that we can make what purchases we please, and an exchange of prices has been established. So I expect we will soon see lots of curios. "Ohio" means "good morning" in Japanese, and we were saluted with an "Ohio" today on every side. The shops were all open and the people very kind and sociable, sociable pantomimically.

April 29th

Some of our men went ashore today on liberty, and amongst them one of the Messenger Boys named Knight. The whole party came off drunk and this boy Knight only 13 years of age was as drunk as a beast, and when the First Lieut. spoke to him, he called Glisson all the bad names he could think of. They locked the little rascal up, and Glisson ought to take him in his room and give him a sound flogging. They all got drunk on Sakee of course. Sailors would drink anything that would make drunks come.

Everything that is bought here has to come through the hands of Lasonoski one of the Governments two sworded jockies, unless it is purchased clandestinely. Some say that by going through Lasonoski's hands we only pay the true value, others that it costs double in that way as yet we can't tell much about it. All the silk offered for sale, so far are in quality inferior to the Chinese, but we hope to see better before we leave.

April 30th

This morning it rained and at Nine o'clock I went ashore and during the morning I made a few purchases. Two pairs of sandals, three pipes, two fans and two tobacco pouches. These articles were not worth buying, but I could not rest until I possessed some of Nipons manufactures. The whole caboodle cost me a little over two dollars.

According to the value of a dollar as established by Commodore Perry it is worth 1200 cash, in China it is worth 1400 cash. Now from reliable sources I learn that the relative value of silver and copper in Japan is such as to make a silver dollar worth 3200 cash! This of course Perry did not know when he established the 1200 valuation, and now he says that he will not do anything more in the true value will be established. He also says that officers know it and if they choose to buy let them do it. Of course for this reason everything comes to a high price, but when we return here from Hakadada things will work more congenial.

Someone has reported to the Commodore that Mr. Kellogg could draw, and he has received an order to go on shore tomorrow and take dimensions of a Junk that is building there and make a drawing of her. We have to keep what we do know from Old Brutus. He is sure to come down on us for the use of our knowledge. I believe he is going to publish a book.

May 1st

This morning I received an order per Mr. Sewell, from the Commodore to take from the Engineers Log a statement of the repairs and alterations on the Engines and Boilers from the time we left Norfolk up to the present. The order was given to me because Mr. King whose duty it is, was on shore. Now an abstract was made the other day and the number of days the ship was detained in port of necessary repairs &c. put down at 25, and Sewell wants the number of days in repairs so as required by the order to embrace 26 days. To do this I have been puzzling my noodle to do it and I find it impossible. So to get out of it I passed the order to King tonight and he says he will put down everything that has occurred. I am out of it anyhow.

Old Perry is "down on" this ship and wants these items to make a report to condemn the ship. The Old Humbug thinks that the *Mississippi* is the only Steam Ship afloat. He is an old fogie.

May 2nd

This morning I took another stroll ashore in company with some of the other Steerage Officers and some from the *Mississippi*. We had a pic-nic with about the same routine that we had the other day, but in different directions. We took the beach around the harbor and first stopped upon large rock on the beach where we rested. We found a house and in a cave in the rock we found a small rock arrangement or temple. These temples are the same as those on Lou Chou, containing images, stands and a trashy paraphernalia that begs description. The Priests have shaved heads and live by the contributions. In one of the Temples, the largest I ever seen here I noticed some expensive and well-constructed stands but I cannot "for the life of me" say where they were either beautiful or expensive. I was so impressed at the time and since then I have not considered the subject.

In my peregrinations through the towns and country I have often met a two sworded Mandarin strolling pompously along with a sword bearer and a hat bearer behind, and sometimes a train of from 2 to 6 soldiers carrying very long spears as "protections." Instill into these people an idea of liberty, if that could be done, and a revolution must ensue.

I saw today a pond of water enclosed by a wall of hewn stones, and by clapping your hands alongside the pond a large quantity of gold and other fish would immediately swim to the top. At the head or at one end of the pond was the common executioner block, where offenders' heads are chopped off with but little ceremony (according to writers and the Japanese version), but I saw no trace of blood or "gory locks" about and I have seen performed many acts by some Japanese here, that according to others, would hurry the head off their shoulders.

I paid another visit to the Simoda Bath House as I returned to Simoda from Coxsackie and saw again the same promiscuous intermingling of men and women in the state of nudity. The place we held forth today was about two miles from the town of Coxsackie which by the way is a most dirty filthy village I've seen since leaving Cumsingmoon.

The *Macedonian* arrived here from the Bonin Islands this afternoon. A large sea turtle weighing about 250 pounds was sent to our Ward Room Mess as a present from Dr. Woodworth.[64] I understand there are about 60 more on board of her and we are fixing our mouths for turtle soup and turtle steaks.

May 5th

Sometime since I mentioned that the coal account of the *Lexington* fell short, and it appears that in all stores received from the Naval Store Keeper at Hong Kong and Macao[65] there has been some defect and the Commodore is now investigating the subject and 'tis believed that he will be able to "bust up" the house of DE Silver & Co. That house having for its head this Naval Store Keeper.

In Squadrons, signals are made in the morning when the sails require drying, for all ships to loose sails and when they are dry which generally occurs in the afternoon. Signal is made to full sails and considerable rivalry exists between the different ships about getting through first, and the whole business of furling is nothing but a race and hurry. This afternoon we made signal to furl sails and as usual all was a race.

In the hurry a man named Parrish[66] fell from the Fore Topsail Yard to the deck, a distance of 74 feet and broke his right leg, badly fractured his shoulder blade and broke his left arm and some of his ribs. He lived about two hours and then died. He was perfectly conscious and in the most intense pain. He gave his clothes &c. away a few moments before he died. The broken bones forced themselves through the flesh and clothes and made on the deck where he fell two holes, one nearly an inch deep! The fracture of the shoulder was the most horrible one I ever saw. He is to be buried tomorrow. This is the second death on board our ship since we have been in commission.

May 6th

We have been living on turtles ever since the arrival of the *Macedonian*. The *Macedonian, Vandalia*, and *Southampton* sailed this morning as was anticipated yesterday. The man who was killed yesterday was buried this afternoon in one of the Japanese burying grounds. His name was Geo. W. Parrish, aged 21 years and from New London Connecticutt.

Saturday Night, May 7th

Danby and Mr. Haggarty saw the two Japanese that I mentioned the other day as having come on board and made a request to be retained on board, and stated that they wanted to go to America. Well, these two customers were seen caged in a cage just large enough to allow them to sit down in one position and to lay down in another, and from the motions &c. that they made were soon to have their heads taken off. On the Commodore hearing this he sent Mr. Williams and Mr. Bent on shore this morning offering to bring them off, but they had gone to Yedo to be executed. That is to have their heads chopped off.

May 9th

Yesterday morning Messrs. H[e]ine, Bent and Nicholson took a stroll into the country designedly to be gone two days, having the Commodores permission and their guns along to shoot any and what game they could. Towards night they became tired, and the people in the country being afraid to, gave them asleep or a place to sleep they made for the town of Simoda where there arrived about eleven o'clock last night and went into a temple to rest until morning. They had not been long here before they walked up on by a number of Mandarin Soldiers who insisted upon their leaving and going on board the ship, which they refused to do, and as the Japanese were our officers loaded their guns and revolvers and drove the crowd away, who at once came on board and made a report to Commodore Perry and requested him to send for the gentlemen at the temple which the Commodore refused to do. So they went off with "glass in their ears."

This morning at Six o'clock H[e]ine and the others came on board, and at nine Bent and Nicholson accompanied by Williams and Portman, the interpreters went on shore to investigate the matters. [. . .] This evening Messrs. Bent and Nicholson have returned.

They saw the Prefect on shore and represented the affair last night as an insult, outrage, &c. and this worthy wanted to see Com. Perry when he was told that Com. Perry was too high for him to see, that Com. P. could talk with no one below their Emperor, and that an instant apology was needed to prevent a ship being sent immediately to Yedo. They made at once the most humble apologies and said that the conduct of the officers was unauthorized (I mean by officers the Japanese officials). They were then told that a repetition of anything of the kind would lead to Com. Perry's sending a guard of Marines on shore to arrest such as might be engaged in it, and that they would be punished on board ship! So we need fear no further molestation if by chance any of us have to remain on shore all night. Perry knows exactly how to manage these cowardly effeminate people. They are truly like so many children. They have no firmness or stability of character, but if they see that they have the advantage they will domineer and tyrannize to a full extent. They have been much overstated by all the writers on Japan.

May 10th

Today we have had a continual rain and the Steerage Hatch being covered in consequence it made it very warm and uncomfortable below, and to go on deck was to contract rheumatism and colds. So all and all we have passed a most uncomfortable day. When it rains all hands have been in the habit of smoking on the starboard side under the Hurricane Deck. The portside being blocked up by the Carpenters Bench and inhabited by the men. We have in the Ward room a Lieut. Nicholson. That is, he is a Passed Midshipman acting Lieut. and another worthy named Lowry, also a Passed Midshipman and Acting Master.

These two "High Mandarins" have been finding fault about the Steerage Officers smoking on the starboard side and several times an order has passed by the First Lieut. prohibiting the offensive act, but no attention was ever paid to it. This morning the First Lieut. said that so much fault had been found about it that he was compelled to insist upon the order for the Steerage Officers to smoke somewhere else, and so far the order has been obliged. A great many of the Steerage Officers are of course deservedly agonized about it but to no purpose. One of these complainants (Lowry) will probably be in the steerage before he goes home, for there is a Passed Mid out here that ranks him. The injustice and arrogances of the affair you can well conceive. As I smoke but very little and when I do it is general on the Hurricane Deck it affects me but in principle.

May 11th

This afternoon I went ashore, and may it be the last time unless a change is made. There I saw nothing but disgusting obscenity, and although of strong nerve I really felt sick at my stomach. On the occasion of my looking into the Bath House which I have described before I saw that a great many had scars and sores on their backs, and on my way to the wharf I looked into a house and saw a man lying on his breast naked and another burning his back in different places or spots. This is a mode of breaking affections of the eye and I believe other diseases. So much for the enlightened spirit of Japan. Oh glorious humbug! And most grand deception. The Japan expedition of '52, '53, '54 and perhaps 55 will be elapsed by posterity with Patient Medicines, Fire Annialators [*sic*] and those of Barnum[67] Noteriety [*sic*] experiments.

North Pacific Ocean off the Island of Nippon., May 14th

Today the Commodore has been in a dreadful fever about the coaling. The poor old *Mississippi* could not keep up with us although we were running very slow, and at first the Commodore reduced our furnaces, and now (after sundown) she has caught us, and we have resumed our speed. The Commodore had a long talk with our first Lieut. today and he is awfully "down on" Sewell because Sewell won't "boot lick." Today he sent for the Engineer of the watch and asked questions of him. Then passed all orders through his orderly immediately to the Engineer of the Watch, treating Sewell badly. This afternoon he said that when we arrived in Hong Kong he was going to leave us and that the *Powhatan* was the best steamer he had ever been in and vastly superior to the *Susquehanna*. This was a free open acknowledgement.

May 15th

Today has been one of the best days for Steaming I have ever seen, and we have been going along very nicely. The *Mississippi* keeping her position very well. She was allowed by the Commodore one furnace more than us and no restriction of coal, whereas we were restricted to a low measure. We have seen large quantities of Sperm Whales today spurting, spouting and garbling on the water.

I had the watch from noon until three and just before three o'clock the Commodore sent for me (as Engineer of the Watch) and wanted to know where "that steam came from." "Surface blows, sir." "I know better," said he "Very well sir, 'tis never the less the surface blows," and then followed a series of questions and answers too trifling for a thought and he is Commodore. He wound up by saying he knew a d[amne]d sight better and I went below and the surface blows made as much steam as ever, and Commodore Perry can stop the engines, but he can't stop that. He was tight as "full as a tick."

May 17th

Yesterday we had a most beautiful steaming day and in the afternoon we made the land but not knowing our position exactly with regards to the harbor we laid to during the night. Sometime during the afternoon the wire to the Engine Room bell broke and Perry saw it. He at once sent for Sewell and told him to keep his bells in order. Sewell said they were in order! So Sewell is suspended and for no cause whatever. Perry was drunk, and made a perfect show of himself. Sewell told me he would not write a letter or notice it any way whatever. He has no just fault to find with Sewell and his enmity arises from the fact that Sewell is too independent for him. He told Sewell that he played the gentleman too much in the Ward Room. It would do no good to continually repeat what this man says and does, but he is the "head and front" of us out here, and a great tyrant head he is.

This morning I had the Watch from 4 to 8. During the fore part of the watch we were enveloped completely in a fog and the bells and steam whistle were kept going so that the *Mississippi* could keep clear of us. At about six it cleared up and the *Mississippi* was very close to us. The land was in sight and we "put for it." Before eight the ships *Vandalia, Macedonian*, and *Southampton* were discovered and about 10 we came to anchor in the Harbor of Hakodada. This is the best harbor we have seen yet. Almost perfectly land locked and very large.

The people here know nothing as yet of the Treaty as the Interpreter Namora has not arrived. He is expected every day, and until he does come very little, if anything, can be done. The country looks bleak and barren. On one side of the harbor it looks like a sand desert backed by high snow clad hills. The other parts are all high and the snow is plainly seen on the mountains. It is very cold. The harbor abounds in fish. The seine has been hauled and some salmon, porgies, and flounders caught. The place is in Latitude 41° and some minutes, and Longitude 141° some minutes East.

The town of Simoda lies on a neck of land or mountain running apparently from the main land into the Ocean. Instead of sculling their boats like they do at the other places in Japan that we have been, they row with a kind of awkward twist combining a screw idea with all their motions of propelling. The day has been very hazy and the shore, town, &c. cannot be seen from the ship very distinctly, so I'll quit for the night and give you my views as they impress me.

May 18th

This morning the Commodore sent a party of Officers ashore to make known to the authorities that a treaty had been made and that he would send his Officers ashore to walk around. The authorities here having no information whatever of our transactions with their Government. Some few went on shore and report that the place is far superior to Simoda. That the streets are wider, the houses larger and better build and that the Temples of Worship are very beautiful. The people were polite and hospitable, but I have not been ashore yet and I'll defer until I see for myself. An opinion and description will then be attempted.

In consequence of some noise in the other steerage last night a mandate has been issued not by the Commodore, by the Captain, decreeing that the lights in the Steerages shall and must be put out at nine o'clock. Now we have had them until ten o'clock on ever since we left the United States. Well it's the Navy as Purser Barry[68] says. Nothing has been done yet with Sewells case and he walks the deck now with white kid gloves on just for fun.

We have had an idle rumor afloat today that Old Perry is going to leave our ship and go to the *Mississippi* before we leave this harbor. This place is where Capt. Golowin[69] of the Russian Service was so long in captivity. We received some chickens and eggs today. I mention this because they constitute the best of the food that we get. Oh give me back my Native Land!

We anticipate remaining here some three weeks, but for what purpose I know not, and as I am so thoroughly disgusted with Japan that I must say I don't care. Never mention Japan to me. Glorious bubble. Emphatic humbug. Worthless, corrupted and lost Empire. Thy paraded [revision?] and brilliant wealth. Thy knowledge, politeness, and strangely supposed content and happiness is but a mass of ignorance, superstition, want, degradation, disease, and imbecility. But Time, Old Father Time will tell, and tell to the discredit of the Empire of Japan, for her wealth and resources so magnificently portrayed will show but a poor miserable Island.

May 19th

Today Commodore Perry left the ship officially for a short time and held an interview on board the *Mississippi* with the Officials of Hakadade, the result of which I have not thought worthwhile to inquire about for there has been already so many interviews with the same results that they have become a bore. So if any different result should issue from any of future interviews I will unfold them.

This place is a great fishing place and fine Salmon are caught at the mouth of a fresh water river that runs into the Bay. I have not tasted any yet. But poor unfortunate mess! How well will we be able to appreciate a cup of coffee and a beef steak smothered in onion! Roast Beef! Ah what a sound is that. Potatoes, fish, potatoes what a luxury. Hard tack, Beans, salt horse, rice and dried apples no more. Don't you think I'm getting fat on such grub? A few months more and the inner man will be treated.

The people of this place have all deserted, or had, thinking that this array of ships was a kind of Piratical Expedition, having heard nothing whatever about our arrangements with their government.

May 20th

This morning I went ashore and landed at a place called the reception house, and which surpasses everything of the kind in beauty, style and furniture—besides in the politeness of the Officers in charge, that I have seen in Japan. We were furnished with very good tea and treated handsomely. From here I took a stroll through the town, which is as far superior to Simoda as New York is to Portsmouth. The streets are wide and the houses well-built of wood. The roofs of which are covered with stones to prevent their blowing off. Some of the roofs are tiled and the tiling of the principal Temple here is the best work of the kind I have ever seen. This Temple is a very large building and the beams supporting the roof, the columns and the mouldings were carved more elaborately and deeper than any I have yet noticed. The heavy guilding and massive brass storks standing on the backs of tortoises form marked feature in the arrangements.

May 22nd

An order was issued this morning by the Commodore to the Officers who got swords yesterday to return them tomorrow. What the immediate circumstances attending the order are I don't know.

May 23rd

This morning those swords were handed over to Mr. Bent the Flag Lieut. per orders of Commodore Perry. A signal was run up about nine o'clock saying "no communication with the shore." Old Hog went ashore himself and made considerable purchases amounting as I hear to one hundred and fifteen dollars. He didn't want to be disturbed in his purchases and that accounts for no one else being allowed to go today.

Mr. Williams the Interpreter says that the Japanese have made no particular complaints about the swords, but that they have complained of Officers visiting their shops and taking off articles without paying for them. We have undoubtedly men mean enough to be guilty of this, but the real trouble in this case is their not being able to pay for them. The men or owners of the goods refusing to take the money and also the Mandarins. [. . .] At any rate a great many of the "American Navy" have been very indiscreet, and the reading of the manner in which Japanese Stores were entered and their goods overhandled by the "Americans" would entail an idea that their object was pillage and plunder!

An edict has been issued that no Steerage Officer shall go ashore until after the Ward Room Officers have made all their purchases! What do you think of that! A Bazaar is to be opened here too! Well, let 'em buy. The greatest "curios" that can be bought home is the "Almighty Dollar."

Perry is an exceedingly just man! He will be President of the United States. He will. He has stopped the Liberty of all Steerage Officers! He has insulted almost every officer in the Squadron! He has proved himself to be unqualified for his post. He is no gentleman and ignorant of his own immediate business as a sailor.

May 29th

Another man died yesterday on the *Vandalia*. His case was typhoid fever. Our ship has been exceedingly fortunate. The only man lost was Parrish who fell from aloft. There is to be an Ethiopian Concert on board our ship tonight. The bills were printed this morning. Mr. Misch is now a regular printer. The printing office is in our Steam Chimney room.

Tuesday May 30th 1854

Last night according to announcement an Ethiopian Concert was given on board our ship. All the Japanese Officials of Hakodade, and some High Officers from Matsmai, and Jeddo were on board, and Officers from all the ships in the Squadron. I enclose you a bill of the performances printed on a Japanese Ladys pocket handkerchief. Those who witnessed the performance were well pleased. A great many did not see the performance but remained in the Ward Room and Steerages enjoying a very regular spirit, and almost everybody got tight. Our steerage was almost afloat with liquor, and even now there is half a dozen talking of the scenes. I never in my life witnessed so many ridiculous and ludicrous scenes in so short a time in my life. Poor Danby, he turned in, in my bunk perfectly gone. This morning at six o'clock I got a boat for him and sent him on board. Don't say a word about it. It was a night of revelry and even the men were allowed liquor.

One thing only occurred to mar the hilarity and good feeling of all, and that was occasioned by Mr. Fauth who is Caterer of our Mess, he took a bottle from the table and emptied the liquor into the Slop tub. Mr. Faron rushed for the bottle and Kellogg interfered and high words and almost blows entered when I was called for and what a scene! I rushed in and separated the parties and pacified them. This morning Mr. Faron spoke of it and Fauth told him that he would give him any satisfaction that one gentleman could ask of another! Faron back down. Whether it is at an end or not I can't say, but presume it is. This little spree was well put in. You cannot imagine how moody everybody was getting, and the "little spree" has made sore heads and strange to say, glad some faces! Everything appears to have been transmogrified.

Give my love to Mother and all, and with unfaltering fidelity, I as ever, remain your devoted and loving husband. George

Hakodado [Hakodate], Island of Iesso [Hokkaido],
Empire of Japan, May 31st, 1854

My Dearest Lide,

We have a kind of large boom rigged out forward for the purpose of sounding as we "go long" this is only indicative of what we can only express by the word "humbugging." We have lived better here than at any place since leaving China. What do you think of eating Muscle [*sic*] Soup and fried muscles [*sic*]? Strange taste, but they are really very good, and I am willing to compromise for them until we get back to civilization.

June 1st

There has been a grand talk this afternoon on board our ship between the officials from Yedo and the Commodore. There is some misunderstanding or else the Japanese feeling themselves rather large are endeavoring to humbug Old Perry but he is obstinate and will make them cry "pecavie" [*sic*] before he is done with them. All these interviews and conclusions interest me but very little, my thoughts run on home and you.

June 2nd

The misunderstanding that I spoke of yesterday was nothing more than the neglect of the Officials from Jedo to call immediately upon His Highness Comodore Perry. They did so, nevertheless yesterday afternoon where I suspect everything wrong was made right. The Commodore had boats lowered, the Marine Guards out, the Sailors "armed to the teeth" this morning for the purpose of calling on these fellows on shore, but it rained and the visit abandoned.

June 7th

Here we are in the Harbor of Simoda again where we arrived about one o'clock this afternoon. We expected to get in on Monday evening, but being disappointed we made sure that we would get in on Tuesday morning but it rained on Tuesday and thickened up so that we could not see anything. This morning at five o'clock it cleared up and the Commodore allowed us ten furnaces and as much coal as we wanted. The *Mississippi* being allowed all her furnaces and as much coal as she wanted, nevertheless the Old *Powhatan* "walked away" from her and left her some six or seven miles astern. As soon as we anchored we made signal "no communication with the shore." The only vessel here besides the two steamers is the *Supply*. The Japanese and Capt. St. Clair[70] of the *Supply* had some little difficulty about one of the soldiers pushing his clerk. They were told that Americans were not Dutchman, and that though peaceably disposed no insult would be tolerated.

June 9th

Another visit was paid ashore by the Commodore today. Seven Princes from Jedo had arrived here even before us, and things look as if the Japanese wanted to end this "party" and get us away. I have just finished some on our safety values and from the use of a hammer one of my fingers is somewhat blistered, so slips of the pen must be excused.

Our Purser received a list of the Commodores attaches this morning and with it an order to make out their accounts to be transferred to the *Mississippi*. This looks as if Perry intended to leave us soon, and therefore every face is glad today.

June 10th

Sewell was sitting in a chair on the Hurricane Deck when the Commodore saw him and sung out "Sewell, Sewell, Sewell, Sewell go below and attend to your Engines, don't sit up here in that way. It is not a proper position!" Sewell went below and remained a few moments and there returned on deck and was met again by the Commodore who hailed him and said "go below and examine your boilers, you are getting too big for your business!" Sewell touched his cap and said "yes sir" and went below. Danby was on board and heard the first part of it, and he was perfectly astounded.

At about a quarter after six Sewell sent for me and said that he wanted me to notice that he examined the boilers in accordance with the order. Whilst I was down there Mr. Glisson came down and said, "Mr. Sewell, the Commodore wants you to make out a written report of the condition of the boilers, and he says that he will examine them tomorrow himself." "Very good, Sir." Sewell had the man hole plates and the connexions cleaned out last night after the occurrence though the men had knocked off work some time before. Up to this time (noon) the Commodore has not examined the boilers. He insults Sewell in this way so as to make Sewell commit himself, but Sewell is too wide awake for him. He and his host leave us next week, and Fortune be praised for it.

Another visit was paid to shore yesterday and the Japanese made presents to the Commodore and the President of the United States. I saw some of them and the lacquer ware cabinets and boxes are truly magnificent. Nothing like them can be bought.

This afternoon Mr. Glisson our First Lieut. and Mr. Boudinot another Lieut. had some words on the Hurricane deck. The 1st intends to prefer charges for disrespect and disobedience of orders. Now I was unfortunate enough to overhear them and if there is a Court Martial I will probably be subpoenaed as a witness.

June 11th

The affair between Mr. Boudinot and Mr. Glisson was investigated this morning by Lieuts. Maury and Bent who were ordered to do so by the Commodore. I was called on and lead off for the defence. As the interested parties agreed to abide by the decision of these two gentlemen and after they had heard the matter through they decided that both were wrong and both should make apologies. So Mr. Glisson withdrew his letter about it to the Commodore and the affair is settled.

June 12th

Last night I had the Mid Watch and during the first hour of the watch about six bags of coal was hoisted in. The ships men were in almost mutinous condition, my men were all stationed and ready at 10 minutes past 12. I reported the condition of the men to Mr. Haggerty who had the deck and he is such a "lackudaisy" that the men pay no attention to him. Cursing and growling during the whole watch by the "gentlemen sailors!" They heaped all kinds of oaths on the firemen who of course did not hear it as they were below decks, but they heard of it and this morning they were up in arms and ready to "pitch into" the whole band of worthy sailors. Our men are the only ones in the ship that are in any kind of discipline.

June 17th

Yesterday the Imperial Commissioners from the Court of Jedo visited the different ships. They came on board our ship at about five o'clock and witnessed a mock fight or in other words we went to General Quarters and exercised the Guns, fire apparatus &c. We had steam on the Boilers and moved the Engines for their edification. From our ship they went on board the *Mississippi* where the Commodore had an entertainment set out for them and our "Serenaders" gave a concert. I went.

Sunday, June 18th

This morning the Commodore left the *Powhatan* for good! But the Broad Pennant flies at four mast until tomorrow morning where it will go up on the *Mississippi* and she will be the Flag Ship again.

Mr. Arnold turned fool the night of the Entertainment on the *Mississippi* and got drunk. Not satisfied with that he kept it up yesterday and was suspended in consequence. As he will make no concessions, he will have charges preferred against him and be tried by a Court Martial perhaps. Some of our men lift boat that was on shore yesterday and they got some Sakie which made them drunk and violent, so a row was kicked up between them and some Japanese which ended in a man named Mordite getting cut badly across the hand and a Japanese across the leg. So it ends. I am so heartily disgusted with Japan that I hate to write anything about it, or what occurs in it.

June 19th

At eight o'clock this morning the Broad Pennant of Commodore Perry "Special Ambassador from the United States to the Court of Jedo" and "Commander in Chief of the U.S. Naval Force in the East India, China and Japan Seas" (!!!) was hoisted on board of the *Mississippi* and hauled down on the *Powhatan*. The narrow pennant of Capt. McCluney now flies at our mast head. When Perry left yesterday he regularly sneaked off. No one saw him over the side and although entitled to a guard of Marines, a full turn out of the officers and three rolls of the drum, he didn't get even the pipe of a Boatswains Mate. He was emphatically driven out of the ship!

This morning when the "Broad" went up on the *Mississippi* and came down on us, our men really cheered. Never has a man made himself so unpopular as Commodore Perry.

June 22nd

We finished coaling today. This morning a signal was made to "settle all bills and prepare for sea," so in a day or two we bid farewell to Japan. The difficulty on the *Mississippi* about the Masters Mate or articles missing with the Passed Midshipmen was settled today by Commodore Perry who ordered a bulk head to be erected so as to divide the Steerage. The Passed Midshipmen are hopping mad about it, but there is no use kicking against the bricks. My days duty tomorrow. Good Night.

Japan, June 23rd, 1854

This morning while I was mustering the men I received an order to fire the boilers and start the fires. So about half past ten we had steam and unmoored the ship and took our position ahead of the *Southampton*. The *Mississippi* followed and took a position outside of us distant about half a mile. We finished all this about twelve o'clock since then we have been under banked fires. We are to start for Lou Chou tomorrow with the *Southampton* in tow. I have the Mid Watch tonight and by the time I get up in the morning I suspect we will be fifty or sixty miles from Japan. We may have to return next fall, but I doubt it. Soon we will have news from home! All of us can't receive good news, some must be disappointed, but I am anticipating. I hope these may be the last times I shall have to pen in Japan. So good night.

Chapter Four

July 3–December 28, 1854

Lou Chou, Nappa Kiang Harbour. July 3rd

The *Lexington* is here, and a new missionary in the place of friend Bettleheim.[1] [. . .] When the *Lexington* first came here, her officers were treated very badly. They could get no provisions, water or anything. This was in consequence of a report having been made by a Japanese who came in a Junk from Japan that the Americans had been driven out. Afterwards a difficulty ensued on shore and some time after the Lou Chouans brought off the body of one of the *Lexington's* men whom they said was found drowned.[2] But upon examining the body the skull was found to be fractured and badly bruised. The affair has been reported by Capt. Glasson[3] of the *Lexington* to the Commodore and this morning the affair is being investigated. Old Perry will probably demand the murderer.

Yesterday morning Old Bettleheim preached on board our ship. I suppose he will return to Hong Kong with us. The Russian Fleet was in here some time ago before the arrival of the *Lexington*. I went on board the *Mississippi* yesterday and had a long talk with Arnold. I advised him to secure the services of Mr. Spaulding,[4] who is a very good lawyer, and he half promised that he would. Capt. Lee and Mr. Lanier[5] insist upon his being tried this week.

July 5th

Yesterday was the glorious fourth. We celebrated it by a salute of 17 guns at noon and "Splicing the Main Brace." In the afternoon I went on board the *Mississippi* and enjoyed myself very much. All communication with the shore is prohibited. This is consequent upon the affair of the murder which is being investigated thoroughly. It appears now that the man was in the act of committing a rape and was driven off by a party of Lou Chouans with clubs and stones. All is yet uncertain, but it is certain that nothing will be left undone to secure every redress. About the matter there is great diversity of opinion.

July 6th

The Court Martial in Arnold's case convened again this morning and all the evidence on both sides concluded. I was called for the defence and testified as to general character. Sewell was then called and testified about the same thing and the Court adjourned to meet tomorrow morning at eleven o'clock when his defense will be read and the case concluded. As yet he can form no idea of what the sentence will be. The charges were preferred by Jesse Gay and not by Capt. Lee, who was at first one of the Court but on convening was ruled out. The Lou Chouans were to give a decided answer as to the murder case this afternoon, but as they did not do so, the Commodore has ordered 24 Marines under Capt. Tansill to occupy the Hospital ashore under arms. They left the ships, 12 from the *Mississippi*, and 12 from our ship about 4 o'clock this afternoon.

July 7th

The Lou Chouan authorities brought a man whom they said was the ringleader of the party who murdered the man from the *Lexington* stating that they had in jail 12 more who they would also bring off. The Commodore ordered the man taken back and remanded to the authorities and to be punished by them. So the affair is ended. Now whether the guilty will be punished or whether any punishment at all will result depends upon the authorities ashore. The Marines have been recalled from the shore and the Artists &c. have again taken up their quarters.

Sunday, July 9th

About eleven o'clock yesterday morning all hands were called to muster, men and officers and the finding and sentence of the Court Martial in Arnold's case was read. He was found guilty and sentenced to be publicly reprimanded by the Commodore (which reprimands was read) to be dismissed from the Flag Ship and ordered to some other steamer, and to be kept on board ship and not allowed to go ashore for two months! Now the sentence is very mild, but I think, and so does many others that the reading of the sentence before the men was unjust. That the Officers alone should have been mustered. Arnold wrote a letter to the Secretary of the Navy about it and sent it to Capt. Lee to be forwarded, but at the solicitation of Capt. Lee he withdrew it. In conformity with the sentence of the Court he has been ordered to our ship, and yesterday afternoon he came on board with "bag and baggage." So, we now have eight assistant engineers, and as this will give us 8 watches and it will make it much more easy.

July 10th

Yesterday afternoon Capt. Tansill of the Marine Corps was detached and left our ship and joined the *Mississippi*. Lieut. Jones[6] who came out in the *Macedonian* and joined the *Mississippi* upon Major Zeiland going home has taken Capt. Tansill's place on board our ship. We are all very sorry that Tansill has left us. We have a rumor that we leave here Saturday next for Amoy and Ningpoo.[7] We are coaling again today and 'tis said now that between the two steamers all the coal that is ashore is to be taken off. The Missionary who preached on board yesterday is an Englishman named Mor[e]ton.

July 11th

Yesterday afternoon I went ashore and was disgusted. Saw the stone over Crosby's[8] grave erected by his mess mates and it is a shameful affair. Badly done and worse than none.

July 12th

I have been reading O'Meara's *Napoleon* and Hazlitt's *French Revolution and Life of Napoleon*. I am a great admirer of that man. Think that he possessed more talent than any man that ever died mortal.

July 15th

The Commodore sent an expedition to an island about 10 miles distant from here, and where the Lou Chou women of immoral character are banished to. They have returned but saw none of the women. There are no prostitutes in Lou Chou. At the age of 10 years every male takes a mate so from that age they commence operations. If a women is caught guilty of inconstancy she is banished and any who choose to visit the place of banishment have perfect liberty to "go in lemons." In Japan I sincerely believe that promiscuous intercourse is as common as rice eating. The formation of the Lou Chou women is much better than the Japanese. Though the Japanese are whiter and better looking, but all are forbidding. I did see a few Japanese women that were somewhat tempting, but no Lou Chouans. The particular sing is in favor of Japan. The generality in favor of Lou Chouans.

United States Steamer *Powhatan*, At Sea, July 18th, 1854

My Dearest Wife,

We left Nappa Harbor, Lou Chou in company with the *Mississippi* yesterday morning and about nine o'clock we parted company. We bound for

Ningpoo and she direct to Hong Kong. About three o'clock yesterday afternoon we made a Dutch Boat and made her "heave to." We sent a boat on board to learn what news one could. The Captain said that he left Shanghai nine days ago and that then the *Susquehanna* and *Vandalia* were at that place. That the rebels had possession of Shanghai and in consequence everything was very dear there. That war between Russia and Turkey was progressing.[9] He had no newspapers or any small stores to part with. After detaining him about half an hour we let him go and proceed on our way.

July 21st

This morning a "bum boat" came alongside filled with peaches, pears, water melons and other fruits peculiar to that place which were delightful. I spent a dollar and have been reveling in luxurious fruit all day. Such pleasures! Besides, we have received fowls and vegetables of every description. Even green corn! Then without exaggerating some of the best beef that I have seen since leaving the United States. Indeed 'tis a treat to get good grub once more.

Yesterday afternoon a fleet of Portuguese Lorchers, small boats, armed, about 50 or 100 Lou Chouans, passed our ship and dipped their colours to us. This morning we heard the reports of guns and did not know what to make of it. About 10 o'clock the Capt. received a notice from Mr. Pegram who went up to Ningpoo yesterday morning in command of the boats that the Portuguese had joined the rebels and were bombarding the town of Ningpoo. A file of Marines and a boat's crew were immediately started off in one of our launches for the [sound] of war and we got up steam and proceeded about five miles and anchored off the town of Chin hai [Zhenhai] at the mouth of the river Yung.[10] Ningpoo is seven miles up the river. We have all kinds of reports about the "war and damages," but nothing certain yet. Old McCluney is a "fighting man" and will protect the "American Interests."

July 22nd

This morning I got the Captains permission to go ashore, and about two o'clock in company with Sewell and Kellogg took the "bum boat" and landing on a point about 2 miles from the grand city. After about an hour's walk through the sand we reached the city outside the walls. I can say nothing more that it is a "Chinese built" city. Narrow street and houses as described in Canton, but no Europeans or American articles for sale in the stores. Nevertheless almost anything can be bought except liquor. I bought a piece of blue crape, 19 yards, for eleven dollars and five pieces of yellow nankeen[11] for two dollars and a Chinese pipe and some fruits.

We received intelligence of a difficulty between the *Plymouth* and some of the Chinese rebels, and that some of the *Plymouth*'s men were killed. The difficulty as we hear it originated by the Chinese invading neutral grounds. We will learn more about it when some of our Officers return from Ningpoo. We hear too that this great "Japanese Expedition" is recalled.

July 24th

This morning about half past five we got underway. I made a mistake in my statement that the Portuguese had joined the rebels. These Portuguese under guises of suppressing piracy carry on a system of it themselves, and the difficulty at Ningpoo was in consequence of the Chinese authorities refusing to pay them a sum of money demanded on a count of their services. They fired into the town, but the Chinese did not return it. The Portuguese Commander was made to understand that he would be held responsible for any damage done to Americans and he kept quiet. We are on our way to Lou Chou.

July 26th

This morning we made the land and about eleven o'clock we anchored, under the lid of an island some twenty miles off the mouth of the river. Minus the mouth of the river being 10 miles from Lou Chou town. This is what I call anchoring at sea. Just after we anchored we fired a gun and hoisted the Jack for a Pilot, but up to this time (after 8 o'clock) we have not seen a human being. The Island is small and completely barren. It is one of the "Two Dogs."

August 2nd

Yesterday morning about nine o'clock we got underway from Lou Chou and after a most delightful run we anchored off the city of Amoy (where we now are). This morning about ten o'clock, here we have received fruits, provisions &c. and the ship has been swarmed with Chinese Merchants anxious to sell all kinds of goods, among which I noticed second hand Mandarin dresses of silk and of very gaudy appearance. I bought a cloth and a pair of carved bracelets. We fired two salutes, one for the English Consul[12] and one for the American Consul.[13] A boat was sent ashore with the Consul and whilst waiting for some papers six of our men jumped out and ran away. Several came off drunk and they are now "forfeiting" at this stanchion.

The outside appearance of Amoy, like all the China coast barren.

August 5th

On the morning of the 3rd, the runaways spoke of above came on board and were punished by being put in irons for 40 hours. We made an examination of the piston and found it loose. We tightened it without much trouble and are ready for sea.

This place is now in possession of the Imperials who took it from the Rebels in March last, after which followed an outrageous and extravagant decapitation. Every week or so some Rebels are taken and beheaded. Today nine of these poor wretches were beheaded on the beach abreast of our ship, and we could see the whole affair. Truly revolting and barbarously brutal. The victims get on their knees with their hands tied behind their backs, in a row like birds perched on a fence. The executioner steps up with an axe, the culprit bows his head towards the ground, the axe falls on the back of the neck, off comes the head, and the next one in the line bows like his neighbor now dead and thus until the line is finished. All disperse. The heads and trunks remain with none to watch or care for them for a few hours. A few of the officials and coolies then return to the ground, dig a hole, throw the heads and bodies in and all is done with no more excitement or apparent feeling than I seen at the killing of a sheep.

July [August] 11th

The whole North Pacific Surveying Expedition Fleet are here. Commodore Ringgold[14] has gone crazy and Old Perry has charge of the vessels composing his squadron. Capt. Rolando[15] of the *Porpoise*[16] has had charges preferred against him by Jno. Van McCollum,[17] and he is to be tried on board our ship tomorrow. I have seen McCollum three or four times and had some good old talks of old affairs.

The Rebels have possession of Shanghai and outside of Canton, so it is necessary to have large forces there to protect the American Interest, and tomorrow a detachment of Marines and Sailors from our ship go up in the *Kennedy*.[18] I have not yet seen or heard directly from Whipple, but I learn that his bronchitis is much better, but that he has chronic diarrhea and that he will be sent home. But everything is so mixed up and so many rumors afloat that I cannot get head nor tail of it. I know that we remain here, and I suppose ere this you know it for I saw it in a New York paper as an official document.

I forgot to mention the arrival today of the ship *Shooting Star*[19] from New York with a new shaft for the *Susquehanna*, 700 tons of coal for the Squadron, and papers, letters, registers &c. She was 105 days from New York.

Whether the shaft will be put in or not we cannot tell, but if they do put it in it will take them at least three months to do it.

I have just seen a Register and from the Act of Congress as passed with regards to the Engineers being examined &c. and the decision of Mr. Jefferson Davis,[20] sustained by the Attorney General, I feel satisfied that we cannot get our back pay, but that we can get our date and rank. Now what do I care for rank? And I think it a piece of rank injustice ever since I have been in the Navy I have done either First Assistant or Chief Engineers duty, and that too combined with a portion of 3rds duty. As a Second, I have always played the part of First, but there is no use growling. I see there is no luck for me in the Navy, and my study shall be to leave it.

Hong Kong, China, August [25th], 1854

My Dearest Lide,

Since Mr. Pegram has become Executive Officer he has made some radical changes, and a complete revolution has commenced. Steerage Officers will feel the change. No consideration whatever will be indulged for their comfort. We will see.

Too hot for anymore tonight so, Good Night.

Aug 28th

Early yesterday morning the *Macedonian* was discovered at anchor in the harbor having arrived sometime during the night Saturday. In the morning about eleven o'clock of yesterday the *Mississippi* arrived from Macao with the Minister. All the Squadron are now here except the *Vandalia* at Shanghai.

The presence of a large Naval force in China is absolutely necessary at this time. The disturbances of the Rebels and Imperialists are beginning to effect the "Barbarian" interest, and there is no telling what these long tailed wretches will do or attempt. There is no trusting them. At Canton from 60 to 80 heads are cut off every day, and the bodies throw[n] into the river, and these bodies float down and often run against and stick to the ships at anchor there.

Aug 30th

Yesterday I went on shore and played several games of billiards. In the evening I saw some officers of the English Steamer *Rattler*[21] who informed me that they had been out in search of Chinese Pirates and that day before yesterday they destroyed 17 Junks and killed 160 Chinamen. Mr. Whipple is on board of the *Lexington* at present. The Commodore not yet having given him orders as to what ship he is to go home in.

I have the worst case of "prickly heat" you ever saw. My hands even are covered. Good Night.

Sept. 2nd

Two years in commission today! This morning Mr. McLane[22] came on board and was received with all the honors and a salute of 17 guns. They have had the stern house enlarged and handsomely fitted up and furnished for a reception room. Many changes have been made in the ship and we now are a clean, beautiful Man O' War.

Commodore Ringgold was on board our ship today, and I saw him for the 1st time. He is rather a fine looking man, and is getting quite rational again. He has been (and gets fits of it yet) completely crazy. He will go home with the *Susquehanna*.

The Commodore (Perry) has ordered that all Chinamen shipped on board any of the ships going home must be discharged. He fears they will be unable to get unemployment at home and will therefore become paupers. Now these poor devils make the very best of servants, and some of them under the notion that they were going to the United States cut off their tails.

On Monday morning the *Susquehanna* with the *Southampton* in tow got underway and left for home. As she passed the different ships she was cheered. When she passed the *Mississippi* the band struck up "home sweet home" and but for that I could stood it, but it seem so plaintive and so touched me that I had to run below into the Steerage to hide my tears.

Whampoa, Sept 8th

Well we got underway from Macao with these folks on board, and for their edification and amusement our Japanese Minstrels were brought out and gave a concert. At midnight we came to anchor at the "Bogue." This morning at nine o'clock we got underway and about twelve we arrived here Whampoa Reach Canton River. The Steamer *Queen* was waiting for us and as soon as we arrived took the ladies, the strange gentleman, the Minister, Capt. McCluney and a couple of officers of our ship on board and left for Canton. Coming up the river some six or eight headless bodies were seen floating close by us. Whampoa is in possession of the Rebels, and at Canton the Rebels and Imperials are fighting day and night.

I went ashore this afternoon and the desolate appearance of Whampoa Bamboo town[23] and Newtown is indeed striking. The stores so full of everything when we were here last, present nothing but barren shelves. Some few trifles to keep up appearances. These Rebels go to the Rich Chinamen and make them pay a certain sum. If they refuse their goods and furniture are seized. This the Chinamen call squeezing, and to avoid it the[y] have removed their most valuable of their goods to Hong Kong and the vessels in the harbour. This place is not only infested with the Rebels, but the most murderous set of villains in the world, who go in bodies and attack weaker ones, and not them. They are neither Rebels nor Imperialists but a set of regular pirates, and these fellows are feared more than the organized Rebels. I was talking to an Imperialist today and he offered me fifty dollars apiece for every live Rebel I would bring him and twenty dollars for one's head! How ladies can live, inhabit, or remain in China is a mystery to me, but now 'tis more than that. 'Tis no place for them. 'Tis disgusting and absolutely sickening.

Give my earnest love to all and accept for yourself my dearest love, my all in sincere affection. George

Closed 8 P.M. Whampoa, Sept. 8th 1854

U.S. Stea. *Powhatan*, Macao Roads, Sept. 15th 1854

My Dearest Lide,

This morning about ten o'clock we left Macao with the American and several attaches, Sec. of Legation, two others, a Chinese interpreter and one Lady. We arrived here about half past three. That is at Hong Kong.

Mr. Bell,[24] the Gunner of the *Macedonian*, whilst that vessel was at Manilla deserted her, and I learn that the American Consul[25] there has arrested him and has sent him over here. He is now on the *Macedonian* awaiting a trial by Court Martial. We have new American Consul[26] at this place. He was on board this afternoon. I neither got a sight at him, neither have I learned his name. My arm has got quite well and I am on duty again.

Sept. 18th

We leave here tomorrow morning with the American Minister for Shanghai. The French Minister,[27] and the English Minister sailed in Her Majesties Steamer *Rattler* day before yesterday. So the Ministers Plenipotentiary of the three greatest Nations on the globe will see what they can do towards accomplishing a treaty with the Long Haired Celestials. From what has been said and heard from the Minister and those who know I judge that we will remain away from Hong Kong about four months. Then return here, take the Minister to Siam, and start for home! This will happen next February, but as we have opportunities to write once a month from Shanghai I will as usual keep you advised.

The *Macedonian* is in the harbor, the *Vandalia* at Shanghai, and the *Powhatan* will be tomorrow on the briny deep pointed for the latter place. Commodore Perry having left without a relief. Capt. Abbott of the *Macedonian* of course assumed command. The Surveying Squadron have all sailed. The Steamer *Jno. Hancock*[28] for Shanghai. Where the others have gone I don't know. McCollum is of the *Jno. P. Kennedy* at Canton. Dr. Stewart is on board the *Porpoise.*

We have a fine ship in the harbor called the *Lady Pierce*[29] just in from the Japanese Islands. Her officers don't think much of Joe Pan. So we got some extra pay for our service I care but little for our country is great enough without any assistance from Japanese.

Tuesday Morning, September 19th, 1854

I expect that Follansbe[30] has gone to sea in the *San Jacinto.*[31] I will do my best to get attached to one of the new vessels to be built. I would like Philada. more than any other place. I have now more sea service on the Register than any of my date and more than a great number of the First Assistants. I don't like this playing and getting the credit of First Asst. Engr. and getting only the pay of a second, but I think that will all be made right. At least an effort will be made for it.

Accept my best love and wishes for your health and prosperity and believe me most truly and affectionately your devoted Husband. George

U.S Ste. *Powhatan,* Shanghai, China Oct. 4th, 1854

My Dear Wife,

Well we started for Hong Kong, and the first four days out were the hardest, roughest and really worst that I have ever seen at sea. We made about a mile an hour against a most tremendous sea and heavy gale of wind. And we poor Engineers in three Watches made it certainly tough. I had no Engineer on with me. Took a man named [Deloache?] and learned him the "tricks." We tore away by butting into the sea much our light and some heavy work on the bow, and a sea struck one of the wheel houses and that was made a half wreck of.

On the 21st we arrived here, and the next day Mr. Pegram, our First Lieut. wished to move the ship nearer the town. The Pilot remonstrated, but Pegram thought he could do it, and in the attempt run into an English Clipper ship named the "*Cairn Gorm*"[32] and carried away her Fore Yard, both our Main and Fore Yards and otherwise injuring both ships. Getting clear of the Clipper we swung into a Danish Brig and knocked her "cold" and then into the Flag Ship of the Imperial Chinese Squadron. The latter was not hurt much. The damage done in all will take some 8 or 10 thousand dollars to repair. This keeps, or would keep us back, but on Monday I took up the air pump cover of the Port engine and found the piston rod of the air pump very much eaten. The brass of the rod being completely gone for a space around the rod some 15 inches long. Since then we have been making preparations to repair it, and tomorrow we try and cast. It has kept me in the Engine Room the whole time since, except meal hours and about 8 hours to sleep. One of those sleeping hours I now employ as you perceive. As I have got my letter started I am all right.

Oct. 11th

Again you have been neglected, and that for a week. My excuse, the work on the air pump piston rod already spoken of. We made a successful cast, but left too much metal, and did not get through until one o'clock yesterday, and then steam was up, and we proceeded down the "Yangs Tse Kiang"[33] as far as "Woosung"[34] where we remained until this morning when we got underway, and shortly after took the Steamer *Jno. Hancock*, and Schooner *Fennimore Cooper*[35] in tow. The English Steamer *Rattler* is in company with us. On board the *Rattler* is the English Minister and report says the French Minister. But of that there is some doubt. We go as near as Pekin as possible, to either make a treaty or make arrangements for renewing the old treaty. None of us have any idea how long we will be gone. I can't say within three weeks. However we are on our way and my hope is that it will not be a Japan stay.

I went ashore Saturday afternoon and looked at Shanghai. Didn't see the Chinese part, only the Foreign, and that is very home like. I remained but a short time. Saw Mr. Schaffer who came out in our ship as Masters Mate and left us at Hong Kong. He left of his own accord and he is marked deserted or rather looked upon as a deserter. He is now a regular pilot on the Yangs Tse Kiang and makes some 2 or 300 dollars a month. The weather is getting cold and that suits me you know.

One day last week Lieut. Rolando of our ship and Lieut. Barbot[36] of the

Vandalia dined with "Alin"[37] the Rebels Chief and just after dinner an onset was made on Alins' house and one of Rolando's shoulder straps was bruised by a bullet. [. . .] flew around for nearly an hour when the firing ceased and the two Americans made a retreat. The attack was ascertained to be from a party of Rebels on Alin. Their having considerable jealousy between him and some of the other leaders. As they have got to fighting amongst themselves, the Imperialists will soon retake the City. My [—bute] opinion about the Rolando affair is that he and both of them were more [scared] than hurt. In consequence of it, the Capt. of our ship made a request that none of the officers would go into the Rebels City.

In Shanghai we can buy five dollar gold pieces for $3.50, and we get a hundred Mexican dollars for 80 Carolus. Exchange at home is in favor of Shanghai to the tune of 50 pr. ct. Now would be the chance to double ones money if he had a few thousand to spare. The ship trembles so much I can scarcely write!

I made a hasty calculation of the amount damages were done. The amount was near 3000 dollars. I thought it would be 10 of them.

Yellow Sea, October 12th

This morning I learned from a satisfactory source that the French Minister was not on board the *Rattler*; he refused to accompany the [tripartite] Legations (as it would be) in consequence of not being able to get a Steamer of his own to take him. We have had on board with us a French count[38] who is the French Ministers interpreter and his presence with us is to look after the French Interest.

Gulf of Pe-chilee[39] near the mouth of the River Peiho and some distance from the Capital of China, Pekin. October 15th

Here we came to anchor this afternoon about half past one o'clock. Last night we anchored and were under banked fires until six this morning.

Our Minister visited the *Rattler* this afternoon and Sir Jno. Bowring[40] afterwards visited us or Bob as we call Mclean, and as the Matelos are now getting out the launches I imagine that an early start is intended on the boats tomorrow for Pekin.

October 20th

Yesterday Mclean and Sir Jno. Bowring took a boat and went to the mouth of the river and without landing and returned. A Chinese boat came up and presented to the ship some sheep, pigs &c. of course we will get none, and what is more we don't want any as we have enough to eat for weeks to come. The *Cooper* has been ashore and got off. She is ashore again. Quite a humbug.

Oct. 21st

Old McCluney and Bob McLean paid a visit to Jno. Bowring today, and as the wind kicked up no inconsiderable sea ship had some difficulty in getting on board the ship from the boat. Jerusalem! But it is cold. To keep us poor devils within the tropics all summer and then send us North in the winter makes it severe.

Peking, Sunday morning, October 22nd, 1854

Today we have been in this most detectable place a week and the whole of that week has been occupied humbugging with the United States Steamer *John Hancock* and the United States Surveying Schooner *Fennimore Cooper*. The latter vessel is over the bar at last and will be in the mouth of the river Peiho when weather moderates.

It is so cold this morning that I can scarcely write. They have a stove in the Cabin and one in the Ward room of course, us poor devils who do all the work must keep ourselves from freezing by bundling clothes on or exercise. This Navy is a great place for "youngsters." The thermometer stands at 36°. Cold enough when one has gradually emerged from hot to cold, but to indulge in such sudden transitions suffices to shake the stoutest nerves. Then the Old fogies or young ones either who have their bread buttered look daggers and feel astounded if the outsiders complain or ask to warm their frozen toes! What equanimity in the distribution of the "good things" is practiced in the Navy.

On the Quarter Deck as far aft as possible there was built by Commodore Perry a home called the After House. If a Captain would have occupied it the name would have been a "poop cabin," but as it was built for, and occupied by Commodore Perry Artists it received the Soubriquet of After House. Now after Commodore Perry left and with him his troupe of Artists, clerks, secretaries, &c. this became a kind of common property and we used to occasionally assemble there, and Kellogg made it his sleeping apartment. All this went on until the news boarded us that Mr. Minister McLean and suite were to come on board the *Powhatan*. Then Cap. McCluney ordered the house to be enlarged which of course was done, and the rooms &c. contained in it were elegantly furnished, carpeted &c. It is now occupied by Dr. Parker,[41] Secretary to the American Legation, and the one on the Port Side by Count Koskiousquenttlesgass (interpreted skouse kettle). This Count is, as I understand it, connected with the French Legation. He has with him a Chinese Teacher from who he is learning the Celestials language. What his business is on board our ship is more that I know, but I suppose he is a "chile among 'em, takin notes" for the French Minister.

In the Cabin is Capt. McCluney and Bob McLean. Dr. Parker messes with them. The Count messes in the Ward Room. In the Ward Room we have First Lieut. Pegram who came out with us. Second Lieut. Rolando who came out Captain of the *Porpoise*. Third Lieut. Passed Midshipman Bennett who came out in the *Susquehanna*. Fourth Lieut. is Passed Midshipman Lowry who came out in the Steerage of the *Plymouth* and Fifth Lieut. is Passed Midshipman Carter who came out as Actg. Lieut. on board one of the Ships of the Surveying Squadron. Master is Passed Midshipman McCauley who came out in our starboard Steerage. Maxwell and Schriver, the Doctors came out with us. Eldredge, purser, came out with us. Sewell, engineer, came out with us. Craig, private secretary to Mclean, picked up in Hong Kong. Jones, Marine Officer, now at Canton, but attached to our ship, came out in the *Macedonian*. Read a passenger to Pekin belongs to the *Vandalia*. In the stabd. Steerage Mr. Dudley, Pursers Clerk, and Mr. Bibby Capts. Clerk. A passenger, Mr. Whettlesy, Capts. Clerk of the *Vandalia* is with them. In our Mess, Faron, King, Kellogg, Fauth, Arnold, and myself. Stamm is at Canton on the *Queen*. Forward Officers are Butler, the Carpenter, came out with us, Whiting the Boatswain, came out with us. Parker the Sailmaker came out with us and Roach the Gunner who was made from a Quarter Master, and fills the place of City gone home.

Oct. 24th

The sickness on board is cold, rheumatisms, catarrhs &c. Some few incurable diseases amongst the men. Scrofula, Syphilitic rheumatisms &c. It is almost heart rending, at least truly painful to see the effects a little indulgence with "loose characters" has produced. Some men who were strong hearty men, with iron constitutions completely helpless. Gone-gone-going.

October 25th

Lide, my own dear Lide, you know not how much I love you. Yet you know my love is deep, sincere and true. You know that it is all yours, and yours undivided. What more could one loving heart, one true being ask or expect from another? Is this all? Indeed 'tis all that I can express, but something more, a feeling more penetrating, and influencing, my every thought is yours, but what it is I know not. But you don't love this kind of harangue or you would write to me likewise and as 'tis dull as above. Good Night.

October 27th

Another expedition with Dr. Parker and Mr. Midhurst[42] in charge left the ships today. Whether to insist on an interview or not I don't know. I learned last night that the authorities emphatically denied giving us an interview and this was stated in the letter received last night. There is this certain, that the weather is getting so cold that we must retire soon. May hold out one month longer. Another week will let us up some.

Sunday, October 29th

Well here I am again I learn that the launch returns tomorrow to the River and that the answer from Pekin received this evening agrees to let the "Barbarians" go up the river where an interview will be held. That they will be ready to receive us in eight or nine days! Confound the Chinese and Japanese too. I wish I would never have seen any of them, or their country. But I suppose it is all for the best. But it's trying my patience rather severely. For want of better humour &c. I'll stop for tonight. This news has given me the blues worse and worse.

I have just learned something about the treaty. It appears that heretofore the Governor General of Canton has communicated with the Emperor at Pekin and authorized to treat negotiate &c. with Foreigners. And that same Governor General has been from time to time insolent and overbearing to Minister's. Now the first answer to McLeans letter referred him to the Governor General, and McLean wrote back that he would not have anything to do with such a man, that he was unworthy the position he held &c.

The answer to this is what was received tonight and it agrees to appoint Commissioners to meet our Minister and the English Minister at Ling sin or Tin sin.[43] This is a place about 70 miles up the river. It is said that the Governor General is to lose his button, to be degraded, lose his office &c., and that it is believed that he has not kept his government correctly informed with regard to Foreign Relations. These are the facts as I can gather them. But there is no reliable authority for them, but it seems a correct version to me. Tomorrow no doubt the whole affair will be talked over and balancing the say so's of the one and the other, with the avenues of information I may be able to get at the Chinese Treaty as being negotiated. Good night.

Pekin[g], China, November 1st, 1854

The version I gave you Sunday evening with regards to the Treaty and the "loosing of the buttons" by the Governor General of Canton seems to be correct. The boat returned to the River on Monday with Dr. Parker and party and we expect them to return this afternoon or evening. The next party that leaves will no doubt be the Ministers and when that happens we can begin to calculate upon their getting back and our consequent getting away.

On the return of the last boat from the River some of our men got fighting, and one named Stevenson had his tongue bitten off. He can talk a little only.

November 3rd

Early this morning the boats from our ship taking the Minister, Messrs. Pegram, Rolando, Elldredge, Carter, Dr. Parker, Roach, Dr. Schriver and Craig left the ship under caring or rather tow from the *Hancock* for the Peiho River, at the mouth of which the Commissioners from Pekin are to meet them and enter into negotiations regarding a treaty. They have a fort at the mouth of the river and just inside near the fort a tent has been erected where the business is to be transacted. Now how long it will take to get through none of us can tell, but all indulge the hope that 'twill soon be over and then for the land of news! The *Rattler* boats and Sir Jno. Bowring of course accompanied the party.

November 4th

Last evening about eight o'clock the whole party returned from the Peiho River unable to accomplish anything. They went expecting to meet a Commissioner or Commissioners vested with full powers to negotiate, but on meeting but the one individual they wanted to know what they wanted! And when informed said that he would inform his Government and give another meeting and answer in 5 days. How vexatious, what conformed duplicity. Here we have to lay 5 days longer without coming any nearer to the Treaty than we did the day we arrived here. Well well it's all in the cruise.

November 8th

This afternoon our boat returned from the river and brings the news that the Chinese will have nothing at all to do with us here. They say one must treat with them at Canton, so we have rumors that we are to get underway and leave this "gay and festive scene" tomorrow. There is some talk that we will go to the Great Wall which is about 40 miles distant. As that is something worth seeing I would like to go. But tomorrow will tell us something definite and I'll drop the subject until then. I am in exceeding ill humor to night. Feel troubled.

November 9th

Efforts have been making all day to get the Schooner *Cooper* out of the river but the wind being unfavorable they have not yet succeeded. Capt. McCluney says that he will go to sea as soon as she gets out if it is at midnight. We fear that they will be unable to get her out before tomorrow night. And we anxious to get away.

The efforts made to secure a Treaty were all vain. The Chinese Emperor refused to have anything to do with either English, American, of the Foreigners, and I judge that the yarns about the Governor at Canton were all made. I heard today that Mr. McLean said that he would have nothing further to do with them and that he could turn the whole affair over to government and they could do as they pleased. So much for our visit to Pekin.

The next pigeon will be Cochin China[44] probably. But we shall see. At any rate we will soon be on our way to Shanghai and the land of news, and god grant that we may start for home. I am sick to the very heart of this Country and Navy. I think I would rather work as a labourer for one dollar per day than go to sea anymore. Good night.

November 10th

Here we are in the Gulf of Pe-cheli (pronounce Pee-chee-lee) yet. They have been unable to get the *Cooper* over the bar and here we are waiting for her. We remain because our men have to assist in getting her over, and our boats are employed lightening her. The British Steamer *Rattler* with the Lorcher sailed today. Confound that *Cooper*. Was it not for her we would be off too. The Minister has said that he wants to be in Hong Kong by the 21st so as to catch the mail that leaves there about that time. This will make our stay in Shanghai very short and I am somewhat glad of it for I would rather be in Hong Kong than anywhere else out here.

Nov. 11th

About nine o'clock last night our launch returned in company with the *Cooper* and orders were given to start the fires. Upon getting up steam the lower steam side pipe nozzle of the Port Engine busted, and steam had to be blow off so as to repair it. At twelve o'clock I went on watch. The fires were banked and the men at work on the damaged nozzle. Sewell asked me if I saw certain nuts screwed up. I told him no!

Now the current report on board the ship, and it is believed by all but a few of the Engineers, is that the burst was occasioned by sudden expansion. It was caused by the nuts spoken of above being screwed up too tight and preventing the gum packing from expanding, and Sewell blamed me for it! I told him that this was not the first time that I had been charged with neglect of duty and that in this case he himself gave the man orders to screw up the nuts as hard as he could. Thereby taking the work off my hands. He said he gave no orders about it. I said all that I know is that the man says you did. Now there is no doubting but that I should have seen the nuts screwed up myself. This I did not do. But when Mr. Sewell is to blame and then attempts to shove it on me or when any man attempts to shove a fault on me undeservedly I speak. I told Mr. Sewell that I would never be attempt to screw up gum cold. And he knew I had a trial of gum expansion on the *Michigan* for I had previously told him of the Sanford affair. There are some excuses for my not looking out for this work. The person who did it is one of our most trust worthy men and the day before had done the same kind of work on the other engine.

By half past six this morning the damage was temporarily repaired and we got underway leaving the *Hancock* and *Cooper* in the Gulf of Pechili. We have some islands to go through and we are now running slow until the moon gets up. The weather is fine. The sea like a mill pond.

Nov. 13th

As I had the watch from 6 to 9 last night I was compelled to forego my usual habit. And as it is smooth today. I will let you see what I am about. Sewell told me yesterday that he had a talk with McLean and learned from him just the contrary to all the rumors afloat with regard to the Treaty. McLean is perfectly satisfied with what he has done and says that all he wanted was a month or six weeks to complete a new treaty, but as the season was getting so late he had to abandon it and will go to Pekin in the Spring.

The Chinese are willing to make a Treaty, and all they ask is reciprocity, and the security of mutual advantages. They wish to have their interests &c. equally protected in the U.S. as ours is in China. McLean thinks that a treaty will be made in the spring which will be of much benefit and advantage to the United States. The story about the Imperial Commissioner at Canton is true. He is to loose his "buttons."

Nov. 15th

Here we are off Gutslaff.[45] Gutslaff is a rock at or near the mouth of the Yangstse Kiang River and the only land mark in view. We arrived and anchored here yesterday afternoon at two o'clock, and we have been waiting ever since for a Pilot, and no signs of any yet. The *Rattler* was passed by us, day before yesterday, and after all our delays and her start ahead of us (in all 26 hours) we arrived some hours ahead of her at the mouth of the river, but towards evening yesterday she came up and passed on up the river. We draw more water than she does and it is necessary for us to have a Pilot. She can go safely to Woosung without one, so in the end the *Rattler* has beaten us. She saw us at anchor here and will probably send a Pilot down and we may get up to Shanghai tomorrow.

This morning the exhaust nozzle of the lower port steam chest gave way!! This is singular. It was slacked up when the Steam broke, and gave no indication of rupture until it burst this morning. Strange things will occur.

November 18th

The Allied English and French have had a fight at a place called Petropaulski[46] or St. Peter and St. Paul in the southern part of Kamtschatka with the Russians, and the English and French were defeated with a serious loss and both admirals killed. We have a vessel in port that was present during the engagement and she received some shot. The English here don't believe it, but 'tis nevertheless so.

The Chinese Pirates took and plundered a Peruvian Bark just outside of Hong Kong and then burned her. She had a cargo valued at a hundred thousand dollars. Captain Abbott of the *Macedonian* put about 50 men on the *Queen*, and the English put about 80 in the *Mary Wood*,[47] a merchant steamer, and went in search of the pirates but they don't find 'em of course.

The Imperialists and the Americans here have had another little fight but after a little firing on both sides the Imperialists retired.

Nov. 18th

Shanghai is not quiet at all. The Rebels on one side and the Imperialists on the other. The French are building a kind of wall which is obnoxious to the Imperialists and the Chinese have fired on the workmen several times and some blood has been spilled. These things hardly interest me. My every hope and thought being on our getting home.

November 19th

I hear that the *St. Mary* Sloop of War[48] is in Hong Kong and that the passengers of the vessels plundered by the pirates outside of Hong Kong have been rescued. Amongst them a French Lady. I went ashore this evening and there was a row at a Hotel between some English officers belonging to the *Rattler*, and some Merchantmen. I interfered and became the hero of the fight. They called me "Old Powhatan." None of them knew my name or what I am. I left and others will gather the glory. All the credit I deserve is that for making peace.

U.S. Ste. *Powhatan*, Shanghai, China, Tuesday November 21st, 1854

My Dearest Lide,

The Rebels and Imperialists are fighting daily without doing much harm. I was ashore yesterday and heard a report that the Rebel Chief Alin had fled. Some think that he has been captured. In either case the Rebels cannot hold out much longer, and when they fall there will of course be butcheries and the river be choked with dead bodies.

Minister McLane intends giving a party on board this week and sailing for Hong Kong about Saturday next. Dr. Parker told Mr. Bibby this morning that Mr. McLean had taken passage in the next steamer from Hong Kong for home and that will be about the 11th of next month. I have also heard that McLean has received answers to his requests with regards to sending this ship home, and the sum up in the flattering (?) news that this ship will go home as soon as relief can be sent out. We can tell nothing about it ourselves and only hope.

Nov. 23rd

One of the *Vandalia*'s men had his throat cut day before yesterday by some Chinamen. I made inquiries about the Rebels Chief Alin, but could learn nothing about him. Somebody gives a party on shore tonight and all the Ward Room Officers except one or two have gone. Extensive preparations are being made for the File to be given by Mr. McLean on board here on Saturday night. Capt. McCluney is very sick with his old complaint.

We have heard of the failure of the *San Jacinto*. I hope she will be ordered out here to relieve us if we are not ordered home before. Good Night. God Bless.

Nov. 27th

On Saturday the *Powhatan* was draped in flags and wreaths. In the evening the "Minstrels" gave a concert before the "Haut ton" of Shanghai who had assembled on board en masse. Amongst them the ladies and gentlemen of the Mission who were well pleased with the serenade. After the Concert the guests adjourned to the Ward room and partook of supper. After supper the dancing &c., commenced on the Quarter Deck, but none of our missionary friends danced.

Yesterday I went ashore and altho' against orders I went into the Rebel City. Saw lots of Rebels and asked to see the Chief. After leading me through caves, and gardens I was ushered into a large Court and then into a fantastically furnished room. Was seated and word came back that he was in another place. We were then lead through more queer places and ushered into another home. An Officer waited on us, and after going out, apparently to ascertain, told us that Alin was asleep. That he had been up all night and they did not like to wake him &c. I got angry and told them to give me a guide at once to the gate. I did not come to be humbugged or beg to see Alin, so we were accordingly showed the way back and didn't see the Chief. Just as we got outside the walls we saw the Rebels have an Imperialist whom they had caught, and the poor fellow looked imploringly at us and begged, but we could not interfere. No doubt his head is off ere this.

The Imperialists and Rebels met on Saturday Afternoon and had a battle. Six of the former were killed and four taken prisoners. These prisoners were beheaded by boys about 12 years of age. They got two dollars for their trouble. One Rebel killed and the Imperialists ran. This morning the Imperial Chinese Governor of this province with a large train visited our ship. He was saluted with three guns. The Rebels let their hair grow long all over the head.

At 3 o'clock we got underway from Shanghai, and about sundown the Pilot boat got adrift. Consequently we came to anchor just below Woosung where we now are under banked fires. A large party of gentlemen came as far as Woosung with us in company with the Minister. We have 4 passengers with us to Hong Kong.

At sea. Nov 29th

Yesterday morning at daylight we got underway from Woosung and we are ploughing the "mighty deep" on our way to Hong Kong, where we fondly hope to receive good news. Just as we reached the mouth of the Yangs Tse Kiang we met the Mail Steamer *La[d]y Mary Wood*. We stopped and sent a boat to her to get our mail, but there was none for us. A newspaper was received and all the news we got was that an attack had been made on Sebastopol (if that is spelled correctly) with a loss to the Russians of 12,000 killed and 3000 of the Allies![49] If this is true, what a sacrifice of human life! We heard too of the passage of the bill increasing the pay of sailors and others in our Navy. Now as no mention is made of Firemen and Coal Heavers in this bill considerable murmuring and disaffection is manifest already in the Department to which they belong.

Dec. 7th

We left Macao on the morning of the 4th and in six hours and a half arrived at Whampoa, where we have been since. The Minister, Captain and some of the Officers have gone to Canton. Yesterday the "Minstrels" went up to Canton in the *Queen*. We expect to leave for Hong Kong tomorrow.

December 10th

We got underway from Whampoa on the afternoon of the 8th and ran about 20 miles and came to anchor, waiting for the *Queen* who was to bring our Captain, the Minister, and Minstrels down. We remained at anchor under banked fires until half past six last evening when the *Queen* arrived and we got underway. Just after starting we were met by the Mail Steamer from Canton and we gave her a race. We beat her badly, and arrived here (Hong Kong) about midnight.

Whilst we were at Whampoa the mail from home arrived, but brought us but little news. [. . .] The *Susquehanna* and *Mississippi* have both arrived at Honolulu, Sandwich Islands. One of them will no doubt be kept as Flag Ship of the Pacific Squadron. The *Mississippi* had a terrible time in a Typhoon.[50]

McLean goes home or rather to Paris for his family and returns here. Dr. Parker formerly Charge' d' Affairs is left with full powers as Commissioner. Good Bye. God Keep You.

Hong Kong, Sunday Evening, Dec. 10th, 1854

My own Dearest Wife,

Mr. Drinker of the firm Drinker & Co. is completely busted up, and the house carried on by Messrs. Armstrong and Lawrence. Mr. Drinker has entered the service of the Imperialists, and is Admiral of the Imperial Fleet in the Canton River. The arrangements entered into sums up thus: that the Imperialists furnish Drinker vessels and everything he wants, and give him one hundred thousand dollars to dislodge the Rebels who have command of all the forts along the river as far up as Canton, and who threaten every day to attack the city.

Last Thursday the U.S. Str. *Queen* came to Whampoa from Canton with a warrant for Mr. Drinker from the U.S. Commissioner, Robert McLane; so he was arrested taken to Canton and promised under bonds to withdraw from the Imperial Service and have nothing to do with either Rebels or them. McLane has issued a notification to all American Citizens to abstain from giving aid or in any way interfering or intervening with either party, and that any citizen of the United States in any way connected with the "War" shall be arrested and fined not less than, I mean, not more than 10,000 dollars and imprisoned not more than 3 years.[...] Good night! God bless nd protect you.

U.S. Stea. *Powhatan*, Whampoa, China, [December 22nd, 1854]

My Dearest Lide,

We left Hong Kong on the 14th and the same day fell in with the *Macedonian*. She having sailed the day before and took her in tow, a few hours after fell in with and passes the Flag Ship of the English Squadron, the *Winchester* in tow of the Side Wheel Steamer *Styx*.[51] Shortly after, in consequence of low water we anchored, so did they, and the next morning all got underway save the *Styx* who proceeded up the river to Canton, in an hour came to anchor here in Whampoa.

On the 12th when Robert McLane left the ship to take passage in the Mail Steamer for, or en route for Paris, and in my opinion from there home, we saluted with 17 guns, or rather 20 for the firing of the guns was managed badly and produced excitement. The 1st Lieut. being predisposed to attacks of the kind and by authority general order forgot his count! The band played "Sweet home" and that confounded (as the King would say) tune affects my nerves. Well Bob has gone, and we of course remain and for how long none of us can tell.

We have had a Court Martial in session on board our ship since the 16th and Passed Midshipman Walcutt[52] has been tried for drunkenness and disobedience of orders, one man of the *Kennedy* for theft, and one on our ship for striking Passed Midshipman McCauley.

The Rebels are yet threatening the City and the Imperialists beating gongs and using squibs in great quantities. If both armies would meet and emphatically annihilate each and every member composing the combined forces, and swallow up in general massacre at least five millions of Chinese, a blessing would be conferred on the World! Such wantonness, degradation, pollution, licentiousness, beggary and crime never burdened any nation, country or state since the day of good old Adam, and the arrogation of the Tartars certainly tends to increase the misery. The abrogation of whose authority is the chief aim of the Rebels, but these Rebels enroll themselves in small bands and by petty acts of piracy, wanton sacrifice of human life and controversy and confliction amongst their leaders do no other act to better the condition of the people and only interrupt foreign trade and entail additional misery upon the whole class of people.

An immense Naval Force of English is at anchor off Canton, and the Americans have the Store Ship *Kennedy* and hired Steamer *Queen* there. The movement of the English Flag Ship and the *Macedonian* and *Powhatan* from Hong Kong to this place was no doubt for some purpose, and as I understand it the Imperialists insist upon the proviso in the Treaty with America and England to assist them in putting down piracy. They call the Rebels pirates and fear the taking of Canton. The English and Americans could prevent it, but on an attempt being made by the Rebels it is difficult to say whether the Christians would interfere or not.

I understand that the English Minister, Sir Jno. Bowring has demanded an interview with the Mandarins inside the walls, which they have refused to grant, and if they persist in the refusal and the Rebels make the attack Canton must fall in which case no good would accrue to anybody, and all trade for the present stopped.

[Dec. 22nd 1854]

We have great hope in the next mail, and as Captain Adams will likely come with the mail and bring with him the Ratifications of the Japan Treaty incurring thereby the necessity of a visit of one of the ships to Simoda, the sanguine and anxious hope that the Captain will have orders for the *Powhatan* to go there with him and from there home. [. . .] Now all I ask is to get started or pointed, and I don't care which way we go. A more disgusted hombre never lived than myself. Some say that we will go to Shanghai very soon. Others, in the event of the Captain Adams not bringing orders for us think that we shall remain at Hong Kong. The *Powhatan* settled the Borneo business,[53] helped to settle the Japan humbug, was the vehicle of Minister McLane, and now tool of Old Daddy Abbott. Something will be known after next mail.

Capt. McCluney is sickly. The men are sickly. We buried two poor fellows this week. One named Thomas Serato, formerly Ward Room Steward and was married in Norfolk only a short time before we left there. The other was a man named Millett, a very quiet man.[54] Dr. Maxwell says that this ship has passed through five epidemics. 'Tis shameful. Outrageous to keep a ship longer than six months on this station, but our only hope nevertheless is in Capt. Adams. The unsettled state of China certainly requires ships of war here. And if have to wait for a Steam relief. 'Tis hard to tell when one will get home. Is this not enough to make one "tear his sheet?"

The Carpenter of the English Steamer *Barracouta*[55] at Canton was on shore and seen drunk a few nights ago, and yesterday morning he was found floating by the *Kennedy*. Having no doubt been murdered by some of the "Celestials" for his watch. Mr. Saml. Craig, late secretary of McLane, has made application for an appointment as Masters Mate on board our ship. Quite a come down.

Saturday Night, Dec. 23rd

Yesterday the China junks around us kept up a beating of gongs and firing of guns and fire crackers all day. The Chinamen say it was their Christmas! A story came down in the *Queen* this morning that the Rebels had surrounded a city some 10 or 12 miles from Canton, locked the gates and set fire to the city, and that in the affair some 4000 Imperialists perished! My opinion is that the affair is exaggeration.

I'm "down on" the Navy worse than ever, and one year ago I really expected to be home two months ago. "Hope deferred maketh the heart sick," and that is my case now. I must speak plainly, My Dear Lide, because I have nothing to hope now for but the orders and when they will come I cannot say. We look for them every mail, and as every mail is now a month apart, imagine how those months pass. It seems like an age since we left Shanghai. Time drags so heavily.

At Shanghai I did enjoy myself a very little, and at Hong Kong one can go ashore and see signs of civilization, and the sight to a very limited extent relieves the drag and monotony. Mr. Craig has accepted the appointment of a Masters Mate, and will join our ship in a few days, unless Mr. Bibby who is a great friend of his, persuades him to show up the appointment. I would not like to see him come on board in that capacity, for as he is a high spirited fellow, he will certainly get himself into trouble. We shall see.

Hong Kong, December 26th

Yesterday we had a *merry* Christmas at Whampoa. In the morning it rained, towards noon it cleared up, and the *Queen* arrived from Canton. The Court Martial convened and soon after dissolved. Mr. McCollum dined with us, and we had a good dinner. The comprador did get us a Turkey. The other fixings consisted of all the delicacies of the season and the market. The firemen and coal heavers of our ship got into difficulty with the sailors. All hands being drunk. And "black eyes" and disfigured visages were quite numerous this morning. Sailors will get rum somehow.

I saw a paper (a N.Y. Herald) of the 5th of October, and learned that Capt. Adams left N.Y. for China and Japan that morning in the Steamer *Pacific*.[56] We expect soon to see him and get some news. Many of our Officers threaten to resign in case we don't get orders to start for home before the 1st of next June. Everybody is complaining, Officers and men. For myself, if I had money enough to pay my passage home in Clipper Ship, and I could not resign, I would make arrangements quietly and "run." Dr. Maxwell says that he would not remain out here another year for twenty thousand dollars!

This morning we got underway at seven O'clock, and at two we anchored in this place. Mr. C[raig] our new Masters Mate entered upon the discharge of his duties yesterday.

Dec. 27th

This morning the Calcutta Mail arrived, and by it I received your letter mailed on the 25th of September enclosing the Talbotype or Mezzograph[57] as you call it of yourself.

I am much pleased that you have sent it. I have looked steadily at the picture for a half hour. I have examine it thoroughly and am much pleased that you have sent it, would rather than any sum to have it! I have shown it to all on board who know you. But it cannot possibly look like you. I have compared it with the daguerreotype and I must be candid, have concluded that 'tis much inferior. It makes me more anxious to behold the original.

I begin to feel very indifferent about the brats. Every nigger, chinaman, and beggar can make babies; but it takes great men to indulge in exercises pertaining to their manufacture and result in nothing! Don't fret about the babies, for I am too old now to find pleasure in clouds, cradles and little yellow chairs with tin pots introduced in the seats.

Chapter Five
January 1–June 27, 1855

Whampoa, Jan. 1st 1855

Yesterday the sentence of the men who were tried by the last Court Martial were read. O'Donnel, the man tried for kicking McCauley was sentenced to forfeit all the pay now due him, to be disrated to a Landsman on half pay, to be confined for 30 days at the "Stanchion" in single irons and fed on bread and water, and at the expiration of the 30 days to be ignominiously discharged and towed ashore on a grating. The latter part of his sentence will no doubt be performed with a tune in accompaniment called the "rogues march." The other prisoners received the simple sentence of double irons and bread and water for 30 days. As to Passed Midshipman Walcutt we don't know only hear it rumored that his sentence is dismissal from the Navy.

Hoping that we may have a kiss in '55. I will bid you a good night.

January 3rd

Our fondest hopes have been dispelled. The mail and Capt. Adams have arrived and we are ordered, not home but to Japan! With this mail we learned the painful particulars of the loss of the *Arctic*.[1] I was again one of the fortunate, for I received your letter of the 29th of October, and a good long letter it was, but feelings almost unnatural filled me at intervals.

Capt. Adams went up to Whampoa yesterday to deliver his dispatches to Capt. Abbott. Unless the orders are positive for us to go to Japan we will not go, for Abbott wants to go himself in the *Macedonian*.

I was so angry yesterday when Capt. Adams stated that he had not orders for us to return home that I immediately wrote my resignation and consulted Sewell about it. Faron agrees to send his in with mine but he backed out. I went ashore to see about a passage to California which will cost two hundred dollars and no ship to sail for a month or more. I would have to run, and the next mail may bring something. 'Tis hard to extinguish hope, and as a rash act might keep me longer from you and at the nearest only a few months sooner than the *Powhatan* would consummate it. I conclude that a "bird in the hand is worth two in the bush," and that patience, perseverance, coolness and quiet philosophy will in the end do the best, and I cannot but hope that in eight months we will have a chance to see each other. Whether I'm home earlier or not I can't tell, but I can tell that arm full as you are, I could give you some squeeze.

January 4th

Rumor states that the Japan Treaty as sent home by Commodore Perry was not ratified and that Capt. Adams is appointed a kind of Ambassador to negotiate further. Some additions and alterations having been made in the original paper. Now if these are of any consequence we will be a month or more humbugging in a Country where we can get nothing but grass water and a very few eggs. I hope we will be spared as it will be awful cold and I didn't think of that last night, but the best way is to make up your mind to be contented, and that is what I shall do. We are now nearly two years out and confound their rusty shins, to do their worst they can't keep us out another year. I am sanguine and will hope in spite of them.

I understand that some difficulty has occurred between Capt. Abbott and Mr. Sturgess,[2] Consul at Canton, with regards to some movement of the *Macedonian*. What it is I can't learn, but a few days ago the Rebels and Imperialists had a fight at Whampoa in which the latter got the worst of it, and I opine that it was in some way connected with it as the *Macedonian* is at Whampoa. [. . .] The French and the Rebels are having a "mess" at Shanghai.

Sunday Evening. January 7th

We received news from Whampoa today stating that Capt. Abbott hoisted the Broad Pennant on board the *Macedonian* yesterday. So he is now Commodore Abbot. This no doubt chafes Capt. McCluney, for at no time McCluney ranked Abbott, and it was only by a kind of lottery that Abbot got ahead of him. Moreover McCluney has seen more service and is undoubtedly the best man of the two. It is certainly unfair to make McCluney sail under Abbot as a Commodore, but 'tis Navy as Purser Barry would say.

News came down also that the *Macedonian* was to be relieved in six months and that the *Colorado* or *Minnesota*[3] would relieve the *Powhatan* as soon as they or either of them could be built. Now we think it would be better for Congress to appropriate a sum to build an extra steamer for the relief of the *Powhatan* and then we need not be so hurried about getting home. Might get home in about nine years! But joking aside. The sanguine hope to receive some news with regards to us by the next mail, we have heard nothing since our return from Japan. We shall see, and "what can't be cured must be endured."

The difficulty between the Canton Merchants and Commodore Abbot arose from his non-interference last week when the Rebels attacked the Imperialists at Whampoa and a very slight injury occurred to some of the shipping there. The Rebels gave notice that they intended making the attack and if any of them got hurt, in my opinion, it served them right, for they should have got out of the way. These same Merchants think they own the whole Navy, and that the only use of it is to protect them in their swindling operations, and do just as they say. If Old Perry was here he would "give 'em rats." We have all kinds of rumors about going to Japan, but nothing positive has come out yet. At any rate we will not start until after the arrival of the next mail.

January 9th

This afternoon the sad pipe of "all hands bury the dead" was again echoed whom [*sic*] the stentorian voices of the Boatswain and his Mates! A man by the name of Shultz[4] who was shipped only a few days ago at Whampoa took sick shortly after, and altho he gave no signs of approaching dissolution at a late hour last night, this morning he "gave up the ghost" and now the cold earth covers the wooden box containing his lifeless corpse. This makes the third death on board our ship that I have had to record in this letter. The general health of the ship is nevertheless very good. The spectacle of the uncovered assemblage of Officers and Men on the Quarter Deck, the Band playing a solemn dirge, the Marines draw up under a "Present Arms" and the slow sad step of the bearers of the dead and the meager procession of the deceased few messmate, is indeed a melancholy one.

January 11th

The *Queen* arrived yesterday morning bearing the broad pennant of Commodore Abbot and we saluted it with 13 guns. Afterwards the *Winchester* saluted it and we returned it. It has been decided that we go to Japan from there to Shanghai and there relieve the *Vandalia*. She comes down here and relieves the *Macedonian*, and she then leaves for Shanghai to relieve us. This will occupy about three months. Rumor states that we are to leave on Monday, but that is uncertain as McCluney wants to wait for the next mail before starting, and they have not yet secured an interpreter for the Japan pidgeon. Nevertheless we are ready for sea. We will undoubtedly have heavy weather, and it does seem so very strange that we always got to northward in winter and come south in the summer.

Our trip to Japan will not be a very long one this time. Hoping to get some solid news by tomorrow. I will close this evening with another good night to you.

January 12th

This morning Capt. McCluney received orders from Commodore Abbot to proceed to Simoda, Japan, as soon as the Commissioner, Capt. Adams, was ready. This afternoon he said Adams came on board and stated that he would be ready on Tuesday morning, so as we started for that country just one year ago on the 14th, and Tuesday will be the 16th it is fair to suppose that in a year hence we will be—just where ever the United States Government chooses to put us.

I had forgotten to mention that the *Vincennes*[5] was at Shanghai and that she had waited 30 days at the Bonin Islands for the *Porpoise* with whom she parted company in a Typhoon, and then she went to Lou Chou, but the *Porpoise* had not been heard of, so it is pretty certain that she is lost. The only person you know on her was Dr. Stewart. The vessel was a small tub unfit for heavy weather. I knew her Captain and several of her Officers. Again, Good night.

U.S. Ste. *Powhatan*, Harbor of Simoda, Japan, Jan. 28th, 1855

My Dear Wife,

Here we are again in one of the harbors of the world so long closed to all but the queer race who own it. We left Hong Kong about ten o'clock on the morning of the 16th and arrived here on the afternoon of the 26th. Thus making the run in a little over 10 days. The first eight days we had head winds and heavy weather, and I again experience those horrible sensations of sea sickness. The day was fine and mild when we arrived and just as we anchored a Japanese boat came alongside containing a pilot, we of course didn't want him. He was too late. Shortly after some Japanese Mandarins came on board and an interview ensued between them and Capt. Adams.

Simoda was visited with an Earthquake on the 23rd of December last and out of more than one thousand houses only sixteen were saved. 200 lives were lost! Simoda is now one mess of ruins! I was on shore yesterday and was completely lost. They are building very rapidly and in a year the town will be as large as ever.[6]

The Russian Frigate *Dianna* was in this harbour at the time and she was whirled around as if in a whirlpool. She struck the bottom, and sprang a leak. They took her guns out of her and landed them.[7] Then they got underway for the purpose of taking her about 20 miles from here to beach her and repair damages, but just as they got outside she commenced sinking and the officers and crew had barely time to escape in the boat without saving anything but what they stood in. The whole party number 450 men. The crew are encamped about 40 miles from here. Some officers are here and dined on board our ship yesterday. The Russian Admiral is with the men but will be here in a day or two. To leave them here would be brutal, and humanity dictates the course for McCluney to pursue. That is take them away, but rumor has it the [*sic*] McCluney is afraid and says that if he takes them he will violate our neutrality. If they were English he would take them without a murmur. But if he does refuse, it will be the worst thing he ever done. If he takes them the world will praise him, but we can't all yet. Every Officer on board our ship is in favor of taking them with us to Shanghai. The Russian Capt. who was on board yesterday stated that they commenced dancing for joy when we gave them all the newspapers we had. They speak (that is the two Officers I saw) English very well.

It appears we will be here about two weeks. Poor Simoda! I looked for the bath house but it was gone. I looked for my little "Onango" but I couldn't find her. We found a couple of stores but the prices are outrageous and I wouldn't buy anything though I saw some very pretty articles. This whole town is one mass of stones, loose timber and straw. It looks dreadful, and the smoke arising from the burning of the rubbish the way they get rid of it almost blinds me.

If I should ever reach home, show me the following sentence when I again get orders to sea. I would rather work as a common laborer. I could find more pleasure in carrying the load. One year at sea injures one's health, and tends more to impair one's mind than ten at home, and if I go to sea again you can charge me with not loving or caring for you, and that I am heartless unfeeling wretch and afraid of my own abilities to get a living. I am determined never to go to Sea if I can make a half dollar a day. I am disgusted, disheartened and almost a maniac. One half hour with you would be more pleasure to me than I have had for almost two years! I am in no humor to write. I feel sad and could only find comfort in your bosom. Great God! Forgive me if I again entail this misery upon myself. We must soon meet my Dearest Lide, and after our first gush of pleasure, after we have that long embrace then I can tell you calmly all my troubles. Good Night.

Jan. 29th

Last night I had the nominal watch from 8 to midnight, and feeling lonely and dis-spirited I walked with the Boatswain and at half past ten was leaving the deck when the ship commenced trembling! Everything was still and the water smooth, but the ship rattled and shook terribly. It was the strangest sensation I ever experienced. All the Officers and men in shirt tails and night gowns were on deck in a jiffy. Sewell met me and ordered me to get everything ready to get up steam, which I did. It was an Earthquake![8] And a more scared party I never saw. After everything got quiet Sewell came below and told me to never mind running up the boilers. So I told the men to turn in, and went on deck where I met Mr. Whiting who asked me to feel the lead line, and I had no more than got hold of it when another shock took place and everything trembled again! But not so severely as first. I immediately ran below and resumed running up the boiler and continued to do so until twelve o'clock when I was relieved by Mr. King. I was for leaving immediately. The people on shore felt it and "zamad" that is they run for the mountains. It appears that there is no end to excitement here.

This morning about eleven o'clock a ship made her appearance off the mouth of the harbor bearing French colors, but soon pulled them down, and ran up the Yankee ensign. We sent a boat on board of her and she proved to be a French Whaler with two ship wrecked Japanese on board. Capt. McCluney sent an order on board for her to pull down the American flag, but the order was not complied with for I saw them up after sundown. Towards evening a boat from the Whaler came alongside of us and brought on board the two Japanese who both talk English, and remain with us. They were picked up at sea by an American Ship and have been absent 3 years and they return to see their parents.[9] The Frenchman no doubt has learned of the presence of the Russians here and will put to sea tonight. I would like for the Russians to catch him! The Captain of the Whaler states that he ran up the American Flag because the Japanese would not allow him to come into the harbor with any other colors. McCluney ought to have sent a force on board and pulled down the Yankee flag! He will be very much censured for his conduct both as regards his actions towards the Russians and the suspicious whaler that now is anchored off the mouth of the harbor.

The Japanese say that they felt the earthquake on board the French Ship last night and that they were six miles from land. The Capt. assumed that he was aground. I never want to feel another earthquake. The sensations are dreadful.

Capt. Adams had an interview with some officials today and a dispute arose about the time to exchange the ratifications. The Treaty distinctly states that they shall be exchanged in 18 months or sooner if practicable. The Japanese hold that it means after 18 months. What a humbugging set they are. Uncle Sam had better give them a thrashing or let 'em alone for what they are worth. I will not venture opinions yet, but merely state the facts so that I can dilate when all is dull. Now everything is excitement. Good night and God Bless you my Dearest!

Jan. 31st

Yesterday afternoon I went on shore at Coxsackie and visited the Russians. I had some conversation with the Russian Capt. and learned from him that he sent for a force to the Admiral which would be here in the morning, but all of course would be too late as the French Merchantman got underway about 9 o'clock on the evening of his arrival and thus evaded the "fat eaters."

This morning the Admiral and a large force of Russians arrived, and encamped on shore. No doubt they are much chagrined at the departure of the Frenchman, as the taking of her would not only be complete "ruse de guerre" under the circumstances, but be a most effectual and entirely fortunate affair for them in aiding the shipwrecked condition.

February 1st

Russian stock is up. Capt. McCluney has really offered to take all the Russians to Shanghai, but they are afraid to go. They have no provisions except what the Japanese furnish them and that is not the kind they have been in the habit of using, so the Capt. has ordered all the beef, pork &c. that we can spare to be given to them, and this afternoon we sent a considerable quantity ashore. Some half a dozen Russian Officers dined today in the Ward Room and everything was done to make them comfortable and drunk. Gen. Keenan from Pennsylvania Consul of the American Government at Hong Kong is a passenger with us, and as the Russians will not accept our offer to take them from here, the General (who by the by is a white man) intends having an interview with the Admiral of the Russians and is disposed to act as an agent for the purpose of securing a conveyance for them from this place. The nearest Russian harbor is Petro Paulaski [Petropaulski] and where they want to go but that place is now blocked up with ice and there is no certainty of getting there until spring. So the unfortunates will have to remain here 2 or 3 months yet.

The earthquake and Russian excitement has thrown our immediate cause here (the exchange of ratifications) entirely in the shade, so that we don't know how affairs in that particular progress. A more disgusted hombre than your husband, Geo Gideon, the writer of this miserable epistle does not live.

Sunday, Feb. 4th

The party of Russians brought over by the Admiral are the largest finest body of men I have ever seen in any service. The place where the Russians are encamped is about 40 miles from here and is called Hzdee.[10] They are negotiating with the Japanese and are in a fair way to conclude a Treaty with them.[11] The Japanese furnish them with Temples to reside in and such provisions as the Country affords.

We have undoubtedly had more excitement in Japan the last week than we had the whole 6 months we were here with Perry. When the news reaches home I expect the Herald will have a large notice "Highly Interesting from Japan—Destruction of Simoda by an Earthquake." Loss of the Russian Frigate *Diana* in the harbor. Escape of the Russians in boats! &c. &c. &c. Save the account of it for me if you see one. Good night.

Feb 8th

Today a great quantity of Japanese have been on board and I hear through our Interpreter, Mr. Lobshide,[12] that we will be able to get away from here in about a week. We have been busy all day braking out provisions and sending them ashore for the Russians. I hear a rumor that the Russians are to pledge their guns, which they saved from the *Dianna*, to the Japanese for the provisions which the latter furnishes them with. With more to write about, I have said less on this sheet than any I have before written.

Simoda, Feb 9th

Simoda was, previous to the destruction by the earthquake on the morning of the 23rd of December last, a flourishing and rather neat little town containing from 7 to 10 thousand inhabitants and some twelve hundred dwellings and temples. The houses mostly of wood with thatched roofs or tiles interspersed occasionally with a better kind off [*sic*] house with fantastic fronts of a kind of plaster. The temples are or were large dwellings for the purpose of worship and used as a kind of Hotel for visitors and strangers.

Now instead of the neat dwellings and temples, the quiet and cleanly aspect of the well-defined streets, the well-constructed bridges crossing the creeks and streams, the gates at the intersections of the streets, and the well-known houses where we were sure to find hospitality are no more. In the place of all this the houses and temples razed, the streets in common with an immense waste can no longer be defined, and in place of the bridges may be seen a dilapidated boat or plank. The air filled with a blinding dis-agreeable smoke arising from the burning of the old straw which once formed the roofs of the houses, and the entire place a mass of ruin and desolation.

I have seen large junks full three miles from the harbor. Others are where homes once were and when they are not absolutely irrepairable men are busy getting them in order, placing them on [mags?] and inching them towards the water. Small houses are rapidly going up but much inferior to the old ones. It is pretty certain that but 16 houses out of over one thousand were all that were saved, and they only partially. I cannot learn correctly the number of lives lost. The lowest statement is 200. The largest is 400.

The harbor is a dangerous one in a blow. Nothing but steam saved the *Powhatan* on Wednesday. I don't care about being left here for several months and loosing what "dry goods" I have got. But I do care about getting home and I'm willing to start tomorrow. Good night Dearest.

Feb. 12th

This night two years ago was our last one together! Tomorrow we will have been gone two years, and during that time what have we not suffered. Oh Lide, this separation is unnatural, but I must not indulge these reflections, they make me too sad. I have been reading another Novel today and I have such a chicken heart that I was compelled to put it aside to prevent blubbering. I think I will cry when I meet you, but everybody won't see it. No, I don't know what I will do. I'll be happy I well know, and you, what will you do? The time must soon come now.

Some Japanese are on board and I think settling the ratification business. The Russians have concluded a Treaty with these people and get the two ports that the Americans have and Nagas[a]ki. This gives us the latter by our Treaty with them.

Feb. 13th

Two years from home! The most unhappy two years of my life, and getting worse every day. This afternoon an official interview was held between the Japanese and Capt. Adams on shore, but I have been unable to learn with what success the Japanese cavil about the time. The eighteen months they say must elapse before the exchange, and to do away with that idea we have remained here already over two weeks. Without an exception I think these people the greatest humbugs in the world! They have already cost me two years imprisonment. I'm sick, tired and disgusted. I will rejoice when I get or hear orders to leave this interesting part of the globe. Good night again. These are the most interesting words I write now.

Feb. 14th

The interview between Capt. Adams and one of the Commissioners of Japan resulted in the promise to have everything signed and delivered in a week. This Commissioner wanted to sign himself but it requires the Emperors signature, and they state that he never had a pen in his hand; then they were told that he must authorize some person to sign for him, and that in case it was not finished in seven days this ship would return to the United States and report the refusal which would induce the President to send a large fleet out here to destroy all their towns and cities. This threat had the desired effect and the promise was made to "hurry up the cakes." It has always been my idea to frighten these humbugs into measures.

Since writing the above I have heard from another source that the Commissioner stated that the Emperor had no authority to sign, that it was a mistake about his not being able to use a pen &c. Now so they get through, which they will do according to the best authority on Tuesday next. I will be very much obliged to them.

Feb. 15th

A day or two ago the Russian Admiral took his leave and when parting he almost cried. They have gone to Hadee which is some 40 miles from here and where their Frigate went down. Before leaving the Admiral presented the Ward Room Mess with two large Japanese bowls and it was decided by lottery that Dr. Maxwell should have them.

Feb. 21st

This morning preparations were made on an extensive scale to go ashore and receive the Japanese Treaty, but the wind blew very strong and it commenced raining, so the affair dwindled down to one boat with Captain Adams and another with several other Officers who went ashore and finished the business!

The Japanese came off this afternoon in great numbers. Amongst them some of the "biggest boys" of Japan, with presents for the Officers and men. The men have received theirs and the Capt. and Ward Room officers theirs. The Engineers have not been served yet. So the Japan "pidgeon" is settled and we are off for Shanghai tomorrow. Several salutes were fired, one of 17 guns for the ratification.

Feb. 26th

Today we have had fine weather and a smooth sea, and all hands feel indeed thankful. On Saturday afternoon the 24th the wind commenced blowing strong and by dark we had a terrific gale called a Cyclone. The ship rolled tremendously, the wind blowing so hard that it was impossible to bring the ship head to it until the Mizzen Storm Stay Sail was set then she became easy. It was necessary for three Engineers to be on Watch at a time and that put us on watch and watch. The sea was truly awful! And the ship was in imminent danger. Never do I wish to see the like, the sight was terrifically beautiful. The noble ship would bound from one sea to another with such ease and so quickly that the monsters were unable to board us. No small vessel could have been saved, and were I a Christian or in the habit of praying I would return thanks to the Preserver of All for allowing us more of this earthly life. I feel indeed grateful, but I must not get hypocritical. To sum up we made a narrow escape.

Tomorrow will be the 27th of February and the anniversary of our wedding. Five years married and no babies yet! Five years married and almost half of them spent away from each other. Good night.

Off the mouth of the Yangstse Kiang river about 55 miles
from Woosung, at anchor, Sunday morning, March 4th

On the morning of the 27th Feb. the wind arose again and soon another gale of wind followed. The blow was little inferior in force than the one on the night of the 24th and lasted until about noon of Friday the 2nd of March. We had a most tremendous sea. The largest I have ever seen, the ship d[o]ing her best could make but 4 miles an hour after the wind subsided. And but a few tons of coal in the bunkers. Old rope, tar, pork, spars and all the wood in the ship was got ready in case the coal would give out, but we fortunately did not have to use it.

On the morning of Saturday about 5 o'clock we got into shoal water and let go the anchor and on defining our position found ourselves where I headed this days remarks, and about 10 o'clock we sent one of our boats in charge of the Master up the river with orders to charter the Steamer *Confucius*[13] to bring us a pilot and 40 tons of coal. Woosung is about 40 miles from Shanghai, and the boat may have to go as far up as Shanghai before meeting the Steamer. She may be here this afternoon and may not until tomorrow. Such anxiety I never saw on board ship. A number of men became so frightened that they could not work.

Now my division is composed of 13 men, and in cases of emergency it is as much as a man can do to fill his place and do his work, but through fright and sickness I was reduced to seven. I took hold myself until I got some of the stronger deck hands, and by dint of whiskey, coaxing and driving I got along very much to my satisfaction. Nothing irritates me so much as men giving out when they are most wanted. I would stand up until I dropped. I have already been so exhausted that I could do no more than hold myself up, and then be able to impressively to do a moments Herculean labor! Often do men imagine themselves sick because death is open mouthed for them. I don't know that any one has turned grey since we left Simoda, but I know that the sea was too high, the excitement too intense, the danger too imminent and my humble services too much required to allow to get sea sick.

On the 2nd of this month we had our first sad ceremony of a burial at sea. On the 1st David Fisk, Fifer, aged 49 died on board with dysentery. On the morning of the 2nd he was sewn up in canvas with two 32 pound shot made fast to his feet, placed on a board and as the words "dust to dust" were uttered one end of the board was raised up and the body slid into the "briny deep" with a strange splashing sound and all was o'er. This man had been in the service 22 years and was a native of Washington.

March 5th

The news is that the French attacked the Rebels at Shanghai and were repulsed with the loss of a few Officers and about 20 men. The Rebels afterwards setting fire to the City and retiring when the Imperialists forces marched in. So Shanghai is now in possession of the Mandarins. We also have news of the great battle near Sebastopool [Sevastopol], but of this anon.

March 6th

Last evening about sundown a vessel was seen approaching us and on hailing her we learned that she was from San Francisco 55 days out and bound for

Shanghai. She dropped anchor and we sent a boat to her. Soon after the boat started a thick fog ensued and we lost sight of boat and ship. We fired cannon and muskets, burned blue lights and rang our bell all night. This morning we got up our anchor and dropped with the tide and about 10 o'clock we saw the ship through the fog, hailed her and learned that our boat was safe alongside of her.

Soon after the boat returned and we received California papers to the 30th Dec., and learned that the *Mississippi* and *Susquehanna* had sailed from San Francisco on the 9th Dec. for home, and that one hundred and eighty of the *Mississippi*'s crew had run while they laid there. The name of the ship is the *Wild Duck*.[14]

U.S. Ste. *Powhatan*, Shanghai, China, March 10th, 1855

My Dear Lide,

I dislike to mention anything about my Mess Mates. None of them suit me. One constant growl and quarrel. I sacrifice a great measure of pugnacity for the sake of harmony and peace. I was very near putting violent hands on Faron the other day. [. . .] I hate to hear him speak. Dislike his looks and would give considerable to be enabled never to look upon his visage. Everyone in the Mess detest him. King has found him out and is the strongest in his expressing of dislike. Sewell is his only chummy. Sewell, too has become known and is liked by none.

In our other Steerage we have but two Officers, the Captain and Pursers Clerk. Neither of whom do I much fancy. The Boatswain is a man of no refinement and with no education, but has a heart without any black spots in it, and I sometimes have a talk with him. Dudley, the Pursers clerk, (you met him at the Ball in Portsmouth) is a strange body. A gifted writer, a man of extensive reading, well posted in affairs of the world &c. but is rather boyish. Butler the Carpenter thinks of nothing else but money and is what neighbors would call a "news carrier." The Ward Room Officers I dislike in a body with the exception of Mr. Carter with whom I sometimes have a conflict.

Shanghai is now all peace and quiet. The Rebels have been conquered and blood flowed freely for some days after the capture of the City by the Imperialists assisted by the French. A reward of three hundred thousand dollars is offered for the Rebel Chief, Alin's head. He escaped, and well for him.

Sunday, March 11th

There small pox is raging badly on shore and several deaths have occurred from it. Mrs. Murphy, the Consuls[15] wife has it. She has a small or rather a young baby to take care of which makes it so much worse. It is an awful disease to get on board a ship.

Sewell has been ashore two nights and a day sponging on the Missionaries I expect. He thinks he is a great lady's man and no doubt he is. He is said to be good looking and all that kind of thing, and appears to amuse and interest the fair creatures with his wit and lively conversation. Never at a loss to have one on his arm when they come on board. He is very attentive. Now all this may be natural talent, education or accomplishment, but when such a man (this now is my opinion only) as G[eorge] S[ewell], who is according to my social views a senseless ass, succeeds so well with women, lady's, if you please, I must say that my notion of the fair sex redounds not much to their credit. I don't believe that more than two women out of every hundred has, compared with man, a proper share of barn yard sense. And that all of them are unable to discern the difference between mockery and reality, of course you are always excepted!

I am rather down on women as a class. But what am I about? I'm writing to one and, Jerusalem! Won't I get rats! But to speak frankly now, I would rather have the good opinion of one man than 40 women.

March 12th

The *Vandalia* sails tomorrow morning for Hong Kong with Capt. Adams who goes home in the next Steamer, overland with the Japan ratifications. Damn Japan. I am thoroughly, heartily, wholly disgusted, and so help me, if I had money enough to pay my passage home I would run and let the Navy go to the devil. Some say it would disgrace me. Let it disgrace and be fiddled. I was a fool, a great big darn fool that I did not quit when I was ordered to this floating hell and ruin my chance for bread. Who gets credit for being attached to this Navy? Those who get big pay and stay at home! I tell you I am done with it, and if I am unable to earn our bread in anything connected with a Steam Engine why I can dig, saw wood or drive a coal cart. And you can help me with your needle.

We will then be together and our world will be our garrett, and the gaudy fools, and heartless hypocrites may scoff and laugh, but not insult. I believe I'm getting angry with myself. But this outrage is to scandalous, 'tis shameful to submit to. Our men's times are expiring and the ship is not more than half Officers. But hope, yes hope. Vain words. Why my heart is sick with hope.

Do not allow these outbreaks to annoy you my own Dear Lide. You know what an impetuous being I am, and when roused I know no bounds.

Believe me truly your own, George.

U.S. Ste. *Powhatan*, Shanghai, China, March 31st, 1855

My Own Dearest,

The French and English learned shortly after our arrival here of the unfortunate position of the Russians at Simoda and a few days since an English Steamer and a French Frigate left here for parts unknown. We suppose they intend visiting Simoda and annoying the Russians. This afternoon the Clipper Ship *Young America*[16] in trying to get out of this harbor got aground. It is hoped that she will get off this evening as she is bound for parts unknown. I think she is going to Simoda to render succor to the Russians and as the *Young America* is one of the fastest and finest Clippers ever built. If she has the least wind why all will be well. I hope she may succeed and that Johnny Crapeau and Jno. Bull may be weathered for the Russians are in a shipwrecked condition and 'twould not be "fair play" to deal harshly with them. In the war I don't care which comes out ahead. Feel rather in favor of the Bear.

Woosung is a place, China town, about 12 miles below here and where vessels sometimes remain to avoid paying Port Duties. Now when sailors desert their ships they generally make this place a rendezvous and kick up all kinds of Barbary. Some have deserted our ship and some others swelling the number of deserters at Woosung to about 60 men. Reports from there have been received stating that some of them starving. Others stealing and keeping up a row and riot. So a Marshall (I can't say whether he be a U. States one or what) came on board our ship got a dozen Marines and an Officer and this evening started off to arrest the crowd. We doubt there will be trouble. Tomorrow will tell.

Monday, April 2nd

Yesterday morning whilst we were at church on the Quarter Deck the boats returned from Woosung where they had gone for the purpose of arresting some deserters. Mr. Wm. Whiting, our Boatswain, commanded the party. They landed at Woosung and arrived in front of a house where the deserters were. On requesting the Keeper open and just as the Marine struck the door with the butt of his musket, from some cause the musket accidentally went off and Whiting being immediately behind the Marine, the whole load went through his body and killed him immediately. He never spoke out the words "I'm shot." Mr. Whiting's body was brought up on the return of the boats, and he is to be buried this afternoon. It will be a difficult matter to fill his place so ably. Everybody liked him and there is but one voice of sincere regret through the whole ship. He leaves a wife and young child in Brooklyn. The death of Mr. Whiting was as pure and clear case of destiny or fate as I have ever heard of.

This afternoon his funeral left the ship and the whole guard of Marines, most of the Officers and as many men as could be spared from the ship together with the band attended, and upon reaching the shore a large concourse of funeral service was read and the body placed in the grave the Marines fired three volleys over it. All the honor was done him, and may he rest in peace. [']Twill be a sad, a terrible blow to his wife, but "such is life," and how true the words, "in the midst of life we are in death." This sad and most melancholy accident has cast a deep gloom over everything.

Poor Whiting only last Friday had charge of the funeral procession that buried one of our fireman.[17] The doleful pipe of "all hands bury the dead" is heard on board the *Powhatan* now almost every week! For two years but one person died on board and that was Lieut. Adams. Death seems to be on board now dealing with all. I trust and pray that all now on board and all who may come on board may be permitted by a Kind Providence to join the friends and families in this world. 'Tis an awful thing to die away from home. No kind friends to hold your memory sacred. No female to speak kindly and softly to the few who may feel it most. And after the grave is covered all's forgotten.

Bibby writes me that Canton is quiet and that the Imperialist are cutting off heads daily. The Rebels having been almost exterminated. Nothing but the wish to leave for home is heard on all sides. Hope lingers. Next mail may tell us something. Good night. God Bless you.

April 4th

The work on the Engines still goes on. The "bushings" were bad and we had to make one out of two. Sewell is quite a lady's man. Plays the gallant admirably. What men can talk about to women who say "yes," "no," "delightful" &c. gets me. I know what they like better and don't I wish I had a chance. Over two years now since I had a pop. That's what I call playing the martyr. Never mind I will make up for it some of these days.

Two French Frigates left here this morning for parts unknown,[18] supposed Simoda and Pedro Paulaski [Petropaulski]. [. . .] A subscription has been taken up for the purpose of erecting a monument to Whiting. Everything seems and is dull and heavy.

April 7th

Yesterday Boatswains Mate Baily received an Acting Appointment to fill poor Whitings place.

We have a "brick" that the *Vandalia* goes to Guam[19] and that the *Macedonian* comes direct here and that we go to Hong Kong. Supposed that we will get off about the 1st of May. Hope still lingers that something may be said of a definite character with regards to our start for home.

Yours Decidedly,
George

U.S. Ste. *Powhatan*, Shanghai, China, April 15th, 1855

My Dearest Lide,

I want you to be very careful how you swallow roast beef, and as you weigh 148 I doubt care about your getting much heavier for you will be catching me.

Now for our news. On Thursday last we put the machinery together in a great hurry got up steam and moved our berth. We are now anchored just far enough from the Bund to swing clear of it. The Bund is the name given to the street fronting the river. Capt. McCluney was induced to thus move the ship by the ladies of Shanghai who wanted to hear our band. Said band is a pretty good one but I'm sick of it. The same old routine every day soon surfeits one. Well here we are and the ladies are satisfied, and they seem very fond of the *Powhatan* for some three or 4 are on board every day. And as ladies ankles will show themselves going up and down the ladders a fellow can't half but look at them. Then the sight of petticoats (clean ones of course) does an hombre so much good. But I am astonished that some of them wear black stockings. The nasty black dye comes off and stains. The pretty white skins of their well shaped . . . Oh! Ankles!

It does me a power of good to see a pretty woman if she has good sense. But I do dislike to see a doll baby. I would sacrifice good looks for good sense, and I would fall in love quicker with a woman with hair on her face than I would with one who looked like an angel if the one knew something and the other nothing. What am I writing about? Why, I am telling you the news. Excessively interesting is it not?

I was on shore yesterday and saw the stone for poor Whiting's grave. It is a very fine one. Every Officer and man on board the ship subscribed, and what is left after paying for the funeral expenses, tombstone &c. is to be sent home to his wife who lives in Brooklyn. A letter came on board for him yesterday and undoubtedly from her. What a blow it will be. We miss him very much.

Mr. Bibby writes me from Canton and informs me that the Rebels have been completely beaten there and driven down the river below Whampoa where a great many of them have been arrested and executed! Chopping off mens heads in China is looked upon with less feeling than cutting a Turkey's throat for a Christmas dinner. It is no common sight to sight to see pigs eating the bodies of dead Chinamen.

Mr. Barbot of the *Vandalia* goes to the *Macedonian* and Mr. [Walcutt] of the *Macedonian* goes to the *Vandalia*. You know that [Walcutt] was tried some time ago by a Court Martial. He was sentenced to dismissal but Capt. Abbott commuted his sentence and it all ends in his exchanging from one ship to another.

Mr. Stamm was offered 175 dollars per month to run the *Queen*, but he could not accept. He is in the Navy, and he was to sign a contract to run the boat six months. Bibby is secretary for Dr. Parker who is Acting United States Minister to China. Mr. King desires me to say to you that he is well and much pleased to hear of you weighing 28 pounds more than he does. Mr. Dudley understands about that honey affair at Portsmouth Ball and he had a good laugh over it. Be certain to write again for I will expect an answer to this next September and perhaps earlier.

April 18th

I have been silent since Sunday in consequence of a slight indisposition. On Monday evening I went on shore in company with Mr. Kellogg and after getting there was induced by some friends to join them at a table where champagne was flowing freely and of course I took some. Afterwards felt the effects of it and became a little sick. But being quiet blue pill and a couple of Seidlitz powders I am all right again. I have been told "that an open confession is good for the soul" and you are my confessor. Now don't pitch into me for if you do I won't tell you when I misbehave again, though I have no fear that there will be an early repetition of it. So much for my negligence and to the rich story I promised you on the other sheet.

Some time ago I hinted to you that I had difficulty with my immediate superior in offices, Mr. Faron, and that the said difficulty was settled by his crying. I never after mentioned the subject to him nor do I think I ever will. Now this same gentlemen has had trouble with every Officer in the Mess. Lately his overbearing and tyrannical disposition had become almost intolerable, and various have been the discussions about remedying the evil, but nothing was done and he kept in. I said that I was determined to get on harmoniously if I could. The other members of the Mess have been in a much greater ration the recipients of his ill humor than me, and I therefore stood more aloof. He had never attempted to interfere with my duty, but to the story.

About six weeks ago him and King had some words which ended in a coolness between them so that they did not speak to another. Last week at the table Mr. F[aron] took occasion to most outrageously insult King by calling him a puppy and telling him he would, "smack his chops" to which he received the reply that he would have to pay for the language. In the evening K[ellogg] called upon me to wait upon F[aron] and request that he would appoint someone with whom I could consult with regards to satisfaction. I could not deny him so I very politely informed the gentleman of my errand. Of course he was astonished, but refused to apologize or refer me to an individual. I saw him twice after and the affair terminated the next morning at the breakfast table by his making an unqualified and open apology. I felt when I undertook the matter that such would be the end of it, for I knew that cool calm deliberation would scare him and so it did, for he has been as meek as a lamb ever since. He is now on speaking terms with all in the Mess except Fauth.

April 19th

I was thinking today whether it would be possible for me to get a situation on one of the river boats on the Delaware River or whether it would be more pleasant to get on the lakes. You see I am thinking ahead for surely I don't wish to make any more voyages after this one. I may have to go again, but if it can be avoided, and I think it can it shall be. I can exercise no influence in Philada. and but little out West, so all that I have to depend upon is my ability. Then I would much rather get into something where there was no

Steam Engine for I'm sick of Steam, just as much so as you used to be when I would talk about it. How would you like me to run a locomotive?

April 20th

The Steamer *Chusan*[20] left yesterday for Hong Kong via Amoy.

Out of the five Lieutenants who came out with us we have but one attached to the ship. Out of 4 Passed Midshipmen but one and he is the Master promoted in the place of the Master who came out with us. Our Gunner is home. Our Boatswain dead. One Asst. Engr. home. Another attached until lately to another ship. Our Marine Officer gone home. The men's times are out and they are growling. They say they shipped for 3 years and not 5. Is it not time for the ship to home? Who will deny it? What keeps us here? The China Civil War is at end so far as it extended on the coast. The Japan affair signed, sealed, and settled. The Peking farce concluded, and two Sloops of War here to defend the American Interest and protect the dollars of as few nabobs. So what do they want with a Steamer here?

Nothing. Nothing but to burn up Uncle Sam's treasury in the shape of coal at the rate of 40 tons per day and costing to burn it about 50 dollars per ton! Exchange on home 50 pr. cent premium so every dollar paid by Uncle S. here costs him one dollar and a half. There is the keeping of the bone and sinew of the country out here to contract diseases giving to benefit the country? It's wrong. All wrong. False economy and ingratitude. I tell you I'm up in arms. I want to go home! I'm tired, disgusted. Sick at heart.

I can't do my duty as it ought to be done. The Government Officers are blind to the general interest, and I go in for ousting the whole cabinet. I'm down on Democracy. I'll turn Whig for I really begin to think they do more good for the people than the "undefiled." "The greatest good for the greatest number." I believe sincerely that Commodore Perry's influence with the representations keeps the *Powhatan* out, and I believe that he could have had the ship ordered home, and that he would have had her ordered home had he not fallen out with Capt. McCluney. And the fault is all with Capt. McCluney, than whom a greater and more egotistical ass does not live. A complete dotard. I'm down on him. I have run off at a terrible rate tonight. So good night. Must stop to play ucre.[21]

Sunday Evening, April 22nd

Just as I stopped on the last page Messrs. Jones and Adams of the *Macedonian* came down the ladder having arrived here in a Pilot boat. Jones is the Marine Officer that relieved Capt. Tansill, but up to this time he has been at Canton with the Marine Guard of the *Macedonian*, and the rebel disturbances having subsided there thus dispensing with the use of the Marines he has been ordered back to our ship. So he joined us bag and baggage this evening. Adams is a son of Capt. Adams and Secretary to "His Highness" Commodore Abbott. He comes up for "look see" as the Anglo Chinese express it.

The news is, that the *Macedonian* is anchored off Woosung where she will have to remain some five days in consequence of the tides being too low to admit of her crossing the bar. That she is to remain here about three months when she will go to Japan. That we are to visit Guam. That a report was current in Hong Kong that the *Powhatan* was to start for home next month, at any rate that the *Powhatan* was the first ship to be relieved! Then again it is stated that an extract of a letter from the Secretary of the Navy states that no ship attached to the East India Squadron will be relieved before November next, and perhaps not until 1856! Pleasant, flattering. Excellent! Ask me if I will even vote the Democratic ticket. Ask me if I voted for the present administration and I can say no! But this very agreeable intelligence does not end with this.

April 23rd

I had an offer today of a situation ashore which I could save twenty-five hundred dollars per year! If I was offered 50 thousand dollars I could not leave. I'm tied, to talk of running or deserting, unless to make good you plans to escape in a ship is nonsense. To talk of resigning is worse. It's absurd. They would think no more of accepting than jumping overboard in a gale of wind.

Stamm is anxious to resign and so is Arnold. This China is a great place for making money and also spending it. The salaries of the Officers of ships are a mere nothing compared to wages of able men on shore. The Chinese government has bought some Steamers and five hundred dollars per month is offered for Engineers! And none to be had. Forty dollars a month for sailors in Merchant Ships. Money seems nothing and Chinamen can live and enjoy considerable luxuries for four cents a day. So good night. God Bless you.

May 3rd

The *Macedonian* arrived up day before yesterday and an interview has been held between the Commodore and our Captain. The result is that we are not going to Guam, and to leave Shanghai for Hong Kong about the 15th of this month. So say those who make pretensions to knowledge of these things. Our work has progressed finely and we can be ready for sea in 24 hours.

A Mr. Lewis[22] who was a Masters Mate on the *Macedonian* has received the appointment of Captain's Clerk on the *Powhatan*. He is said to be a very fine young man. Bibby was afraid that McCluney would request him to return, but I have put him on easy legs about it.

Sincerely Your Devoted George

Shanghai, May 10th

My Own Dearest,

I finished a novel called the "*Money Lender*" today and this evening took up *Rienzi*. The very idea of reading *Steam and Mechanics* disgusts me, and when I convince myself that to read such and study their teachings helps me in the detestable business I have adopted to earn my bread, and sternly resolve to study. The book is opened and so are my eyes for only a very short time for I am sure to fall asleep!

The last news from the Secretary is that we may be relieved next spring! Arnold offered his resignation the other day but Capt. McCluney refused to forward it. Should I offer mine, I know that it would be forwarded. Now I am one of the sanguine kind and altho every mail dampens my ardor I hope still. I must hope, I will hope, and oh that blessed day when I again have you seated on my lap with your arm around my neck. Hard indeed must be my fate if in all the world a spot cannot be found where we can live and be with one another. I feel very loquacious to night and will stop. So good night, and may angels bless and protect you.

Sunday Evening. May 13th

Yesterday the Races came off and I was there. Now all the respectable people here, save the Missionaries attend. As they do not do this at home some explanation seem necessary, so you must understand that the ponies and horses are ridden by gentlemen, and it is about the only general sport the folks have. I was much pleased, but standing all the time and the long walk in the sun made my headache so that I did not write any last night.

May 15th

Mr. C[raig] joined our ship today as a Master Mate. Mr. Sewell is much better, so much so that he is able to sit up. The Race Club of Shanghai give a ball tonight and the Captain and Officers of the ship have been invited, and strange to relate the invitation has been sent in the Steerage, but no Steerage

Officers in the ship is going but Dudley. Thus you have all the news since I last quit you on Sunday evening.

This evening whilst on the hurricane deck I noticed the evening star and being the first time since I left home I take it as a good omen. I think as I grow old (you know we are growing old) that I grow superstitious or it may be that the nonsense that I read exercises an influence in sympathy, for my nature is certainly sympathetic, and it will not act in unison with machinery or its attributes but with those connections whose tendencies point to domestic happiness. Home and wife! So that where I noticed a connection in superstitious circumstance in my readings, I may be led to form with myself some chain linking the occurrence with my own humble fate.

Amoy Harbor, May 24th

On Sunday last we got up steam and left Shanghai. As we left and passed the town the ladies were at the windows moving handkerchiefs and making all sorts of parting demonstrations.

During the night the ship *Africa* ran into us and did some slight damage. About daylight we again got underway and arrived here about six o'clock this evening. 'Tis very hot. My rheumatism is much better thanks to some cups and a good sweat in the Engine Room. Good night.

At Sea, May 27th

We left Amoy this morning at five o'clock and we are now on our way to Hong Kong where we expect our letters.

This afternoon just after Mr. King relieved me, he in arranging the Port Exhaust Valve got his arm caught between the lifting tow and side pipe and broke it just above the hand. He is in much pain, but stands it like a major. It is well that his arm is a small one or there would have been more than bones broken. As it is, the Doctor fears that he will partially loose [lose] the use of his arm. At any rate he is good for two months at least on the list.

Hong Kong, May 29th

[The following is a letter written to George's wife by William H. King, First Assistant Engineer]

My Dear Madam,

Your dear George has been employed all this long; and as he might term gloomy day, reading "Rienzi" very contrary to my wishes as I have been endeavoring to persuade him to employ his time to better purpose. But I regret to say without avail and as I know of no better way to punish him for his disobedience, I take the liberty of writing you a few lines on the back of this letter informing you that he is getting entirely beyond my control, with the request that you may give him a proper lecture on the subject. I also have to request that you give him a good scolding for his not deigning. As I learn, to mention, even once, in his numerous epistles to you that there was among the occupants of the "Port Steerage" so humble a person as myself.

Pardon the liberty dear Madam I take in addressing you almost an entire stranger, but you will perceive the importance of the subject demands it.

Your friend, Wm. H. King

By the above you will see how much ones privacy is respected in a Steerage! You will certainly excuse the hard cheek of Billy King, and take to heart, no doubt his noble interest in the welfare of your devoted George. Had he have read my remarks last night on my readings no doubt at all that he would have chosen some other topic where with to acquaint you of my waywardness. Excuse him, and believe that the correct deportment of him who stands accused, and of what, is beyond reproach.

Philadelphia can only be my residence as a rich man. As a poor one I will and must be estranged from those whose blood only ties me to them. My first endeavors on getting home will be in search of something whereby I can make my living without going to sea. I have hope, and that very hope keeps me fat! I look well, feel well, and have no red whiskers.

May 31st

In the morning about ten o'clock one of our men named John C. Westgate[23] fell from the Port Crank Pin and injured himself so badly that he died in about two hours. It seems strange that the best men, and those full of health and life should be the first victims. This man was a coal-heaver and was very much beloved by all, Officers and men. He is to be buried this afternoon.

A strange fatality seems attached to the place where this man fell from, for all the men that we have lost had charge of that work. Westgate was appointed to clean it only a few minutes before he fell. The promotion consequent upon the death of Clockerty was offered to two who refused it, and one of our storekeepers afterwards accepted it, but he could not be spared from the storeroom and poor Westgate took the fatal spot with pleasure, and to meet his death in so short a time. Many of our men are very superstitious and it will be with no little trouble that we shall have to get someone to do the office lately filled by Storm, Clockerty and Westgate. Does it not seem strange?

June 3rd

On Friday evening (this is Sunday) I received a letter from my friend Bibby who is thrown out of employment in consequence of the departure home of Dr. Parker. He anticipated employment in the American Consuls Office at this place. Stamm has not joined the ship yet. I have to record the death of another man attached to our ship named Chas. Wilson who died of dysentery this morning and was buried this afternoon.

June 5th

This morning I went on shore and whilst walking on the principal street I detected a Chinaman with his hand on my pocket. I necked him and gave him rats. It would be too troublesome to take him the police office so I whaled him and let him go. These Chinamen are the most notorious pickpockets in the world. It seems as if everybody is getting more sanguine about home. Most of the Officers think we shall get our orders within three months. I can't write tonight.

Evening, [June 6th]

You ask me how I look, and how much I weigh. Well, I think when I'm shaved clean and my head cropped short I'm pretty good looking with my clothes on. But I'm one of the best looking fellows you ever saw stripped. My legs (excuse me, I'm speaking physiologically) are as plump and round as they can well be to have shaped, my arms a perfect model, and the bust, why it's bigger than yours! Talk about mauling me, why woman it would take a dozen ordinary men to put me on my back. And one of my hugs is worse that the strongest bears. Tho' I must confess not quite so hairy. Do you think now, ducky, that you can take me down?

US Steamer *Powhatan*, Macao, June 16th 1855

My Dearest Wife,

I'm full of the prickly heat again. Sewell is getting very well. Faron is taking Cod Liver Oil. Kings arm is doing very well. Stamm has not joined us yet. The men have had liberty at this place and drunkenness, brawls, black eyes and bloody noses are not a few. A Marine named Walker, I knew him when I was a boy, was struck with a belaying pin in the hands of one Mullen the other night and badly hurt. His upper lip was cut completely in two. The men seem to be making the most of this liberty as they are under the impression that 'tis the last they will have in China for all now look to the next mail for something.

Stamm came on board a few nights ago and got a week's leave from the Captain. We expect him now in about 4 days. I went on board the new Steamer "*River Bird*" the other day and I very much dislike her. Engineers are in great demand out here. Almost any kind of one can command over two thousand dollars a year, but I would not remain, if I could, unless you were with me for any sum. You with me I could live anywhere.

Mr. Sewell will never be the man he was, and great and great care will have to be taken of him the remainder of the cruise. He begins to pick up a little but he is not allowed to exert himself any. Faron is weakly and can't stand anything. In fact the whole ships company including officers are worn out—broken down, and 'tis a shameful outing that we are kept in this intolerable climate so long. Mr. Secretary Dobbin is a heartless wretch or an ignoramus! We ought to have started when the other ships did or at least after Mr. McLane was done with us. But even after doing everything and now to keep us here to lay and rot is truly shameful. But hope we must, never despair. Now good night and may I dream of you again. It does me good to do so, even if it is not a good one.

June 18th 1855

This morning we noticed a signal of distress flying from an American ship at anchor here and sent on board to ascertain the difficulty and learned that the crew had refused to work. That is Mutiny. The men stated that they did not get proper food, and the Captain stated that they wanted to be discharged because seamens wages were double here to what they were getting. That they had signed Articles to serve 14 months at the rate he was paying them. On examination it was found that the Captain's statement was correct and the men were ordered to go to work. They said they would, but about two hours after the Captain boarded us and stated that the men still refused to work and he wanted to get underway. So we sent a Sergeant and 13 Marines on board to put them in irons, but rather than go in irons they went to work and got underway.[24]

Yesterday a man named Dennin[25] who had been sick for a long time and at the point of death for the last week drank a bottle of soda water because he was encouraged by learning that he was improving! Consequence was that last night he came within an ace of dying and is yet very low!! The man we lost buried in Hong Kong probably was imprudent for 'tis reported that after his death a fried fish was found in his cot! The villains that furnish the sick with any of these things contrary to the Drs. orders ought to be tried for manslaughter.

June 20th 1855

Dan "The Man" Dennin who drank the soda water died this afternoon. It may be a salutary lesson to those who disobey orders given for their own good. I find that there is too much noise and humbugging in the Steerage to write much at nights. So I think I will try it in the daytime.

June 21st, 1855

And yet another! Today Washington Hickman died.[26] This morning Dennin was buried. Tomorrow Hickman will be. One begins to get hardened to the mournful hymn played by the band on a corpse leaving the ship. One gets accustomed to the sight of a wooden box in the shape of a coffin. Death almost looked upon as an everyday affair and treated as a "matter of course." Well 'tis sad to contemplate.

Saturday Night, June 23rd

The men lately have been getting drunk every day, and every effort to detect where the liquor came from proved fruitless until this morning when some liquor was passed over the side in Mr. Kelloggs name. He was sent for as suspicions were aroused to the fact of so much liquor coming for Mr. K[ellogg]. He of course knew nothing about it, I told K[ellogg] to state that I saw the Ward Room Stewards have three bottles of gin yesterday. I was asked about it and made my statement. So on examination it was found that this fellow with some of the Ward Room boys and the Surgeons Steward were the guilty parties and they were not punished. But the comprador who furnished these fellows with it got pitched into "Night Shift." They could buy the rum from the comprador for 65 cents a bottle and they would sell it to the sailors and firemen for from 3 to 5 dollars per bottle. The affair created a little excitement this morning and we assuredly want something to rear away this dullness that seems to encompass everything.

Then one dollar here is worth at least 1 dollar and a quarter at home, and I would dislike to charge any more for an article than it cost me. Now in Shanghai 20 dollar gold piece can be bought for about 13 dollars. That is Spanish dollars, and we get paid in Shanghai in Spanish dollars, in other places they pay us in Mexican dollars, and these are far more valuable out here than gold.

Hong Kong, June 27th

Yesterday the Asst. Engineers learned that Capt. McCluney had issued an order not to allow but two Engineers to leave the ship at the same time. To this we wrote a joint letter of remonstrance, but got for an answer that he would not write revoke the order. All we can do is to grin and bear it. Tomorrow we leave for Whampoa.

Chapter Six
July 2–December 23, 1855

July 2nd

We are now in Whampoa where we arrived on the 27th having left H.K. the day before. I wrote to Bibby and he came down to see me. We have had a nice time together on board the *Jacob Bell*,[1] a Clipper Ship in which Bibby is going home on and is to start from here in about two weeks.

July 6th

We have just received news from Shanghai and learn that Commodore Abbott has ordered our ship to Loo Choo to investigate some troubles between a Capt. Stone and Chinamen. This Stone it is reported with a ships company killed some fifty of the Celestials, and accordingly we start tomorrow morning for Hong Kong and shortly after for Loo Choo.

I don't weigh as much as usual. I'm down to 160 pounds. The fat must come out in the shape of sweat.

July 7th

This morning at a little after six o'clock we left Whampoa and about half past as we entered the harbor of Hong Kong a tremendous crash was heard and Mr. Kellogg who was on watch in the Engine room immediately stopped the engines. We then discovered that the Starboard Air Pump had completely carried away. The air pump piston rod bent. The air pump beam shaft pillar blocks broken and the caps torn from their places leaving the A.P.B. shaft some 8 inches in the air. The cut off rods bent in all kinds of shapes, the bottom of the bed plate knocked out. The piston bent. The piston rod broken and a general smash up of the Starboard Air Pump. This no doubt from what I have seen will take six months to repair! Certainly we shall not leave Hong Kong until we leave for home!

We are so far as the Engines are concerned a perfect wreck and as yet we have not ascertained the extent of the damage. Tomorrow morning we will take the Air Pump cover up and tomorrow I can tell you more about it. All is excitement. We disconnected the broken engine and with one engine made the anchorage, a distance of about 5 miles. I worked so hard that twice I had to leave the Engine Room. I never before experienced the sensation of fainting or exhaustion. Danby helped me. I brought the ship to anchor and left with pleasure. More of this tomorrow. So now good night and God Bless you.

July 8th

This morning a partial examination of the broken engine was made and we found that the air pump piston rods had broken about an inch below the upper edge of the bucket. Leaving the bucket and valve at the bottom of the pump, and as the valve had canted it obstructed the descent of the rod and first carried away the bottom of the pump which coming up on the bottom of the ship caused the further obstruction which ended in breaking the works above the pump. How far the bed plate, the bucket and valve are damaged we can't yet tell and to repair everything depends much on the facilities on shore. Should our orders for home come out you may depend that there will be no delay on the part of any of us. Without a doubt the accident is the most extensive I have ever seen. The crack was tremendous! [. . .] No one is to blame it is one of those things that will occur. The excitement is intense about it.

Everybody is very anxious. I don't think that new air pump piston rods can be made here. If they cannot they will have to be made either at Manilla or Bombay and one of us will have to go and superintend the making of them. This accident keeps us from doing all the work in these seas as has been the custom, but I'm afraid will keep us out here a couple of months longer than otherwise.

Good bye again. God Bless you my own dearest wife and keep you safe to unite with me again in happiness.

U.S. Ste. *Powhatan*, Hong Kong, July 19th 1855

My Dearest Wife,

In consequence of the excessive heat, the annoyance of boils, sore fingers and prickly heat with the natural excitement consequent upon the breaking down of our machinery I have not been able to muster courage enough to commence a letter to you, and even now the fore finger of my right hand is dreadfully painful. The joint is stiff and I cannot bend the finger. I have two joints on the left hand in the same condition. I have nine boils on the back of my head. Two on my forehead. One on my right cheek and others in other places too numerous to mention. I would indeed like you to see me in this plight, but enough of these torments and to other things.

I took the Port Air Pump to pieces this week and discovered that the piston rod was very much eaten. So much so that the brass casing was loose and we will have to cast a new casing on it for some two feet of its length. We are in a terrible fix and all our ingenuity, skill and constant attention must centre to get us clear.

Sewell continues on the list, and today our Blacksmith ran away. Engineers and men are disgusted. No tools to work with and the weather so hot as to create fatigue even in sleep. My finger pains me very much and I must stop. So good night, love, and God bless you.

July 24th

This is the first day that I have been able to use the fore finger of my right hand. I have suffered terribly with it for the past 5 days by poulticing, leeching and lancing it the Doctor has succeeded in curing it. My left hand was also affected but not so badly. The right hand is yet in a bandage, but I am able to use it.

There was a sorry looking set of Engineers in our Steerage the other day. Sewell, Faron both sick with Bronchitis. King with a broken arm, Stamm with fever, and Gideon with both hands tied up and a head full of boils. I would not go on the list. I am very anxious to do all in my power to get the work along, for I am sorry to say that it progresses very slowly. Scarcely anything done yet above taking the Engines to pieces. But should the mail, which is now due, brings us the good tidings of being ordered home, I have no doubt but we could ready in one month[.]

Yesterday and the day before we had a tremendous blow. A perfect Typhoon. The Hospital ship of the English was unroofed, a small steamer sunk, a large number of junks lost. Some houses on shore blown down, several Chinamen killed and a quantity of damage done. It was a severe blow indeed. We held our own and sustained no damage at all. Good night. I think I will be able now to write a letter every day, but I cannot promise you more than four pages this time. Again good night. God bless you.

July 27th

Mr. Pegram received a letter dated in May stating that the *Powhatan* would be home in nine months from that time. That gives us until about September to start from here. Should this be true I feel content.

August 2nd

Last evening I was on shore and had quite a pleasant time with some brother chiefs. Today I have not felt very well, and dullness seems to reign. The British Steamer *Rattler* left here a few days ago after Pirates. They succeeded in finding their hiding place, but they were unable to reach them in consequence of shoal water, so they returned here today and have made a request of Capt. McCluney to furnish some men and boats, and McCluney has granted. So tomorrow morning allies (American & English) go a Pirate hunting.

August 3rd

At about two o'clock today the expedition after the Pirates left this harbor.[2] The *Rattler* and small Steamer *Eaglet*[3] with 93 of our men, two launches and first cutter composed the party. The Officers from our ship were Messrs. Pegram, Rolando, Jones, McCauley, Kellogg and Dr. Schriver. Kellogg has left with me a sealed letter directed to myself which is not to be opened if he returns. It must be his will. I don't think much blood will be shed, but it is well enough to have everything made right in case of emergency. You can imagine how quiet the ship is with one third of the crew are out of her.

Hong Kong, August 6th, 1855

Last evening the *Rattler* returned from the Pirate grounds bringing with her our three boats and those that were left after the attacks. From the numerous reports I gather the following account which may be looked upon as reliable. On nearing the supposed rendezvous of the pirates flying the Portuguese flag was observed getting underway whereupon Capt. Fellows,[4] the Commander of the *Rattler* and in command of the expedition ordered one of his boats and our first cutter under command of Mr. McCauley with Mr. Kellogg as his aid to intercept her. This they were unable to do until the *Rattler* fired several guns at her when she hove to and was boarded. She had a European Captain who told rather a crooked story and he was detained under the guns of the *Rattler* as a suspicious individual.

In the meantime the small steamer *Eaglet* was ordered to get underway, the *Rattler* having anchored in consequence of shoal water, with our two launches and two small boats from the *Rattler* in tow. She proceeded about five miles when she had to stop on account of the shallowness of the water. The boat then pulled away in the direction of some junks which were under way and firing shot. These junks soon ran aground when they opened broadsides on our first launch under command of Lieut. Rolando with Mr. Craig as his aid. Rolando pulled towards them firing his howitzer and making every shot tell. He soon silenced the guns of one, then another and a third. He then boarded them, and whilst on board, the boat containing Capt. Fellows also boarded and then at the time when the two boats crews and officers were on board, some secreted Chinese piratical miscreant fired the magazine and blew up the junk! Three of our men were killed and eleven wounded.[5] Mr. Rolando being wounded in the hand and blown overboard, but saved. Capt. Fellows was blown overboard without being injured. He could not swim but was saved by one of our men named Taylor who was badly wounded.

Now must have commenced a general fight. The Chinamen throwing stink pots, spears, and firing guns loaded to the very muzzle and our men with the Englishmen fighting like demons showing no quarter. Seventeen junks were destroyed and some 300 Chinamen killed. The *Rattler* lost 4 men killed, six wounded.[6] The Englishmen pay the Americans the highest compliments, and those of our officers who saw the slaughter say that the Englishmen fought like very devils. It was neck or nothing. I hear men talk of taking deliberate aim and shooting Chinamen in the water, of knocking their brains out with cutlasses and muskets. In all, three junks were blown up by pirates themselves.

Aug. 8th

Last evening a man named Adamson, a marine,[7] who was wounded in the attack on the pirates died from his wounds. He was buried this evening. Two more of the marines are very low and little hopes are entertained of their recovery. The whole affair was certainly of a brilliant character on the side of our men and officers with their English friends. Accounts of it will be published in the Hong Kong papers and if I can get one I shall send it to you.

Some of our men secured considerable money from the junks before they were burned. I know some who have from 3 to 500 hundred dollars and one who has over 800 dollars. It is a pity that instead of burning the junks and property they did not tow them to this place and divide the spoils. The affair is now the whole subject of conversation.

One of the pirate prisoners who was brought on board our ship wounded either jumped overboard or was thrown overboard by some of the men about two hour after he got on the ship. He was however rescued. My opinion is that he was thrown overboard, for a more exasperated set of men than ours I never saw in my life. They can hardly treat an honest Chinamen than abusively. It is rumored that another expedition is soon to fit out for the same purpose, but I think that Capt. McCluney will not allow any of his ships company to go.

Chinamen will no doubt look upon the battle as a victory gained by them, for our loss has been very great. Tho' compared with theirs insignificant. In all, up to this time, 8 men have lost their lives and some three lying dangerously. The China loss could not have been less than 300 killed and twice that number wounded. Without a doubt Lieut. Rolando of our ship behaved in the most gallant and admirable manner. In fact all behaved well, and no men in the world could have fought better. I should have liked to have been there and had a look at them.

I put the Port Air Pump together today and in two days the Port Engine will be ready for sea, and in one week the Exhaust pipe will be finished and then if necessary we can go to sea. The repairs in total will not be completed until about the end of next month when I and everybody else hopes to start for home, but of this there is no certainty. I must now wind up. Stamm is off the list. Sewell and King are on yet. Faron is better.

Aug. 9th

Last evening Mr. Pegram asked me to copy his official report of the expedition which I done. This morning I copied another. So much for being good natured &c. Some newspapers with a full account have been ordered and should I get one I will send it to you. The Port engine is ready for sea. Good bye, love. God bless you. Soon now we shall meet. I think when you receive this we will be on our way home. Let us hope so. Keep up love, and that happy time will yet come. Love to all the family. Again good bye.

Ever yours,
Devotedly, George

U.S. Ste. *Powhatan*, Hong Kong, Aug. 11th 1855

My Own Dear Lide,

A man, Marine, named Mullard[8] who was wounded in the attack on the Pirates died this morning and was buried this afternoon. The weather begins to get cooler in the evenings and if it lasts you may get a long letter this time.

The Calcutta mail has arrived and we have news from England up to the 26th of June. The piece of news is the revolt in India[9] which you will see in the papers.

The excitement with regards to the Pirates has not subsided yet. People seem to talk about nothing else. It was undoubtedly a splendid affair, but purchased very dearly, and it thus served to create a feeling of the deepest cordiality and esteem as to institute a profound friendship between the Officers and crews of the two ships, *Rattler* and *Powhatan*. This is some commencement. Good night.

Aug. 25th

Day before yesterday I was in company with some of the Officers of the *Vandalia* and heard their account of Guam which is anything but flattering. It must be one of the most primitive kind of places and one where little variety is to be had, but as I have not seen it I cannot describe so "masker" that.

Last evening I was astonished to see on board Mr. Oliver H. Perry, the son of the notorious Commodore. Of course everybody was anxious to have a chat with Perry in order to get the latest bricks from home, and those particularly with regards to the movements of the *Powhatan*; being a Steerage Officer, and somewhat over punctilious with regards to Officers who live further left I did not get any of the bricks, but this morning he came in our house and he did nothing but boast of the good qualities of the *Mississippi* and what a splendid Engineer Jesse Gay was. He said that the *Powhatan* would certainly go home via Cape Horn, and that we would not start until we were relieved by a Steamer, and that no Steamer would or could come out here until one of those now building was finished! Now I don't believe that he knows any more about it than I do, for he is a perfect gas bag and a regular "nincompoop." He has the appointment of American Consul at Canton, and gets a salary of three thousand dollars a year!

It is very warm tonight—hot—burning, and for the life of me I can't see how people can sleep double in the climate. I know if you and I were to attempt it there would be nothing left in the morning but a grease spot! But that cannot be, so good night love—Angels bless you.

Aug. 26th

Dr. Schriver and Mr. Pegram received letters stating the *San Jacinto* was fitting out for China and was to bring the new Commodore out to relieve us. This is the best news that we have had since leaving the United States. We also learn that the *Merrimack*[10] has been launched. Now from the reports I think that we will leave for home about November and arrive there in April or May, but of this you will be better informed after we know what route we will take and when we start, for altho' the old ship is pretty well used up she is good enough yet to beat the best of 'em.

Sept. 5th

A new Captains clerk has been appointed whose name I have forgotten.[11] On Sunday last the Clipper ship *Sunny South*[12] left the harbor and in firing a salute a premature discharge took place and the boatswain[13] had both hands blown off. The poor fellow was brought on board our ship where he is now. The Doctors think they can save the thumb and forefinger of each hand.

September 8th

One year ago I would have bet my head almost that at this time we would have been home, but the "exigencies" prevented us, or rather Commodore Perry, John C. Dobbin & Co. It will be glorious tidings to us when we hear the good news of "up anchor for the United States!"

I have been thinking of going to Cleveland for a home and if nothing can be done on shore to get a living I could without much difficulty get a situation on one of the boats. Situations out here are very plenty and pay well, but I would not live in this climate 10 years for a fortune, about the time it would take to make one. "Hold on my dear" there is time enough yet for you and I to spend a happy time in some spot on "Mother Earth." Good night. "I embrace you."

U.S. Ste. *Powhatan*, Hong Kong, Septr. 21st 1855

My Own Dear Lide,

Last Friday, a week ago today, Sewell, who is on duty became anxious to try his exhaust pipe arrangement. [. . .] We got everything ready and on Monday morning we started the fires and successfully steamed about four miles and again anchored. The "arrangement" doing very well.

We have today fifty one cases on the sick list! Capt. McCluney is very low and was taken on shore a few days since perhaps never to return! Our First Lieut. is very sick. Faron, Stamm and Fauth are improving. Arnold is very sick. King, Kellogg, and myself are the only Asst. Engineers on duty, and with as much work as we have on hand makes no easy task for us. Should the fever abate we will remain here; should it increase we must leave this place for a while. You may depend that this amount of sickness almost wears the Doctors out and should they get sick it would be awful.

I have become somewhat callous, and feel that injustice can reign but a short time longer, so if orders come I will look upon the event, of course cheerfully, but without surprise or astonishment. If ever a man made me an enemy that man is John C. Dobbin. I would delight to see him imprisoned! He is a heartless unfeeling wretch, a tyrant and an ass! Swayed by Commodore Perry to gratify a personal pique against Capt. McCluney. Excuse me Lide, but my resentment must find vent somewhere, for that North Carolina hog I detest, abhor, hate! Good night.

I have been reading *The Lost Heiress* by Mrs. Southworth and would advise you to get it and read it. Next to *Ernest Maltravers* I think it the best novel I ever read. You must know that something besides work must be done, and so I read novels. Again good night. God bless you my own dearest.

Septr. 22nd

Yesterday I complained of weakness and feeling weary I turned in my bunk. Sewell noticed it and I said I was only a little tired. Shortly after Dr. Maxwell came to me and asked how I was, I told him I was well. "Nothing the matter with me" he felt my pulse, looked at my tongue and gave me an awful dose of quinine which set my head sea sawing and my ears whizzing for the balance of the day. Now why Sewell should have sent the Dr. to me I know not. My position now calls for my superintendence, and whether Sewell is anxious to prevent my getting sick or to put me off duty I don't know, but I do know that should I go on the list now he would have a mighty hard time of it and the end would be sickness to himself. I must say that Sewell has always reposed implicit confidence in me, and jobs requiring care and attention he has given to me. Why this is I know not, but there are others who can do it and should do it. But that's "all in a lifetime."

A few days ago a brig arrived in this harbor in charge of some English Officer [. . .] men belonging to the Squadron now cruising in the North Pacific. This brig is [. . .] Hamburg or Bremin [*sic*] one and was captured flying American Colors. She has onboard of her some 250 of the crew of the *Diana* wrecked in Simoda Bay last December. The Russians were distributed amongst the Squadron and the brig brought here for sale. Pedro Paulaski [Petropaulaski] has deserted and the Allies are destroying towns and shipping up in that direction wherever and whenever they find them. Much anxiety is felt among the English inhabitants of this colony with regards to Sebastapol [Sevastopol]. The majority of them feeling almost assured that the mail now dire will bring the news of its fall. But those things cannot or rather do not interest you, so 'tis idle to speculate upon them. I have my own opinion about the matter of war, but it sides not with the majority of American people.

Septr. 24th

The mail arrived this morning and we have received by it the intelligence of our being ordered home! We know that the orders are here! We know that we will leave China in less than a month! Our orders will reach the Commodore and be back here by the middle of next month, and by that time we shall be ready for a start. I will give you further information at the closing of this because by that time I will have all the "bricks." As it is we are to take the most expeditious route home.

Septr. 26th

We have had tremendous weather for two days. The equinoxial gales have visited us with unusual severity and today we had to eat salt horse and hard tack. Boats from shore not being able to get off with "fresh grub." Good night.

Septr. 27th

The gale broke this morning. The British Brig *Comus* was reported sunk in the Blenheim Reach and the *Rattler* went out in search of her. The reports are vague and uncertain. A few days will give us all the information.

Sunday, Septr. 30th

Yesterday morning about eleven o'clock we got underway with the exhaust pipe arrangement and very satisfactorily steamed around the Island of Hong Kong and anchored about five o'clock close to [town]. Steam was raised in consequence of the sickness, the Doctors thinking that a small run would be beneficial. I hope it will be for this amount of continued sickness is fearful. King is improving and Arnold is convalescent. The Capt. is improving greatly. Pegram is convalescent. McCauley and B[en]net were taken yesterday, and Jim Jones the day before. All the Officers save the two Doctors, Sewell, Craig, Parker and myself have had it. I [sincerely] trust no more will be attacked.

Cape Town, Dec. 23rd 1855

My Dear Lide,

We arrived here about two hours ago, and I have just learned that a ship sails for Boston tomorrow morning and as there is a possibility of her arriving in the United States before we do I embrace the opportunity of sending this. And should you get it before you hear from me again start for Norfolk or Portsmouth at once and await my arrival. We left Singapore on the 13th November and after a most pleasant run without any accident arrived safely at Mauritius early on the morning of the 2nd Dec. remained there until the morning of the 11th and arrived here after a pleasant run, except the last 500 miles as stated above. We have but little to do here as everything connected with the machinery is in good order and as soon as we coal we shall start for Helena. From thence to St. Thomas's and from there home, that is Norfolk. Expect to arrive about the 18th or 20th of February.

Our ship is very healthy. Very few men and not an Officer on the "list." We have the sick of the *Macedonian* on board, but they are generally cases of lameness, rheumatism &c. Sewell is weakly. He cannot stand much. Everybody is in high spirits. From the information received we expect the *San Jacinto* here before we leave. She has not been here yet.

Give my love to all and believe me truly yours, Geo.

Should you get this before seeing me remember that every day after the 20th Feb. I may be looked for.

Geo.

Notes

Introduction

1. Arthur Walworth, *Black Ships off Japan: The Story of Commodore Perry's Expedition* (New York: Alfred A. Knopf, 1946), 229.

2. Samuel Eliot Morison, *"Old Bruin": Commodore Matthew C. Perry, 1794–1858* (Boston: Little, Brown, 1967), ix–x.

3. A phrase the Japanese used to describe how the American ships moved without sail or oars and belched clouds of black smoke. Walworth, *Black Ships off Japan*, 3.

4. John Blair Linn, *History of Centre and Clinton Counties, Pennsylvania* (Philadelphia: Louis H. Everts, 1883), 71, 75.

5. John A. Wolter, David A. Ranzan, and John J. McDonough, *With Commodore Perry to Japan: The Journal of William Speiden, Jr., 1852–1855* (Annapolis, MD: Naval Institute Press, 2014), 1–2.

6. Walworth, *Black Ships off Japan*, 101, 133; John H. Schroeder, *Shaping a Maritime Empire: The Commercial and Diplomatic Role of the American Navy, 1829–1861* (Westport, CT: Greenwood Press, 1985), 153.

7. Walworth, *Black Ships off Japan*, 132.

8. John H. Schroeder, *Matthew Calbraith Perry: Antebellum Sailor and Diplomat* (Annapolis, MD: Naval Institute Press, 2001), 216.

9. Ira Dye, *Uriah Levy: Reformer of the Antebellum Navy* (Gainesville: University Press of Florida, 2006), 201; Schroeder, *Matthew Calbraith Perry*, 172; James E. Valle, *Rocks and Shoals: Naval Discipline in the Age of Fighting Sail* (Annapolis, MD: Naval Institute Press, 1996) 4, 83; Harold D. Langley, *Social Reform in the United States Navy, 1798–1862* (Urbana: University of Illinois Press, 1967), 202–203.

10. Walworth, *Black Ships off Japan*, 226.

11. Wolter, Ranzan, and McDonough, *With Commodore Perry to Japan*, xxi, 231.

12. Edward V. Gulick, *Peter Parker and the Opening of China* (Cambridge, MA: Harvard University Press, 1973), 183.

Chapter One

1. The frigate *Powhatan*, a 2,415-ton side-wheel steamer, was launched at the Norfolk Navy Yard in 1850 and commissioned in 1852. It was 253 feet in length

overall (l.o.a.), and had a beam of 45 feet and a draft of 18 feet. In 1853, under the command of Commander William J. McCluney, the *Powhatan* was assigned to the East India Squadron. It was Perry's flagship when the treaty was signed on March 31, 1854. During the month of August 1855, the *Powhatan* accompanied HMS *Rattler* in a successful raid against the Chinese pirates off Kulan. The *Powhatan* was active throughout the Civil War. After the war, it was the flagship of the South Pacific Squadron from 1866 to 1869, and the Home Squadron from 1869 to 1886. It was decommissioned in June 1886 and sold a month later. James L. Mooney, *Dictionary of American Naval Fighting Ships* (Washington, DC: Navy Department, Office of the Chief of Naval Operations, Naval History Division, 1959–81), 5:365.

2. According to the ship's logbook, The USS *Powhatan* left Norfolk on February 13, 1853.

3. One of the world's finest natural harbors, Hampton Roads is situated in the James River estuary at its entrance to the Chesapeake Bay. During the American Civil War, Hampton Roads was the site of the battle between the ironclads *Monitor* and *Merrimack*. Saul B. Cohen, *The Columbia Gazetteer of the World* (New York: Columbia University Press, 1998), 1503.

4. Madeira is the largest of the Madeira Islands, a Portuguese archipelago some four hundred miles west of the African coast. Ships could acquire ample supplies here and take advantage of the northeast trade winds as well. *Merriam-Webster's Geographical Dictionary*, 3rd ed. (Springfield, MA: Merriam-Webster, 2007), 687.

5. Mortimer Kellogg (1821–70) entered the navy as a third assistant engineer in 1852 and was promoted to second assistant engineer in 1855, to first assistant engineer in 1859, and to chief engineer in 1861. While serving on the USS *Terror* in Key West, Florida, he provoked an altercation on shore with Dr. William M. King, navy surgeon, on November 6, 1870. Dr. King drew a pistol and shot Kellogg through the right lung. Kellogg died from internal hemorrhage. Edward W. Callahan, *List of Officers of the Navy of the United States and of the Marine Corps from 1775 to 1900, comprising a complete register of all present and former commissioned, warranted, and appointed officers of the United States Navy, and of the Marine Corps, regular and volunteer* (New York: L. R. Hamersly & Co., 1901), 308; "The Famous Dead of 1870," *Appleton's Journal: A Magazine of General Literature* 5, no. 96 (January 28, 1871): 112; "The Naval Homicide—Particulars of the Killing of Chief Engineer Kellogg," *New York Times*, December 5, 1870, 1.

6. Built in 1817, Rip Raps is a small, 15-acre artificial island at the mouth of Hampton Roads. Fort Calhoun, later renamed Fort Wool, was built on the island. Valgene Dunham, *Allegheny to Appomattox: The Life and Letters of Private William Whitlock of the 188th New York Volunteers* (Syracuse, NY: Syracuse University Press, 2013), 41.

7. John P. Whipple (d. 1864) received a commission as a third assistant engineer in 1847, and was promoted to second assistant engineer in 1849, first assistant engineer in 1851, and chief engineer in 1855. He died in a marine hospital in Key West, Florida. Callahan, *List of Officers of the Navy*, 581; *Register of the Commissioned, Warrant, and Volunteer Officers of the Navy of the United States, Including*

Officers of the Marine Corps and Others to January 1, 1865 (Washington, DC: Government Printing Office, 1865), 118.

8. William Henry King (d. 1859) was appointed third assistant engineer on February 6, 1851. Twenty days later he was promoted to second assistant engineer and in 1853, first assistant engineer. He died in 1859 in Warrington, Florida. Callahan, *List of Officers of the Navy*, 315.

9. John Joseph Faron (1828–64) received a commission with a rank of third assistant engineer in 1848. He was promoted to second assistant engineer in 1851, first assistant engineer in 1853, and chief engineer in 1859. He was lost on the *Tecumseh* in Mobile Bay in 1864. Callahan, *List of Officers of the Navy*, 189; United States, Navy Casualties Books, 1776–1941 (digital images), Ancestry.com, http://www.ancestry.com/: 2012; New York, Registers of Officers and Enlisted Men Mustered into Federal Service, 1861–1865 (digital images), Ancestry.com, http://www.ancestry.com/: 2014.

10. Henry Fauth received his commission as a third assistant engineer in 1852 and was promoted to second assistant engineer in 1855. He resigned his commission in 1856. Callahan, *List of Officers of the Navy*, 190.

11. LeRoy Arnold received his commission as a third assistant engineer in 1852 and served on the USS *Powhatan*. He resigned his commission in 1856. Callahan, *List of Officers of the Navy*, 28.

12. In the official ship log book, the *Powhatan* was two days out from the island of Madeira. *Logbooks of the U.S.S. Powhatan*, Record Group 24, Records of the Bureau of Naval Personnel, National Archives Building, Washington DC.

13. William J. McCluney (c. 1796–1864), who had served in the Mexican War, took command of the *Powhatan* during the Japanese Expedition. In 1858 he was placed in command of the Atlantic Squadron, and he was commissioned commodore in 1860 before retiring the following year. James Grant Wilson and John Fiske, eds., *Appleton's Cyclopaedia of American Biography* (New York: D. Appleton & Company, 1887), 4:84.

14. The frigate *Mississippi*, a sidewheel steamer, was laid down by the Philadelphia Navy Yard in 1839 and was built under the personal supervision of Matthew C. Perry. Launched in 1842, it was 229 feet l.o.a. and had a beam of 40 feet and a draft of 19 feet. Two side-lever engines operated two paddlewheels 28 feet in diameter, and the masts were rigged to spread 19,000 square feet of canvas. After service in the Mexican War and duty in the Mediterranean Squadron, the *Mississippi* returned to the United States to become Perry's flagship in the expedition to the China Seas and Japan in 1852–54. Arriving back in the United States in 1855, the *Mississippi* returned to the Far East again in 1857. When the Civil War broke out, it was in New York and almost immediately saw action, but in March 1863, during the Port Hudson operation, the ship grounded in the Mississippi River, and blew up and sank while under heavy fire. Samuel Eliot Morison, *"Old Bruin": Commodore Matthew C. Perry, 1794–1858* (Boston: Brown, Little, 1967), 193; Mooney, *Dictionary of American Naval Fighting Ships*, 4: 387–88; Roger Pineau, ed., *The Personal Journal of Commodore Matthew C. Perry* (Washington, DC: Smithsonian Insti-

tution Press, 1968), 225; Stephen Culver Craddock, "'To the Honor and Credit of the Country': A History of the Warships Mississippi," *Journal of Mississippi History* 54 (May 1992): 129–34; Frank M. Bennett, *The Steam Navy of the United States: A History of the Growth of the Steam Vessel of War in the U.S. Navy, and of the Naval Engineer Corps* (Westport, CT: Greenwood Press, 1972), 126–36.

15. The screw-steamer *Princeton*, the second naval vessel to bear that name, was laid down in 1851. Its machinery was installed at Baltimore in 1852, and it was scheduled to rendezvous with the *Mississippi* at Annapolis. While on the way there, it developed boiler trouble and was forced to drop out of the expedition. Mooney, *Dictionary of American Naval Fighting Ships*, 5:384.

16. "Salt horse" was a nautical term for salted beef. "Hard tack" is a simple type of cracker or biscuit, made from flour, water, and salt. Gershom Bradford, *The Mariner's Dictionary* (Barre, MA: Barre Publishers, 1972), 224; John D. Billings, *Hardtack and Coffee or The Unwritten Story of Army Life* (Lincoln: University of Nebraska Press, 1993), 113.

17. William Seaman Stamm (1825–97) entered the navy as a third assistant engineer in 1851. He was promoted to second assistant engineer in 1853, first assistant engineer in 1857, and chief engineer in 1861. He was placed on the retired list in 1887. Callahan, *List of Officers of the Navy*, 516; "William Seaman Stamm," Find A Grave Memorial #86075261, Find A Grave, http://www.findagrave.com.

18. The inventor of the "present signal service system," William E. Boudinot (d. 1889) was appointed midshipman in 1836, promoted to passed midshipman in 1842, master in 1849, and lieutenant in 1849. He resigned his commission in 1858. Martha J. Lamb, ed., *Magazine of American History with Notes and Queries,* vol. 26 (New York: Historical Publication Co., July–December 1891), 451; Callahan, *List of Officers of the Navy*, 68.

19. Robert Selden was appointed to the rank of midshipman in 1841. He was promoted to passed midshipman in 1847, master on 14 September 1855, and lieutenant a day later. He resigned his commission in 1860. Callahan, *List of Officers of the Navy*, 489.

20. Edward Yorke McCauley (1827–94) began his naval career with the rank of midshipman in 1841. He served in the Mediterranean Squadron from 1841 to 1845 and 1847 to 1850. He was promoted to passed midshipman in 1847, master in July 1855, and lieutenant in September 1855. He served on board the *Niagara* during the transatlantic cable expedition in 1857. He resigned his commission in 1859. He reentered the navy during the Civil War with a rank of acting lieutenant in 1861 and in the South Atlantic Blockading Squadron. He was promoted to lieutenant commander in 1862 and served in the East Gulf Blockading Squadron from 1862 to 1864. He was commissioned as commander in 1866 and served as fleet captain of the North Atlantic Squadron from 1867 to 1868. He was promoted to captain in 1872 and commanded the *Lackawanna* on the Asiatic Station from 1872 to 1875. He was promoted to commodore in 1881 and rear admiral in 1885, serving as commandant at League Island in 1884–85 and commanding the Pacific Station during 1885–86. He retired in 1887. In 1882, he published the *Dictionary of the Egyp-*

tian Language. Callahan, *List of Officers of the Navy*, 360; William H. Powell and Edward Shippen, eds., *Officers of the Army and Navy Who Served in the Civil War* (Philadelphia: L. R. Hamersly & Co., 1892), 254.

21. James Monroe Bibby (c. 1830–60) was the captain's clerk on the *Powhatan*. His death was noted in the newspaper: "Died," *Washington Constitution*, March 14, 1860, 3.

22. After attending Harvard, Charles Henry Wheelwright (1813–62) pursued his studies under Dr. George Shattuck of Boston. He earned his commission as an assistant surgeon on 1839 and was posted to the sloop *Marion* in Brazil. In 1842, he reported to USS *Ohio* and in 1843 transferred to the frigate *Independence* in the Home Squadron. In 1844, he was promoted to passed assistant surgeon, and a year later he was posted to the U.S. Naval Hospital at Pensacola, Florida. In 1848, he joined the Mediterranean Fleet at Marseilles. In August 1852, he reported to the USS *Powhatan* in Norfolk, Virginia. In 1854, he was promoted to surgeon. By March 1856 Wheelwright was back with the Home Squadron aboard the *Ohio* in Boston harbor. He died at Pilotstown, Louisiana, while he was in charge of the naval hospital there. Callahan, *List of Officers of the Navy*, 581; *Harvard Memorial Biographies* (Cambridge: Sever & Francis, 1866), 1:31–37.

23. John K. Wilson received a commission as midshipman in 1841, was promoted to passed midshipman in 1847, master on September 14, 1855, and lieutenant on September 15, 1855. He resigned his commission in 1856. Callahan, *List of Officers of the Navy*, 595.

24. Robert Tansill (1812–90) enlisted in the U.S. Marine Corps in 1833 and was promoted to second lieutenant in 1840, first lieutenant in 1847, and captain in 1858. He relinquished his commission in 1861 and accepted a position in the Confederate Marine Corps in 1862 with the rank of captain. During the Civil War he was taken prisoner while near Fort Fisher and was exchanged in 1865. After the war he served as mayor of Manassas, Virginia. Pineau, *The Personal Journal of Commodore Matthew C. Perry*, 231; Callahan, *List of Officers of the Navy*, 698; Bruce S. Allardice, *Confederate Colonels: A Biographical Register* (Columbia: University of Missouri Press, 2008), 364.

25. Built for defense of Lake Erie, *Michigan*, the U.S. Navy's first iron-hulled warship, was designed by naval constructor Samuel Hart. Fabricated in parts at Pittsburgh during the last half of 1842 and carried overland to Erie, Pennsylvania, where assembled, the sidewheel steamer weighed 685 tons with an overall length of 163 feet, a beam of 27 feet, and a draft of 9 feet. It was commissioned in 1844 with Commander William Inman in command. The *Michigan* spent its entire career operating on the Great Lakes. Renamed *Wolverine* in 1905, it was decommissioned in 1912. Mooney, *Dictionary of American Naval Fighting* Ships, 4:350–51.

26. Founded by Portuguese explorer João Gonçalves Zarco in 1421, Funchal is a port city on the island of Madeira, exporting wines, fish, and fruit. Cohen, *Columbia Gazetteer*, 1295.

27. A water jacket consists of a water-filled metal casing built around a mechanism or apparatus, which allows it to remain cool during operation. Frank Gaynor,

ed., *The New Military and Naval Dictionary* (New York: Philosophical Library, 1951), 272.

28. John Howard March (1791–1863) was the U.S. consul in Funchal, Madeira, from 1816 to 1859. John M. Johnson, compiler, *Congressional Directory for the First Session of the Thirty-second Congress of the United States of America* (Washington, DC: Gideon & Co., 1852), 21; John M. Johnson, compiler, *Congressional Directory for the Second Session of the Thirty-second Congress of the United States of America* (Washington, DC: Gideon & Co., 1853), 50; John M. Johnson, compiler, *Congressional Directory for the Second Session of the Thirty-third Congress of the United States of America* (Washington, DC: Gideon & Co., 1855), 42; Robert Morris, compiler, *Congressional Directory for the Third Session of the Thirty-fourth Congress of the United States of America* (Washington, DC: Gideon & Co., 1856), 42; Ronald S. Vasile, Raymond B. Manning, and Rafael Lemaire, *William Stimpson's Journal from the North Pacific Exploring Expedition, 1853–1856* (Tokyo: Carcinological Society of Japan, 2005), 101.

29. Sometimes referred to as South Africa's Mother City, Cape Town lies at the foot of Table Mountain and on the shore of Table Bay. Founded as a supply station for the Dutch East India Company in 1652, the city became the capital of the United Kingdom's newly established Cape of Good Hope Colony in 1801. Cohen, *Columbia Gazetteer*, 648.

30. Saint Helena, discovered in 1502 by João da Nova Costella, a Spanish navigator in the service of Portugal, lies in the South Atlantic twelve hundred miles off the coast of Africa. Taken over by the Dutch in 1645, Saint Helena was later occupied by the British and came under their full control in 1661. Jamestown is its capital and port. *Geographical Dictionary*, 1022.

31. The fourth largest island in the world, Madagascar lies in the Indian Ocean and is separated from southeastern Africa by the Mozambique Channel. *Geographical Dictionary*, 684.

32. *West Wind* was built by Joshua Foster at Medford, Massachusetts. Measuring 180 feet l.o.a., the 1,071-ton medium clipper ship was launched in 1853 with G. W. Elliott as captain. It was sold to the British in 1863 and renamed *Lord Clyde*. Octavius T. Howe and Frederick C. Matthews, *American Clipper Ships, 1833–1858* (New York: Argosy Antiquarian, 1967), 2:689–90.

33. James Cochrane Dobbin (1814–57) was a politician and lawyer who served as U.S. secretary of the navy from 1853 to 1857. *Biographical Directory of the United States Congress 1774–2005: The Continental Congress September 5, 1774, to October 21, 1788 and the Congress of the United States from the First through the One Hundred Eighth Congresses March 4, 1789, to January 3, 2005, Inclusive* (Washington, DC: Government Printing Office, 2005), 966.

34. After serving in the U.S. Navy for thirty-nine years, Robert Field Stockton (1795–1866) resigned his commission in 1850 for business and political pursuits. He was elected to the U.S. Senate, serving from 1851until 1853 when he resigned to serve as president of the Delaware & Raritan Canal Company. During the Civil War, he commanded the New Jersey Militia at the time of the Confederates' 1863

invasion of Pennsylvania. Callahan, *List of Officers of the Navy*, 524; John A. Garraty and Mark C. Carnes, eds., *American National Biography* (New York: Oxford University Press, 1999), 20:814–15.

35. Samuel G. City (d. 1860) served in the navy as a gunner from 1835 until his death in 1860. Callahan, *List of Officers of the Navy*, 114.

36. John O. Butler (d. 1862) began his naval career as a carpenter in 1837. He resigned his commission in 1839. He was reappointed as a carpenter in 1841. He died on board the *Michigan*. Callahan, *List of Officers of the Navy*, 94; *Register of the Commissioned and Warrant Officers of the United States Navy and Marine Corps and Reserve Officers on Active Duty* (Washington, DC: Government Printing Office, 1863), 117.

37. George W. Elliott (d. 1867) entered the navy as a carpenter in 1848 and warranted in 1850. He died at Hampton, Virginia. Callahan, *List of Officers of the Navy*, 181.

38. Oliver Spencer Glisson (1809–90) began his naval career as a midshipman in 1826. He was promoted to lieutenant in 1837 and commanded a schooner in the Mexican-American War. He was promoted to the rank of commander in 1855 and captain in 1862. He served in the North Atlantic Blockading Squadron during the Civil War. He was promoted to commodore in 1866 and rear admiral in 1870. He retired from the navy in 1871. Callahan, *List of Officers of the Navy*, 221; Day Otis Kellogg, ed., *New American Supplement to the New Werner Edition of the Encyclopedia Britannica: A Standard Work of Reference in Art, Literature, Science, History, Geography, Commerce, Biography, Discovery and Invention* (New York: Werner Company, 1903), 109.

39. Table Bay is a northern-facing inlet of the Atlantic Ocean off the Western Cape Province of South Africa. Cohen, *Columbia Gazetteer*, 3780.

40. The 280-ton *Perry* was launched in 1843 by the Norfolk Navy Yard. Measuring 105 feet l.o.a., the brig had a 25-foot beam and a draft of 13 feet and a depth of hold of 12 feet. During the Mexican War, it blockaded Mexican ports in the Gulf of Mexico. From 1847 to 1854, it joined the Brazil Squadron to help suppress the slave trade. During the American Civil War, it was assigned to the Atlantic Blockading Squadron. Decommissioned in April 1865, it was sold at public auction in August 1865. Mooney, *Dictionary of American Naval Fighting Ships*, 5:268.

41. Table Mountain, approximately 3,500 feet high, overlooks Cape Town and Table Bay. The summit is flat and covered by a white mist. Cohen, *Columbia Gazetteer*, 3079.

42. The *Mississippi* anchored at Cape Town from January 24 to February 2, 1853. Wolter, Ranzan, and McDonough, *With Commodore Perry to Japan*, xx.

43. Louis Kossuth (1802–94), leader of the Hungarian insurrection of 1848–49, fled into exile following military defeats and the collapse of his republican government. He visited the United States in 1851–52, where he appeared before both houses of Congress and was presented to President Millard Fillmore. William R. Denslow, *10,000 Famous Freemasons* (Whitefish, MT: Kessinger Publishing, 2004), 2:39.

44. Francis S. Haggerty (c. 1816–99) began his naval service as a midshipman

in 1832. He was promoted to passed midshipman in 1838, lieutenant in 1843, and commander in 1861. During the Civil War, he was appointed commander of the brig *Perry* and the *Vandalia* in 1861. He retired from the navy in 1862. He was assigned the rank of captain on the retired list in 1867. Callahan, *List of Officers of the Navy*, 237; James J. Barnes and Patience P. Barnes, *The American Civil War through British Eyes: Dispatches from British Diplomats* (Kent, OH: Kent State University Press, 2003), 2:60.

45. The USS *Susquehanna*, a sidewheel steamer, was laid down by the New York Navy Yard in 1847. Launched in 1850, it was 257 feet l.o.a. and had a beam of 45 feet and a draft of 20 feet. In 1851, it sailed for the Far East to become the flagship of the East India Squadron. In 1855, it returned to Philadelphia and was decommissioned. A year later, the *Susquehanna* was recommissioned to join the Mediterranean Squadron. During the Civil War, it served in the Atlantic Blockading, North Atlantic Blockading, and West Gulf Blockading Squadrons. It was decommissioned for the last time in 1868 and sold for scrap in 1883. Mooney, *Dictionary of American Naval Fighting Ships*, 6:685–86.

46. Under Spanish rule until 1898, Manila is located on the southwestern coast of Luzon, the largest island of the Philippines. Cohen, *Columbia Gazetteer*, 1811, 1870.

47. Macao is a Portuguese town on the Macao peninsula, 40 miles west of Hong Kong. From 1717 until the nineteenth century, Macao and Canton (now Guangzhou) were the only Chinese ports open to European trade. *Geographical Dictionary*, 680.

48. John Henry Aulick (c. 1791–1873) entered the U.S. Navy as a midshipman in 1809. He was promoted to lieutenant in 1814, commander in 1831, and captain in 1841. In December 1850, he received orders to command the East India Squadron. In June 1851, he sailed to Japan on the *Susquehanna* to negotiate with the Japanese. In February 1853, he was replaced by Commodore Matthew C. Perry to complete the mission. He retired in 1861 and received the rank of commodore while on the retired list in 1867. Callahan, *List of Officers of the Navy*, 31.

Chapter Two

1. Naha is a port on the southwest coast of Okinawa island, in the Ryukyu Islands. During World War II, Naha was virtually destroyed. *Merriam-Webster's Geographical Dictionary*, 3rd ed. (Springfield, MA.: Merriam-Webster, 2007), 787.

2. The USS *Plymouth* was launched by the Boston Navy Yard in 1844. The 989-ton sloop-of-war measured 147 feet l.o.a. and had a beam of 38 feet and a draft of 17 feet. In 1851, it joined the Perry expedition to Japan. In 1854, it supported a British-American expedition against hostile forts near Shanghai. The *Plymouth* served as a training ship for midshipmen from 1855 to 1860, and burned and scuttled at Norfolk in 1861. James L. Mooney, *Dictionary of American Naval Fighting Ships* (Washington, DC: Navy Department, Office of the Chief of Naval Operations, Naval History Division, 1959–81), 5:331.

3. USS *Supply* was a 547-ton, ship-rigged sailing vessel commanded by Lieutenant John Calhoun. Commissioned in 1846, it served as a storeship during the Perry expedition. Throughout the Civil War, the *Supply* supported the blockading squadrons on the Atlantic coast and in the Gulf of Mexico. It was decommissioned in 1884. Mooney, *Dictionary of American Naval Fighting Ships*, 6:679–80.

4. Whampoa (Huangpu) is a city on an island in the Pearl River, lying southeast of Canton, for which it served as an outpost. *Geographical Dictionary*, 500.

5. Cumsing Moon or Chin-hsing-Men is an anchorage north of Macau. Roger Pineau, ed., *The Personal Journal of Commodore Matthew C. Perry* (Washington, DC: Smithsonian Institution Press, 1968), 120.

6. Commanded by Commander Josiah Tattnall, the USS *Saratoga* was built by the Portsmouth Navy Yard, New Hampshire, laid down in summer 1841, launched in 1842, and commissioned in 1843. The 882-ton, 146-foot-long sloop-of-war had a beam of 35 feet and a draft of 16 feet. It served in the African Squadron and the Home Squadron until 1850 when it was ordered to serve in the East India Squadron and participated in the Perry expedition. The *Saratoga* carried Commander Adams with the American copy of the treaty to Honolulu in 1854. After the outbreak of the Civil War, it was recommissioned in 1863 to patrol the Delaware capes and served in the South Atlantic Blockading Squadron. From 1875 to 1907, it served as a school ship at Annapolis and Philadelphia. Mooney, *Dictionary of American Naval Fighting Ships*, 6:336–39.

7. Sho Taimu, the regent of Okinawa, was a member of the royal family and the hereditary lord of Mabuni Village, eight miles south of Naha. As king of Ryukyu, Sho Tai (1843–1901) was only ten years old when Perry visited. Bruce D. Clayton, *Shotokan's Secret: The Hidden Truth Behind Karate's Fighitng Origins* (Valencia, CA: Black Belt Books, 2004), 76; *Encyclopedia of People of Okinawan History* (Naha: Okinawa Bunka-sha, 1996), 42.

8. The 614-ton sloop-of-war *Vandalia* was launched in 1828. It was 127 feet l.o.a. and had a beam of 34 feet and a draft of 16 feet. After service in the Brazil, West Indies, Home, and Pacific Squadrons, it joined Perry's East India Squadron in 1853 and was commanded by John Pope (1798–1876). During the Civil War the *Vandalia* was in the South Atlantic Blockading Squadron. It was broken up in the 1870s. Mooney, *Dictionary of American Naval Fighting Ships*, 7:461; Edward W. Callahan, *List of Officers of the Navy of the United States and of the Marine Corps from 1775 to 1900, comprising a complete register of all present and former commissioned, warranted, and appointed officers of the United States Navy, and of the Marine Corps, regular and volunteer* (New York: L. R. Hamersly & Co., 1901), 440.

9. The 22-gun 1,341-ton sloop-of-war *Macedonian* was rebuilt on the keel of the first USS *Macedonian* at Gosport Navy Yard at Portsmouth, Virginia, in 1832. Launched in 1836, it was 164 feet l.o.a. and had a beam of 41 feet and a draft of 21 feet. In 1847, it carried 12,000 barrels of provisions to Ireland during the famine of the late 1840s. From 1852 to 1854, it was assigned to the East India Squadron under Commodore Perry, and remained on patrol for another three years in the North Pacific. From 1857 to 1861, it served in the Mediterranean and the Caribbean. During

the Civil War, it patrolled in the South Atlantic and the Caribbean. From 1863 to 1870, it served as a school and practice ship for midshipmen at the Naval Academy. It was decommissioned in 1871. Mooney, *Dictionary of American Naval Fighting Ships*, 4:179–80.

10. The USS *Southampton* was a 567-ton storeship in the U.S. Navy during the Mexican War. The *Southampton* was laid down at Norfolk, Virginia, as a sidewheel steamer in October 1841, but its machinery proved to be unsatisfactory and was removed. Apparently purchased by the U.S. government in 1845, the ship was commissioned on May 27, 1845, with Lieutenant Henry W. Morris in command. It was 156 feet l.o.a. and had a beam of 27 feet and a draft of 13 feet. In 1852, it sailed for the Pacific and in 1853 joined the Perry expedition. It was decommissioned in 1855. Mooney, *Dictionary of American Naval Fighting Ships*, 6:564.

11. Located in the Guangdong province in southeast China on the Zhu River in Xi Delta about 80 miles from the sea, Guangzhou or Canton became the first seaport of China to open to foreigners. *Geographical Dictionary*, 454

12. Xiamen, or Amoy, is a coastal city in southeastern China in the Fujian Province, and it lies near the Taiwan Strait at the mouth of the Jiulong, or Amoy, River. *Geographical Dictionary*, 1320; Cohen, *Columbia Gazetteer*, 3500.

13. Dagger Society occupied Amoy from 16 May until 11 November 1853. George Hughes, "The Small Knife Rebels (An Unpublished Chapter of Amoy History)," *The China Review* 1 no. 4 (1872): 244–246; Mervyn Llewelyn Wynne, *Triad and Tabut: A survey of the origin and diffusion of Chinese and Mohamedan Secret Societies in The Malay Peninsula A.D. 1800–1935* (Singapore: Government Printing Office, 1941), 63.

14. The Taiping Rebellion was a widespread civil war in China from 1850 to 1864, led by Hong Xiuquan against the ruling Qing dynasty, in which twenty million people died. Samuel Eliot Morison, *"Old Bruin": Commodore Matthew C. Perry, 1794–1858* (Boston: Brown, Little, 1967), 297; Pineau, *The Personal Journal of Commodore Matthew C. Perry*, 116–17.

15. Lamar is situated in southern Clinton County, Pennsylvania. Saul B. Cohen, *The Columbia Gazetteer of the World* (New York: Columbia University Press, 1998), 2045.

16. Penang, or Prince of Wales's Island, is situated two and a half miles off the west coast of the Malay Peninsula. *Geographical Dictionary*, 916.

17. Born in Wilmington, Delaware, Robert Danby (1821–86) began his naval career as third assistant engineer in 1845. He was promoted to second assistant engineer in 1847, first assistant engineer in 1851, and chief engineer in 1856. Danby supervised the construction of the mile-long railroad tracks gifted to Japan. He was the first person to run the Baldwin locomotive and blow the steam whistle in Japan. During the Civil War, he was appointed fleet engineer of the South Atlantic Blockade Squadron, which consisted of nearly a hundred steam vessels and between three and four hundred engineers. He retired from active service in 1883. *The Brooklyn Eagle*, September 30, 1883, 5; Callahan, *List of Officers of the Navy*, 147.

18. Jesse Gay began his naval career as a first assistant engineer in 1847. He was

promoted to chief engineer in 1848 and resigned his commission in 1859. Callahan, *List of Officers of the Navy*, 213.

19. William Holland (d. 1856) accepted a commission as second assistant engineer in 1848 and was promoted to first assistant engineer in 1851. Callahan, *List of Officers of the Navy*, 271.

20. George T. W. Logan began his naval career as a third assistant engineer in 1848 and was promoted to second assistant engineer in 1851. He was dropped from active duty in 1856. Callahan, *List of Officers of the Navy*, 336.

21. Edward Dunham Robie (1831–1911) began his naval career as the third assistant engineer of the *Mississippi* in 1852. He was promoted to second assistant engineer in 1855, first assistant engineer in 1858, and chief engineer in 1861. He erected and operated the first line of telegraph ever seen in Japan and instructed the Japanese in building and operating the first steam railways. He was chief engineer of the Norfolk Navy Yard from 1874 to 1877 and from 1887 to 1891. He was placed on the retired list in 1893 with the rank of commodore. Callahan, *List of Officers of the Navy*, 466; Erik S. Hinckley and Tom Ledoux, eds., *They Went to War: A Biographical Register of the Green Mountain State in the Civil War* (Victoria, BC, Canada: Trafford Publishing, 2010), 193.

22. George F. Hebard (1826–81) entered the navy as second assistant engineer in 1848 and was promoted to first assistant engineer in 1851. He resigned his commission in 1856 but was reactivated to acting first assistant engineer in 1863. During the Civil War, he served on the USS *Proteus* of the East Indies Squadron. He was given the rank of acting chief engineer in 1864 and honorably discharged in 1866. Callahan, *List of Officers of the Navy*, 258; *The United States Service Magazine* (New York: C. B. Richardson, 1864), 1:443; "George F Hebard," Find A Grave Memorial #46245415, *Find A Grave*, http://www.findagrave.com.

23. Henry H. Stewart (c.1823–93) entered the navy as third assistant engineer in 1848. He was promoted to second assistant engineer in 1849, first assistant engineer in 1851, and chief engineer in 1858. During the Civil War, he served on several vessels in the Atlantic and North Atlantic Blockading Squadron. He served on the board of examiners from 1866 to 1869 and was stationed at Norfolk Navy Yard from 1870 to 1872 and the Navy Yard at League Island from 1872 to 1878. He retired in 1885. Callahan, *List of Officers of the Navy*, 521; "Henry H Stewart," Find A Grave Memorial #38419985, *Find A Grave*, http://www.findagrave.com; Lewis Randolph Hamersly, ed., *The Records of Living Officers of the U.S. Navy & Marine Corps* (Philadelphia: J. B. Lippincott & Co., 1878), 332.

24. John C. E. Lawrence received a commission as a third assistant engineer in 1850. He was promoted to second assistant engineer in 1851. He resigned his commission in 1856. Callahan, *List of Officers of the Navy*, 325.

25. Thomas A. Shock (d. 1873) received a commission as a third assistant engineer in 1851, second assistant engineer in 1853, first assistant engineer in 1856, and chief engineer in 1860. Callahan, *List of Officers of the Navy*, 496.

26. William Henry Shock (1821–1905) entered the navy as a third assistant engineer in 1845 and served during the Mexican War. He was promoted to second as-

sistant engineer in 1847 and afterward served in the steamer *Engineer* of the Home Squadron. He received a promotion to first assistant engineer in 1848 and superintended the construction of the machinery of the steam frigate *Susquehanna*. He was raised to the rank of chief engineer in 1851 and served on the *Princeton* of the Home Squadron. After the Civil War, he served for two years as chief engineer of the Boston Navy Yard and served as engineer-in-chief and chief of the Bureau of Steam Engineering from 1877 until his retirement in 1883 with the rank of commodore. He authored *Steam Boilers, Their Design, Construction, and Management* in 1881, which became a standard textbook in the U.S. Naval Academy. Callahan, *List of Officers of the Navy*, 496; Charles Morris, *Men of the Century, an Historical Work: Giving Portraits and Sketches of Eminent Citizens of the United States* (Philadelphia: I. R. Hamersly & Co., 1896), 155; "Como William Henry Shock," Find A Grave Memorial #120372607, *Find A Grave*, http://www.findagrave.com.

27. Labuan is an island off the northwest coast of Sabah, Malaysia, in the South China Sea. It became a crown colony in 1848. Cohen, *Columbia Gazetteer*, 1657.

28. A "comprador" is a Chinese agent of a foreign business. *Webster's Third New International Dictionary of the English Language Unabridged* (Springfield, MA: Merriam-Webster, 1986), 467.

29. Also known as Ogasawara Islands, the Bonin Islands are a group of twenty-seven volcanic islands in the western Pacific Ocean, six hundred miles south of Tokyo, Japan, that were first colonized in 1830 by a small group of Europeans and Hawaiians. *Geographical Dictionary*, 159.

30. Commander Henry Allen Adams (1800–1869), Perry's trusted chief of staff, was given the title of captain of the fleet. He was to be given much responsibility in conducting conferences and making decisions preliminary to the final treaty negotiations with Japan. He was also placed in charge of carrying the treaty to the United States for ratifications, and in September 1854 he sailed for Japan with the ratified treaty. Adams, it appears, was second in importance only to Perry himself in the conduct of the entire diplomatic affair. He became a commodore in 1862 and died in 1869. Callahan, *List of Officers of the Navy*, 17.

31. Samuel Archbold (1815–90) began his naval service as third assistant engineer in 1843. He was promoted to second assistant engineer in 1845, first assistant engineer in 1847, chief engineer in 1851, and engineer-in-chief in 1857. He resigned his commission in 1861 to become a partner in an iron-ship building company, Reaney & Son (renaming it Reaney, Son & Archbold). Callahan, *List of Officers of the Navy*, 26; Leonard Alexander Swann, *John Roach, Maritime Entrepreneur: The Years as Naval Contractor, 1862–1886* (Annapolis: U.S. Naval Institute, 1965), 52; "Samuel Archbold," Find A Grave Memorial #23286492, *Find A Grave,* http://www.findagrave.com.

32. Pennsylvanian Albert Schriver received a commission of assistant surgeon in 1852. *Register of Commissioned and Warrant Officers of the US Navy* (Washington, DC: Government Printing Office, 1863), 48.

33. Franklin Buchanan (1800–1874) entered the navy as a midshipman in 1815. He was promoted to lieutenant in 1825, commander in 1841, and captain in 1855.

He was dismissed from his duties in 1861 and became an admiral in the Confederate Navy in the Civil War, during which he participated in the battles of Hampton Roads and Mobile Bay. Callahan, *List of Officers of the Navy*, 86; *Merriam Webster's Biographical Dictionary* (Springfield, MA: Merriam-Webster, 1995), 208.

34. Launched in 1847 at Pittsburgh, the USS *Alleghany*, a 989-ton Hunter wheel gunboat, was propelled by two, eight-bladed horizontal wheels. It was 185 feet l.o.a. and had a beam of 33 feet and a draft of 13 feet. In 1851, it was rebuilt as a screw steamer and was slated to join Commodore Perry's expedition but failed the sea trials. Mooney, *Dictionary of American Naval Fighting Ships*, 1:190–91.

35. Taiwan, also known as Formosa, is an island situated in the Western Pacific Ocean and located off the southeastern coast of mainland China. Some Dutch settlements were established in the seventeenth century but the settlers were driven out by the Chinese. It was not available to Europeans again until the Treaty of Tientsui opened a few ports in 1858. *Geographical Dictionary*, 1154–55; Cohen, *Columbia Gazetteer*, 3087.

36. The Bogue, or Boca Tigris, is part of the large estuary of the Canton, or Pearl, River between Hong Kong and Macau. Several Qing dynasty forts, including the Weiyuan and Shajiao forts, were built at Humen Town. Cohen, *Columbia Gazetteer*, 2388.

37. Blenheim Reach is ten miles south of Canton. It was named after the HMS *Blenheim*, which turned the Chinese flank during the Anglo-Chinese War in 1841. J. Willet Spalding, *The Japan Expedition: Japan and Around the World: An Account of Three Visits to the Japanese Empire, with Sketches of Madeira, St. Helena, Cape of Good Hope, Mauritius, Ceylon, Singapore, China, and Loo-Choo* (New York: Redfield, 1855), 178.

38. William H. Rutherford (1828–98) was appointed third assistant engineer in 1849, and promoted to second assistant engineer in 1852, first assistant engineer in 1856, and chief engineer in 1861. In the Civil War, he was attached to the *Pawnee*, the *Mississippi* and the *Wachusett*. He was placed on the retired list in 1874 for disability incurred in the line of duty. "Obituary," *American Machinist: A Practical Journal of Machine Construction* 21, no. 10 (March 10, 1898): 193–94; Callahan, *List of Officers of the Navy*, 478.

39. George Washington Alexander (1829–95), born in Francesville, Pennsylvania, was appointed third assistant engineer in 1848, promoted to second assistant engineer in 1852, and promoted to first assistant engineer in 1855. He resigned his commission in 1861 and offered his service to the Confederacy. He was part of the expedition to capture the *St. Nicholas* in 1862, was appointed assistant provost-marshal of Richmond, and served as the commandant at Castle Thunder Prison and Salisbury (North Carolina) Prison. After the Civil War he was a wanted man and escaped to Canada, spending several years teaching French to children. After the amnesty of 1872 he returned to the United States and worked as an editor of the *Sunday Gazette* in Washington, DC. Callahan, *List of Officers of the Navy*, 19; "Old Castle Thunder: Death of Colonel Alexander, Who Was Superintendent of This Prison," *Richmond Times-Dispatch*, March 3, 1895, 1; Frances Harding Casstevens, *George W.*

Alexander and Castle Thunder: A Confederate Prison and Its Commandant (Jefferson, NC: McFarland & Co., 2004), 1–3.

40. William Bond Slack (1822–95) started his career in the U.S. Marine Corps in 1839 with a rank of second lieutenant. In 1847 he was promoted to first lieutenant, and then quickly was appointed brevet captain. In 1860 he became a quartermaster with the rank of major and held that position until his retirement in 1885. Pineau, *The Personal Journal of Commodore Matthew C. Perry*, 231; Callahan, *List of Officers of the Navy*, 501; "Maj William B. Slack," Find A Grave Memorial #105052106, *Find A Grave*, http://www.findagrave.com.

41. Joseph Harrod Adams (1817–53), grandson of President John Adams and nephew of President John Quincy Adams, entered the navy as a midshipman in 1831 and was promoted to lieutenant in 1843. He died on 4 October 1853 and was buried in the Old Protestant Cemetery in Macao. Callahan, *List of Officers of the Navy*, 17; Pineau, *The Personal Journal of Commodore Matthew C. Perry*, 121, 226; Shyama Peebles, "Old Protestant Cemetery in Macau," *Gwulo: Old Hong Kong*, October 2010, http://gwulo.com/sites/gwulo.com/files/Gwulo-Macau-Old-Protestant-Cemetery.pdf.

42. Robert Baker Pegram (1811–94) received a commission as midshipman in 1829 and served in the Mediterranean Squadron. He was promoted to passed midshipman in 1835 and lieutenant in 1841. In 1855, he participated in a joint expedition of the HMS *Rattler* and USS *Powhatan* against a flotilla of thirty-one piratical junks. He resigned his commission in the U.S. Navy in 1861 to command the Norfolk Navy Yard. Callahan, *List of Officers of the Navy*, 428; Cdr. Robert Baker Pegram, Find A Grave Memorial #93764917, *Find A Grave*, http://www.findagrave.com.

43. Luis de Camões (1524–80) was a Portuguese poet whose epic "The Lusiads" celebrated Vasco da Gama's voyage to India. Illustrations of his cave, or tomb, in Macau are reproduced in Roger Pineau's edition of *The Personal Journal of Commodore Matthew C. Perry*, 129. Magnus Magnusson, ed., *Cambridge Biographical Dictionary* (Cambridge: Cambridge University Press, 1990), 252.

44. James W. Shirk (1832–73) received a commission as midshipman in 1849. He was promoted to passed midshipman in June 1855, master in September 1855, and lieutenant in 1856. Before the Civil War, he served in the Africa, East Indies, Pacific, and Great Lakes Squadrons. He was promoted to lieutenant commander and commanded the timberclad gunboat *Lexington* during the Battle of Fort Henry, Tennessee, and participated in several expeditions during the Civil War. He was promoted to commander in 1866 and worked for the Navy Department until 1872. Spencer C. Tucker, ed., *The Civil War Naval Encyclopedia* (Santa Barbara, CA: ABC-CLIO, 2011), 1:634; Callahan, *List of Officers of the Navy*, 495.

45. Founded by the Portuguese in the sixteenth century, Nagasaki is the capital and the largest city of Nagasaki Prefecture on the island of Kyushu in Japan. *Geographical Dictionary*, 787; Cohen, *Columbia Gazetteer*, 2104.

46. Edward Gideon (1830–1909). M. Patrick Sauer, "King Family Tree," http://person.ancestry.com/tree/89897781/person/75004716816/facts (accessed June 1, 2016).

47. The Zhu or Pearl River forms part of the delta of the Xi and flows from the city of Guangzhou to the South China Sea. *Geographical Dictionary*, 1340.

48. The 1,125-ton clipper *Flying Childers* was built in 1852 by Samuel Hall of East Boston, Massachusetts, and launched the same year. Its first commander was Captain Jeremiah D. White. It was 183 feet l.o.a. with a beam of 36 feet and a draft of 22 feet. Rigged with Forbes' double topsail rig, it was designed with a racehorse for a figurehead but no trailboards. It was sold to Mackay, Baines & Co. of Liverpool in 1863 and was renamed *Golden South*. Glenn A. Knoblock, *The American Clipper Ship, 1845–1920: A Comprehensive History, with a Listing of Builders and Their Ships* (Jefferson, NC: McFarland & Co., 2014), 309–10.

49. A native of Delaware, Charles Duval Maxwell (1806–90) was appointed assistant surgeon in 1837 and promoted to surgeon in 1849. He served through the Civil War, retiring in 1868. He was appointed medical director on the retired list in 1871. Callahan, *List of Officers of the Navy*, 357; "Dr Charles Duval Maxwell," Find A Grave Memorial #49259386, *Find A Grave*, http://www.findagrave.com.

50. Manned by twenty sailors and ten Chinese, the jolly-boat English steamer *Queen* weighed 150 tons and carried an armament of four guns of 4-pound caliber each. Spalding, *The Japan Expedition*, 346, 351.

51. Richard Follins was appointed as boatswain in 1850 and resigned his commission in 1853. Callahan, *List of Officers of the Navy*, 199.

52. Thomas A. Stephens (d.1864) was commissioned as a third assistant engineer in 1849. He was promoted to second assistant engineer in 1851 and resigned his commission in 1853. He reentered the U.S. Navy as a second assistant engineer in 1861. Callahan, *List of Officers of the Navy*, 519.

53. William F. Gorton (d. 1853) was appointed as a third assistant engineer in 1852. He died in Pensacola from yellow fever. Callahan, *List of Officers of the Navy*, 225; United States. Navy Department, *Laws, Regulations, Circulars, Orders, Decisions Relating to the U.S. Naval Engineer Corps* (1871; reprint, London: Forgotten Books, 2013), 65.

54. Alfred Taylor (1812–91) began his career as a midshipman in 1825. He was promoted to passed midshipman in 1831, lieutenant in 1837, commander in 1855, captain in 1862, commodore in 1861, and rear admiral in 1872. He retired in 1872. Callahan, *List of Officers of the Navy*, 535; "Adm Alfred Taylor," Find A Grave Memorial #11717977, *Find A Grave*, http://www.findagrave.com.

55. Humphrey Marshall (1812–72) was a Whig congressman from Kentucky in 1849–52, and U.S. commissioner and consul to China in 1852–54. He later served as a Know-Nothing congressman (1853–54) and was a Confederate brigadier general in 1861–63. Allen Johnson and Dumas Malone, eds., *Dictionary of American Biography* (New York: Charles Scribner's Sons, 1958), 6:310–11; *National Cyclopaedia of American Biog*raphy (New York: J. T. White, 1892), 2:368; George Henry Preble, *The Opening of Japan: A Diary of Discovery in the Far East, 1853–1856*, ed. Boleslaw Szczesniak (Norman: University of Oklahoma Press, 1962), 73.

56. Last of Russell & Company's opium clippers, the 300-ton schooner *Brenda* was launched in 1852 at Portsmouth, New Hampshire, by George Raynes. State

Street Trust Company, *Some Ships of the Clipper Ship Era, Their Builders, Owners and Captains* (Boston: Printed for the State Street Trust Company, 1913), 7, 10.

57. Joseph C. Eldredge (1818–81) served as a purser from 1847 until he was promoted to pay director in 1871. He retired in 1880. Callahan, *List of Officers of the Navy*, 180; Pineau, *The Personal Journal of Commodore Matthew C. Perry*, 212–13; "Some Personal Items," *The United States Army & Navy Journal, and Gazette of the Regular and Volunteer Forces* 19 no. 3 (August 20, 1881): 50.

58. William B. Draper (1830–57) set up the first telegraph system in Japan. In 1862, in the Civil War, he held the rank of mate and resigned his commission a year later. Pineau, *The Personal Journal of Commodore Matthew C. Perry*, 228; "William B. Draper," Find A Grave Memorial #32060663, *Find A Grave*, http://www.findagrave.com.

59. The USS *Jamestown* was launched in 1844 by the Gosport (Virginia) Navy Yard with Commander Robert B. Cunningham in command. The 1,150-ton ship was 163 feet l.o.a. with a beam of 32 feet and a depth of hold of 17 feet. Its first commission was to suppress slave trade off Africa. From 1851 to 1854, it began operations off South America. It served in the African Squadron and the Home Squadron. During the Civil War, it was assigned to the Atlantic Blockading Squadron. After a long naval career, it was destroyed in 1913. Mooney, *Dictionary of American Naval Fighting Ships*, 3:501–2.

60. Commanded by Lieutenant John J. Glasson, the *Lexington* was a converted storeship of 691 tons, 127 feet l.o.a., with a 33-foot beam. It was bringing a printing press and other bulky presents for the emperor of Japan. It was built by the New York Navy Yard in 1825 and was commissioned in 1826. It was decommissioned in 1855 and sold in 1860. Pineau, *The Personal Journal of Commodore Matthew C. Perry*, 136; Morison, *"Old Bruin,"* 316, 353, 356; Mooney, *Dictionary of American Naval Fighting Ships*, 4:101–2.

61. George Beall Balch (1821–1908) began his naval career with the rank of midshipman in 1837. He was promoted to passed midshipman in 1843, lieutenant in 1850, commander in 1862, commodore in 1872, and rear admiral in 1878. He retired his commission in 1883. Callahan, *List of Officers of the Navy*, 37; Jan Onofrio, ed., *Tennessee Biographical Dictionary* (St. Clair Shores, MI: Somerset Publishers, 2000), 55–57.

62. John Matthews (d. 1853) entered the U.S. Navy as a midshipman in 1838. He was promoted to passed midshipman in 1844, master in 1851, and lieutenant in 1852. He drowned on October 25, 1853. Callahan, *List of Officers of the Navy*, 356.

63. John Brokenborough Randolph (1818–54) entered the navy as a midshipman in 1833. He was promoted to passed midshipman in 1839 and lieutenant in 1946. Ten days after returning from Japan, he died of dysentery. Callahan, *List of Officers of the Navy*, 452; "Lieut John Brokenborough Randolph," Find A Grave Memorial #37161516, *Find A Grave*, http://www.findagrave.com.

64. John William Bennett (1822–1902) was appointed midshipman in 1840. He was promoted to passed midshipman in 1846, master in March 1855, and lieutenant in September 1855. He was dismissed from active service in 1861. During

the Civil War, he commanded the CSS *Gaines* from 1862 to 1864 and participated in the Battle of Mobile Bay. Callahan, *List of Officers of the Navy*, 53; "Capt John William Bennett," Find A Grave Memorial #37281262, *Find A Grave*, http://www.findagrave.com.

65. Charles Gray began his naval career as a midshipman in 1841. He was promoted to passed midshipman in 1847 and dropped from active service in 1855. Callahan, *List of Officers of the Navy*, 228.

66. Somerville Nicholson (1822–1905) entered the navy as a midshipman in 1839. He was promoted to passed midshipman in 1845 and master in 1853. He was the navigating officer on the *Mississippi* and was present at the signing of the treaty between the U.S. and Japanese governments in 1854; in 1860, after the treaty was burned in the fire at Yeddo, he was present at the signing of the second treaty in Washington. He was promoted to the rank of lieutenant in 1854 and lieutenant commander in 1862. During the Civil War, he commanded the gunboat *Marblehead* and the steamer *State of Georgia*, engaged in blockading service. He was promoted to the rank of commander in 1863, captain in 1870, and commodore in 1880. He retired in 1881. Callahan, *List of Officers of the Navy*, 407; *Washington Post*, May 2, 1905, 3.

67. John Kelly (d. 1863) began his naval career as a midshipman in 1814. He was promoted to lieutenant in 1825, commander in 1841, and captain in 1855. He received the rank of commodore while on the retired list in 1862. Callahan, *List of Officers of the Navy*, 309.

68. John P. Gillis (1803–73) entered the navy as a midshipman in 1825. He was promoted to passed midshipman in 1831 and lieutenant in 1837. During the Mexican War, he served with distinction at the capture of Tuxpan and in the operations against Alvardo. In 1855, he was promoted to commander, and to captain in 1862. During the Civil War, he commanded the *Monticello* and the *Seminole*. He was put on the retired list in 1864 and attained the rank of commodore in 1866. Callahan, *List of Officers of the Navy*, 219; Robert W. Nesser, *Ship Names of the United States Navy: Their Meaning and Origin* (New York: Moffat, Yard & Co, 1921), 87–88.

69. George's brother-in-law, Daniel Dobbins Ward (b 1823). Carrie Pilto, "Pilto Family Tree," http://person.ancestry.com/tree/9707512/person/-756253332/facts.

70. The flagship of Rear Admiral Fleetwood Broughton Reynolds Pellew, the 173-foot-long, 44-foot-beam HMS *Winchester* was commanded by Captain Granville Gower Loch. The 52-gun, 1,487-ton, fourth-rate ship was launched in 1822 at Woolwich Dockyard. It became a training ship in 1861. J. J. Colledge, *Ships of the Royal Navy: The Complete Record of all Fighting Ships of the Royal Navy* (Mechanicsburg, PA: Stackpole Books, 2003), 358.

71. Sir Fleetwood Broughton Reynolds Pellew (1789–1861) was the son of Sir Edward Pellew, First Viscount Exmouth (1757–1833). Sidney Lee, Leslie Stephen, and George Smith, eds., *Dictionary of National Biography* (London: Oxford University Press, 1938), 15:715–16.

72. The Ethiopian Minstrels were played partly by "Negroes" in Perry's squadron but mostly by white sailors in blackface. The folk-cultural show sprang up in 1843. A

line of banjo players was drawn up with two men, one at either end, "Mistah Bones" and "Mistah Tambo," exchanging jokes and insults. A man called the Interlocutor umpired the two men. The banjo orchestra accompanied popular songs and dances, and the entertainment concluded with a burlesque on some popular play or opera, in "Negro" dialect, such as Bulwer Lytton's romantic play, "The Lady of Lyons." Samuel Eliot Morison, "Commodore Perry's Japan Expedition Press and Shipboard Theatre," *Proceedings of the American Antiquarian Society* 77, no. 1 (1967): 39.

73. John P. Williams (c.1826–57) was the brother of S. Wells Williams. On Williams's tombstone in Morrison Chapel and Protestant Cemetery at Macao, the transcription states that "he assisted in setting up the first magnetic telegraph in Japan in 1854." After the expedition, he remained in Asia and took command of the river steamer *Spark*, which was owned by J. B. Endicott. Lindsay Ride and May Ride, *An East India Company Cemetery: Protestant Burials in Macao*, ed. Bernard Mellor (Hong Kong: Hong Kong University Press, 1996), 101.

74. George Parker (c. 1797–1857) was appointed a sailmaker in 1841. Callahan, *List of Officers of the Navy*, 421.

75. William Whiting (d. 1855) was appointed a boatswain in 1848. On 1 April 1855, he was accidentally killed at Woosung, China. Callahan, *List of Officers of the Navy*, 584.

76. Sir Samuel George Bonham (1803–63) served as the third governor of Hong Kong and chief superintendent of British trade in China (1849–54). G. B. Endacott, *A Biographical Sketch-Book of Early Hong Kong* (Hong Kong: Hong Kong University Press, 2005), 30–35.

77. Lola Montez (1818–61) was an American dancer and adventuress, who, during a dance performance for the Russian Emperor Nicholas I, became very thirsty and asked for some water. She was informed that no artists could eat or drink in the presence of royalty, according to a rule of court etiquette. Upon hearing that her request was denied, she declared she would not go on with the dance. Nicholas I sent for a goblet of water and placed it to his own lips, then presented it to Montez, which satisfied the demand within the rule of court etiquette. *Merriam-Webster's Biographical Dictionary*, 728; Lola Montez, *The Lectures of Lola Montez (Countess of Landsfield), including Her Autobiography* (New York: Rudd & Carleton, 1858), 42–43.

78. Inspired by Melville's vivid description of flogging in his 1850 novel *White Jacket*, the U.S. Congress approved an amendment to a naval appropriations bill to ban flogging on all U.S. ships on September 28, 1850. Langley, *Social Reform in the United States Navy, 1798–1862*, 185–92.

79. Alexander Henderson (1832–1901) entered the U.S. Navy as a third assistant engineer in 1851. He was promoted to second assistant engineer in 1853 and first assistant engineer in 1857. He was a member of the Paraguay expedition in 1858. He was promoted to the rank of chief engineer in 1861. He was fleet engineer of the Asiatic and European stations until 1882 when he became the chief engineer of the Boston Navy Yard. He retired in 1894 but returned to active duty during the Spanish War as fleet engineer of the auxiliary navy. Callahan, *List of Officers of the Navy*, 259; "Alex. Henderson," *Harper Weekly* 49, no. 2301 (January 26, 1901): 97.

80. British sidewheel steamer *Hermes* was laid down by Portsmouth in 1834. Launched in 1835 at Woolwich, it was 170 feet l.o.a. and had a beam of 32 feet. Captained by Edmund Gardiner Fishbourne (1811–87), it was recommissioned in 1850 for the East Indies and China, participating in the second Anglo-Burmese War in 1852. Richard Blake, *Religion in the British Navy, 1815–1879: Piety and Professionalism* (Woodbridge, Suffolk, UK: Boydell Press, 2014), 217; Rif Winfield, *British Warships in the Age of Sail, 1817–1863: Design, Construction, Careers and Fates* (Barnsley, S. Yorkshire, UK: Seaforth Publishing, 2014), 302.

81. William Rufus de Vane King (1786–1853) was a congressman from North Carolina in 1811–16, a senator from Alabama in 1819–44 and 1846–52, and vice president for six weeks in 1853. *National Cyclopaedia of American Biography*, 4:147.

Chapter Three

1. Edwin Fithian (1820–1908) accepted his commission of third assistant engineer in 1848. He was promoted to second assistant engineer in 1851, first assistant engineer in 1853, and chief engineer in 1859. During the Civil War, he served on the USS *Roanoke* in the North Atlantic Blockading Squadron. From 1871 to 1876, he was stationed in the Washington Navy Yard. He was placed on the retired list in 1882. Edward W. Callahan, *List of Officers of the Navy of the United States and of the Marine Corps from 1775 to 1900, comprising a complete register of all present and former commissioned, warranted, and appointed officers of the United States Navy, and of the Marine Corps, regular and volunteer* (New York: L. R. Hamersly & Co., 1901), 195; Lewis Randolph Hamersly, ed., *The Records of Living Officers of the U.S. Navy & Marine Corps* (Philadelphia: J. B. Lippincott & Co, 1878), 333–34; "Adm Edwin Fithian," Find A Grave Memorial #14402402, *Find A Grave*, http://www.findagrave.com.

2. Edward Canty Stockton (1836–80) started his naval career as a midshipman in 1849. He was promoted to passed midshipman in June 1855, master in September 1855, and lieutenant in 1857. He was dismissed from active duty owing to his decision to serve in the Confederate States Navy during the Civil War. He served aboard the CSS *Lady*, CSS *Gaines*, and the CSS *Chicora*. He rose to the rank of lieutenant in the CSN. Callahan, *List of Officers of the Navy*, 523; David Coles and David Hartman, *Biographical Rosters of Florida's Confederate and Union Soldiers, 1861–1865* (Wilmington, NC: Broadfoot Publishing Company, 1995), 5:2004; "Edward Canty Stockton," Find A Grave Memorial #119642047, *Find A Grave*, http://www.findagrave.com.

3. Robert Dabney Minor (1827–71) accepted a commission as midshipman in 1841 and rose to the rank of lieutenant in 1855. He was dismissed from active service in 1861 as he decided to serve in the Confederate States Navy. Callahan, *List of Officers of the Navy*, 384; "Robert Dabney Minor," Find A Grave Memorial #12163367, *Find A Grave*, http://www.findagrave.com.

4. Reuben Harris (d. 1857) entered the navy as a midshipman in 1840 and rose to the rank of lieutenant in 1855. Callahan, *List of Officers of the Navy*, 248.

5. The Rawle family kept a house in Macao, but they moved to Hong Kong in 1846. They were trading partners with several foreigners there, including T. C. Lewis, Wetmore & Co in 1844, N. Duus in 1845, and Sandwith Drinker in 1848. Rawle and Drinker parted company in 1853 to carry on their own businesses. Paul A. Van Dyke, ed., *Americans and Macao: Trade, Smuggling, and Diplomacy on the South China Coast* (Hong Kong: Hong Kong University Press, 2012), 146.

6. George Sewell was appointed to first assistant engineer in 1847. He was promoted to chief engineer in 1851 and placed on the retired list in 1885. Callahan, *List of Officers of the Navy*, 490.

7. Victoria Peak is the highest point on the island of Hong Kong, reaching 1,805 feet. *Geographical Dictionary*, 1263.

8. Peter Wager Jr. entered the navy as a midshipman in 1840. He was promoted to passed midshipman in 1846 and master in March 1855. He was dropped from active duty in September 1855. A commander took offense at the Naval Board dropping Wager, to the extent that he wrote an editorial letter that appeared in the *New York Times* on January 10, 1856. Callahan, *List of Officers of the Navy*, 563; *New York Times*, January 10, 1856, 2.

9. The Rev. Dr. Bernard J. Bettelheim (1811–70) served for eight years (April 1846–February 1854) as the first Church of England representative of the Loo Choo mission at Naha. Born in Pressburg (Bratislava) to a Hungarian Jewish family, he earned a medical degree at Padua in 1836 and served as a cholera specialist in Naples and Trieste, and as a surgeon in the Egyptian and Turkish navies. In 1853 he sent a Japanese translation of the New Testament to London. On his journey back to England after serving in Loo Choo, his ship was damaged near Bermuda, and he eventually settled in the United States. During the Civil War he served as a surgeon of the 106th Regiment Illinois Volunteer Infantry from August 16 to December 28, 1863. His later years were spent in Brookfield, Missouri. B. R. Burg, ed., *An American Seafarer in the Age of Sail: The Erotic Diaries of Philip C. Van Buskirk 1851–1870* (New Haven: Yale University Press, 1994), 103–4; William Leonard Schwartz, ed., "Commodore Perry at Okinawa from the Unpublished Diary of a British Missionary," *American Historical Review* 51 (January 1946): 276; Edmond Papinot, *Historical and Geographical Dictionary of Japan* (New York: Frederick Ungar Publishing Co., 1910, republished 1964, second printing 1968), 768.

10. Samuel Wells Williams (1812–84) began his career in China as a printer to the American Board of Foreign Missions in 1832. Ten years later he was appointed the corresponding secretary of the Morrison Education Society. After returning to the United States, he published "The Middle Kingdom" in 1848. He accepted a position as editor of the *Chinese Repository*, a leading Western journal, from 1848 to 1851. He accompanied Perry to Japan, serving as an official interpreter. In 1860 he was appointed *chargé d'affaires* in Peking and served in this capacity until 1876. In 1881 he was elected president of the American Bible Society. Frederick Wells Williams, *The Life and Letters of Samuel Wells Williams, LL.D.: Missionary Diplomatist, Sinologue* (New York: G. P. Putnam's Sons, 1889), 11, 168, 447, 461; "Obituary—Prof. S. Wells Williams," *Publishers' Weekly* 25 (1884): 243; *Memorials of Protestant*

Missionaries to the Chinese: Giving a List of Their Publications, and Obituary Notices of the Deceased (Shanghai: American Presbyterian Mission Press, 1867), 76–78.

11. Shuri is a port on Okinawa Island. It was formerly a separate city unto itself, and the royal capital of the Ryukyus. Papinot, *Historical and Geographical Dictionary of Japan*, 595.

12. David Ochiltree received a commission as a midshipman in 1839. He was promoted to the rank of master in March 1855 and dropped from active service six months later. Roger Pineau, ed., *The Personal Journal of Commodore Matthew C. Perry* (Washington, DC: Smithsonian Institution Press, 1968), 230; Callahan, *List of Officers of the Navy*, 412.

13. J. Howard March (d. 1858) began his career as a midshipman in 1841 and was promoted to lieutenant in 1855. Pineau, *The Personal Journal of Commodore Matthew C. Perry*, 229; Callahan, *List of Officers of the Navy*, 350.

14. Sidney Smith Lee (1802–69), who became commanding officer of the *Mississippi*, was a close friend of Perry's from the Mexican War. A brother of Robert E. Lee, he supported the South in the Civil War and commanded the naval defenses of the James River. Douglas Southall Freeman in his biography of Robert E. Lee described him as "almost as handsome as Robert and of fine cordial manners." Pineau, *The Personal Journal of Commodore Matthew C. Perry*, 229; Samuel Eliot Morison, *"Old Bruin": Commodore Matthew C. Perry, 1794–1858* (Boston: Little, Brown, 1967), 219, 433, 275; Edmund Jennings Lee, ed., *Lee of Virginia, 1642–1892: Biographical and Genealogical Sketches of the Descendants of Colonel Richard Lee* (Philadelphia: Edmund Jennings Lee, 1895), 408–10; Douglas S. Freeman, *R. E. Lee: A Biography* (New York: Charles Scribner's Sons, 1935), 1:105; Henry P. Beers, *Guide to the Archives of the Government of the Confederate States of America* (Washington, DC: Government Printing Office, 1968), 364.

15. Anton L. C. Portman traveled to Japan with Perry as an interpreter from the Dutch. In 1861 he returned to Japan to assist the U.S. government until 1866, when he accepted a position as secretary of the American delegation. Just before the fall of the shogunate, he successfully negotiated the establishment of a railroad line from Yokohama to Tokyo. Louis-Frédéric, *Japan Encyclopedia*, trans. Kathe Roth (Cambridge, MA: Belknap Press of Harvard University Press, 2002), 776–77.

16. Oliver Hazard Perry II (1825–70), fourth child of Matthew C. Perry, served as his father's flagship secretary after joining the expedition in China. He remained in China after the expedition and was made U.S. consul at Canton in 1855 and served for many years. Morison, "*Old Bruin*," 447; George Henry Preble, *The Opening of Japan: A Diary of Discovery in the Far East, 1853–1856*, ed. Boleslaw Szczesniak (Norman: University of Oklahoma Press, 1962), 395.

17. Mount Fuji is an active stratovolcano just west of Tokyo that last erupted in 1707–8. Cohen, *Columbia Gazetteer*, 1055; *Geographical Dictionary*, 409.

18. German-born Peter Bernard Wilhelm Heine (1827–85) immigrated to New York City in 1849. He served with the Perry expedition to Japan from 1852 to 1854. During the Civil War, he served as a colonel in the 103rd Regiment of New York Volunteers. In 1869 he was appointed consular clerk at the U.S. Embassy in Paris and

served until 1871. William Cullen Bryant II and Thomas G. Voss, eds., *The Letters of William Cullen Bryant* (New York: Fordham University Press, 1992), 5:93–94; Wilhelm Heine, *With Perry to Japan: A Memoir*, trans. Frederic Trautmann (Honolulu: University of Hawaii Press, 1990), 178–84.

19. Oragawa, or Uraga, is about twenty-five miles from Tokyo and has a harbor that is capable of accommodating twelve hundred junks. In 1846 the first U.S. emissaries, under Commodore James Biddle, landed at the port to establish relations with Japan but were repulsed. S. B. Kemish, *The Japanese Empire. Its Physical, Political and Social Condition and History. Japan in English* (London: Ganesha Publishing, 2003), 233; *Geographical Dictionary*, 1244.

20. Izawa, the prince of Mimasaka and the Nagasaki *bugyo*, was "forty-one years old, best looking, quite gay, fond of fun and frolic and had the reputation of being a Lothario, had the most liberal view with respect to foreign intercourse. He resembled Secretary of the Treasury Thomas Corwin." Pineau, *The Personal Journal of Commodore Matthew C. Perry*, 184; Peter Booth Wiley and Korogi Ichiro, *Yankees in the Land of the Gods: Commodore Perry and the Opening of Japan* (New York: Viking, 1990), 391.

21. Junius J. Boyle (c. 1807–70), commander of the *Southampton*, started his naval career as a midshipman in 1823. He was promoted to lieutenant in 1832. He prepared the "Report of an Examination of Volcano Bay," which appears in volume 2 of the *Narrative*. Callahan, *List of Officers of the Navy*, 71.

22. Named by Perry in mid-July 1853 during his first visit to Japan, the anchorage is off present-day Yokosuka Ko. Morison, "*Old Bruin,*" 322.

23. Kanagawa is a subdivision of Yokohama. Cohen, *Columbia Gazetteer*, 1521.

24. François Marie de Guyonneau Pambour (1795–1878) wrote extensively on the theory and practice of steam engines and steam locomotives. Charles Coulston Gillispie, ed., *Dictionary of Scientific Biography* (New York: Charles Scribner's Sons, 1970), 10:286.

25. While on liberty at Cumsing Moon, a Chinese man struck Marine private Robert Williams (c. 1830–54) in the head with a stone. This led to an affection of the brain which caused paralysis of his right side. He was buried at Yokohama. Later his body was disinterred and buried in the cemetery of Gyokusenji Temple in Shimoda. Oliver Statler, *The Black Ship Scroll. An Account of the Perry Expedition at Shimoda in 1854 and the Lively Beginnings of People-to-People Relations between Japan & America, Based on Contemporary Records, with translations by Richard Lane, Ph.D. and scroll paintings in full color by an anonymous Japanese eyewitness* (Rutland, VT: Charles E. Tuttle Co., 1964), 73; Wolter, Ranzan, and McDonough, *With Commodore Perry to Japan*, 106; Morison, "*Old Bruin,*" 369–70.

26. Eliphalet M. Brown Jr. (1816–86) was "a pioneer photographer who gave up a lucrative business in New York to accompany Perry. He brought a daguerreotype camera and an abundance of plates with which he took many 'stills' of scenery and people and some of our illustrations initialed W T Peters or H Patterson were undoubtedly redrawn by these rather obscure New York artists from Brown's daguerreotypes of which most of the originals have been lost." Pineau, *The Personal Journal of*

Commodore Matthew C. Perry, xvii. Before the expedition, he spent thirteen years working for various establishments, including Currier & Ives, producing portraits and historical and marine lithographs. He learned daguerreotype from his younger brother, James Sydney Brown, and made approximately four hundred daguerreotypes during the expedition. He spent twenty years in the U.S. Navy as a master and ensign, beginning in the Civil War, and later was in the Mediterranean as an admiral's secretary. He retired in 1875 and never was active in any area of art or photography. Morison, "*Old Bruin,*" 278, 393, 419, 434; Callahan, *List of Officers of the Navy*, 80; Bruce T. Erickson, *Encyclopedia of Nineteenth-Century Photography*, ed. John Hannavy (New York: Routledge, 2008), 1:222–24.

27. George Jones (1800–1870) was an Episcopal clergyman and chaplain of the *Mississippi*. He also acted as an astronomer and geologist on the expedition. His study of zodiacal lights makes up volume 3 of the *Narrative of the Expedition*. He twice served as chaplain of the United States Naval Academy. Johnson and Malone, *Dictionary of American Biography*, 5:170–71; Pineau, *The Personal Journal of Commodore Matthew C. Perry*, xvii, 52; Morison, "*Old Bruin,*" 279, 424, 434.

28. The *United States* was a 1,576-ton frigate, measuring 175 feet l.o.a. with a 44-foot beam and 21-foot depth of hold. Designed by Joshua Humphreys and Captain Thomas Truxton, it was launched in 1797 at the Philadelphia Navy Yard and captained by Captain John Barry. After a distinguished service hunting French vessels in the Caribbean and serving in the Pacific Squadron, it was decommissioned in 1849 and placed in ordinary at Norfolk. Mooney, *Dictionary of American Naval Fighting Ships*, 7:413–17.

29. A cornet is a short, swallow-tailed pendant indicating a commodore's ship in a squadron; a signal for all hands to report on board a naval vessel at once, or for every ship to prepare to receive a message. Dean King, John B. Hattendorf, and J. Worth Estes, *A Sea of Words: A Lexicon and Companion for Patrick O'Brian's Seafaring Tales* (New York: Henry Holt, 1995), 334; Gershom Bradford, *A Glossary of Sea Terms* (New York: Yachting, Inc., 1927), 42.

30. Edmund C. Bittinger (1819–89) served as a chaplain in the U.S. Navy from 1850 to 1881. Morison, "*Old Bruin*," 372–73; Callahan, *List of Officers of the Navy*, 59.

31. Jacob Zeilin (1806–80) entered the Marine Corps as a second lieutenant in 1831 after several years of study at the United States Military Academy. He was promoted to first lieutenant in 1836. He served on board the USS *Columbus* and the USS *Congress* from 1842 to 1848. In 1847 he was promoted to captain and appointed military commandant of San Diego. In 1852 he was appointed a fleet marine officer attached to *Mississippi*. He was the second man to set foot on shore at the formal landing at Yokohama in 1853. Although he received a rank of brevet major in 1847, he was appointed in 1861 to the regular rank of major and given command of a company of Marines. In 1864 Zeilin was appointed colonel commandant of the Marine Corps and assumed command of the Marine Barracks at Portsmouth, New Hampshire. In 1867 he became the Marine Corps' first general officer when he was promoted to brigadier general. After the war, Zeilin officially approved the design of the "Eagle, Globe, and Anchor" as the emblem for the Marine Corps. He retired in

1876. Pineau, *The Personal Journal of Commodore Matthew C. Perry*, 232; Callahan, *List of Officers of the Navy*, 679; Alan Reed Millett and Jack Shulimson, *Commandants of the Marine Corps* (Annapolis, MD: Naval Institute Press, 2004), 85–96.

32. Rama IV (1804–68), known in English-speaking countries as King Mongkut, was the fourth monarch of Siam, now Thailand (r. 1851–68). He was made famous in the West by Margaret Landon's 1944 book *Anna and the King of Siam* and the 1956 film musical *The King and I*. William H. Harris and Judith S. Levy, eds., *The New Columbia Encyclopedia* (New York: Columbia University Press, 1975), 1812.

33. Francis S. Haggerty (c. 1816–99) began his naval service as a midshipman in 1832. He was promoted to passed midshipman in 1838, lieutenant in 1843, and commander in 1861. During the Civil War, he was appointed commander of the brig *Perry* and the *Vandalia*. He retired from the navy in 1862. He was assigned the rank of captain on the retired list in 1867. Callahan, *List of Officers of the Navy*, 237; Barnes, *The American Civil War through British Eyes*, 2:60.

34. David Stockton McDougal (1809–82) received a commission of midshipman in 1828. He was promoted to passed midshipman in 1834 and lieutenant in 1841. He served in the West India Squadron and in the Mexican War. He was promoted to the rank of commander in 1857, captain in 1864, and commodore in 1869. From 1861 to 1864, he was in command of the USS *Wyoming* and later in charge of Mare Island Navy Yard. He was placed on the retired list in 1871 and rose to the rank of rear admiral in 1873. He died in San Francisco. Callahan, *List of Officers of the Navy*, 365; David Shavit, *The United States in Asia: A Historical Dictionary* (Westport, CT: Greenwood Press, 1990), 321.

35. Albert G. Slaughter (d. 1853) began his naval career as a midshipman in 1819. He was promoted to lieutenant in 1827 and commander in 1848. He commanded the *Bainbridge* from 1848 to 1850. He died in Warrenton, Virginia. Callahan, *List of Officers of the Navy*, 501, Mooney, *Dictionary of American Naval Fighting Ships*, 1:85.

36. The *Bainbridge*, a 259-ton brig, was launched in 1842 by the Boston Navy Yard. Commissioned the same year, it joined the Home Squadron and with Lieutenant Albert G. Slaughter commanding, patrolled the African coast for slave runners in 1848. It was 100 feet l.o.a. and had a beam of 25 feet and a draft of 14 feet. During the Civil War, it was assigned to Rear Admiral DuPont's South Atlantic Blockading Squadron in the summer of 1863. In August 1863, it encountered a severe storm and capsized off Cape Hatteras. Mooney, *Dictionary of American Naval Fighting Ships*, 1:85.

37. Son of Captain Henry A. Adams, N. B. Adams was the clerk to the captain of the fleet. William G. Beasley, *The Perry Mission to Japan, 1853–1854* (Richmond, Surrey, England: Japan Library, 2002),1:9.

38. A mariner from the Ryukyu Islands standing 5 feet 4 inches, Kamata Nōju (b. c. 1821), nicknamed Jake Canoe by the Americans, known also as Jackalow, Jack Lowe, and John Lord, sailed to America on the *Mississippi*. He was convicted of robbery on the high seas in 1860. While employed on board the sloop *Spray*, he allegedly murdered Captain Jonathan Leete and his brother Elijah Leete. Francis Vincent, ed.,

Vincent's Semi-Annual United States Register: A Work in Which the Principal Events of Every Half-Year Occurring in the United States Are Recorded, Each Arranged under the Day of Its Date (Philadelphia: Francis Vincent, 1860), 218; F. Calvin Parker, *The Japanese Sam Patch: Saga of a Servant* (Notre Dame, IN: Cross Cultural Publications, 2001), 75.

39. Alban Crocker Stimers (1827–76) was appointed third assistant engineer in 1849. He was promoted to second assistant engineer in 1851, first assistant engineer in 1853, and chief engineer in 1858. In the early months of the Civil War, he was a member of the board that examined engineer candidates. In 1861, he supervised the construction of the *Monitor* and operated the *Monitor*'s turret during the Battle of Hampton Roads. He served as the general inspector of ironclads from 1862 to 1864. He resigned his commission in 1865. Callahan, *List of Officers of the Navy*, 522; William H. Roberts, *Civil War Ironclads: The U.S. Navy and Industrial Mobilization* (Baltimore: Johns Hopkins University Press, 2002), 29–30.

40. Bushrod Bust Taylor (1832–83) was assigned a position as midshipman in 1849. He was promoted to passed midshipman in June 1855, master in September 1855, and lieutenant in 1856. He was an instructor for the Naval Academy before the Civil War and served in the Gulf, West Indies, and Western Gulf Squadrons during the war. From 1866 to 1869, he again was an instructor at the Naval Academy. He was promoted to captain in 1879. Callahan, *List of Officers of the Navy*, 535; Wilson and Fiske, *Appletons' Cyclopaedia of American Biography*, 6:42.

41. John K. Contee served Perry as flag lieutenant and aide. He was utilized frequently in conferences and preliminary negotiations with the Japanese. The *Narrative of the Expedition* alludes to making use of a journal kept by Contee but does not identify it specifically. His naval career ran from 1832 to 1854. Callahan, *List of Officers of the Navy*, 127.

42. Amami-O-Shima is the largest island in the Amami-Gunto island group in the Ryukyu Archipelago. It lies roughly halfway between the islands of Okinawa and Kyushu. During the Perry expedition, it was apparently named Preble Island. Cohen, *Columbia Gazetteer*, 89; *Geographical Dictionary*, 40; Preble, *The Opening of Japan*, 202.

43. Amos G. Gambrill (d. 1854) graduated from the University of Maryland School of Medicine in 1826. He entered the navy with the rank of assistant surgeon in 1829. He was promoted to passed assistant surgeon in 1835 and surgeon in 1838. Callahan, *List of Officers of the Navy*, 210; Eugene Fauntleroy Cordell, *Historical Sketch of the University of Maryland School of Medicine (1807–1890)* (Baltimore: Press of Isaac Friedenwald, 1891), 175.

44. The town of Matsumae is located on the extreme southwest peninsula of Hokkaido on the Tsugaru Strait, which separates Honshu to the south and Hokkaido to the north, and provides passage between the northwest Pacific Ocean and the Sea of Japan. Cohen, *Columbia Gazetteer*, 1918.

45. Ki Hayashi, Daigaku no Kami (1799–1858) served as the prince counselor. The lord rector of the University at Edo, he was "about fifty-five years old, well formed, of middle size, of grave and reserved deportment. He might be likened in

appearance to Maryland Congressman Reverdy Johnson." Pineau, *The Personal Journal of Commodore Matthew C. Perry*, 162, 184.

46. Satohiro Ido (d.1858), the prince of Tsushima and one of the Uraga *bugyo*, was "about fifty years old, tall and rather corpulent with a pleasant expression, resembling the Minister of London James Buchanan." Pineau, *The Personal Journal of Commodore Matthew C. Perry*, 184.

Masoyoshi Izawa, the prince of Mimasaka and the Nagasaki *bugyo*, was "forty-one years old, best looking, quite gay, fond of fun and frolic and had the reputation of being a Lothario, had the most liberal view with respect to foreign intercourse. He resembled Secretary of the Treasury Thomas Corwin." Pineau, *The Personal Journal of Commodore Matthew C. Perry*, 184; Wiley, *Yankees in the Land of the Gods*, 391; Sho Sakanishi, ed., *A Private Journal of John Glendy Sproston, U.S.N.* (Tokyo: Sophia University, 1940), 8.

47. Shimoda is a port southeast of Izu Peninsula. Papinot, *Historical and Geographical Dictionary of Japan*, 572.

48. Hakodate is a city and port located on Hokkaido, Japan. It is the capital city of Oshima Subprefecture. *Geographical Dictionary*, 467.

49. William L. Maury (1813–78) began his naval career as a midshipman in 1829. He rose to the rank of lieutenant in 1841 and resigned his commission in 1861. Maury Island was named after him during the 1841 Wilkes expedition. Callahan, *List of Officers of the Navy*, 357; Pineau, *The Personal Journal of Commodore Matthew C. Perry*, 229; Morison, "*Old Bruin,*" 316, 360, 419.

50. The breed of the dogs was the Japanese Chin or Spaniel. William Speiden Jr., purser's mate of the *Mississippi*, recollected that one of the dogs, Master Sam Spooner, died in January 1855, while the other, Madame Jeddo, died in the month of February. They were put in shotted canvas bags and buried at sea in sailor fashion. James Watson, *The Dog Book: A Popular History of the Dog, with Practical Information as to Care and Management of House, Kennel, and Exhibition Dogs; and Descriptions of All the Important Breeds* (New York: Doubleday, Page & Co., 1906), 2:733–34; Wolter, Ranzan, and McDonough, *With Commodore Perry to Japan*, 162.

51. William W. Bleecker (d. 1854) received his appointment as midshipman in 1827. He was promoted to passed midshipman in 1833 and lieutenant in 1838. He was lost on the *Albany* in 1854. Callahan, *List of Officers of the Navy*, 62.

52. Silas Bent (1820–87), the flag lieutenant on the *Mississippi*, was appointed midshipman at age sixteen and served in the navy for the next twenty-five years, during which he became well versed in the science of oceanography. In 1849 he was promoted to lieutenant. During the expedition to Japan, he made hydrographic surveys of Japanese waters and published his findings in 1857 in *Sailing Directions and Nautical Remarks: by Officers of the Late U.S. Naval Expedition to Japan*. In 1860 he was detailed to the hydrographic division of the Coast Survey, but he resigned from the navy a year later at the outbreak of the Civil War. Mooney, *Dictionary of American Naval Fighting Ships*, 6:505; Callahan, *List of Officers of the Navy*, 53; Edward L. Towle, "Lieutenant Silas Bent's Device to Eliminate Variation Correction in the Magnetic Compass, 1849," *American Neptune* 25 (1965): 93–98.

53. Joel Abbot (1793–1855) began his naval career as a midshipman in 1812 and took part in the battle on Lake Champlain. He rose to the rank of captain in 1850 and succeeded Commodore Perry as commander of the East Indies Squadron with a rank of commodore. He died in Hong Kong. Callahan, *List of Officers of the Navy*, 15; John W. Jordan, ed., *Colonial and Revolutionary Families of Pennsylvania: Genealogical and Personal Memoirs* (reprint; Baltimore: Clearfield Company, 2004), 676.

54. John Pickens Abbot (1828–86) was a purser in the navy for a time and then a physician. He served in the Civil War, rising to the rank of captain. *Representative Men and Old Families of Rhode Island: Genealogical Records and Historical Sketches of Prominent and Representative Citizens and of Many of the Old Families* (Chicago: J. H. Beers & Co., 1908), 2:1166.

55. Yokohama was a fishing village in 1854, eighteen miles southeast of Edo on the west shore of Tokyo Bay. *Geographical Dictionary*, 1331.

56. Jan Cock Blomhoff (1779–1853) was director of Dejima, the Dutch trading colony in the harbor of Nagasaki, Japan, from 1809 to 1824. During his second stay in Dejima in 1817, his wife Titia Bergsma, and Petronella Muns, her Dutch wet-nurse, were the first Western woman to set foot in Japan. Rudolph Effert, *Royal Cabinets and Auxiliary Branches: Origins of the National Museum of Ethnology, 1816–1883* (Leiden: CNWS Publications, 2008), 65–66.

57. Known also as Natsu Shima, Webster Island is a partly wooded island about one and a half miles south of Koshiba Zaki, or Fillmore Point, in the "American Anchorage." United States Hydrographic Office, *Asiatic Pilot: Volume II—The Japan Islands* (Washington, DC: Government Printing Office, 1920), 2:164; Pineau, *The Personal Journal of Commodore Matthew C. Perry*, 165; Morison, "*Old Bruin*," 322.

58. Samuel H. Houston (d. 1854) received a commission as third assistant engineer in 1851 and was promoted to second assistant engineer in 1853. Callahan, *List of Officers of the Navy*, 277.

59. Probably Garret V. Denniston (d. 1858), who entered the U.S. Navy as a midshipman in 1840. He was promoted to passed midshipman in 1846, master in March 1855, and lieutenant in September 1855. Callahan, *List of Officers of the Navy*, 159.

60. Nicknamed after an American stuntman named Sam Patch, Sentaro (c. 1831–74) was rescued along with the rest of the crew of the cargo junk *Eiriki-maru* by the American bark *Auckland* in the Pacific Ocean in 1851. After spending some time in San Francisco, he accompanied the Perry expedition to Japan on board the USS *Susquehanna*. He returned to the United States after the Japanese treaty was signed and stayed with U.S. Marine Jonathan Goble, who gave him lessons in English and taught him Christianity. In 1860, Sam Patch accompanied Goble to Japan to start work for the American Baptist Free Missionary Society. He was the first Japanese to enroll in Colgate University (then Madison University) and the first Japanese to be baptized as a Baptist. Belle M. Brain, *All about Japan: Stories of Sunrise Land Told for Little Folks* (London: Fleming H. Revell Co., 1905), 143–45, 152; Parker, *The Japanese Sam Patch*, 100, 200, 203, 204.

61. Born in New Hampshire, Thomas Cochrane Dudley (b. c. 1830) served as purser's clerk aboard the *Powhatan*. "Thomas C. Dudley Papers, 1853–1856, 1925," Pea-

body Essex Museum, Salem, MA, http://www.pem.org/library/finding_aids/MH85_ThomasCDudleyPapers.pdf.

62. Kidder Randolph Breese (1831–81), born in Philadelphia, began his naval career as a midshipman in 1846. During the Mexican War he served with Commander Farragut on the USS *Saratoga* and later on the USS *St. Mary's, Brandywine*, and *St. Lawrence*. In 1855 he was promoted to master and lieutenant. During the Civil War he was appointed fleet captain of the third division of Porter's Mortar Flotilla and participated in the attack on New Orleans and Vicksburg. In 1862 he was promoted to lieutenant commander, and after the war he was ordered to the Naval Academy and served until 1866 as assistant to the superintendent. In 1866 he was appointed commander; in 1870 he was ordered to the command of USS *Plymouth*, and he was commissioned as captain in 1874 in charge of the Torpedo Station. Callahan, *List of Officers of the Navy*, 75; Wilson and Fiske, *Appleton's Cyclopaedia of American Biography*, 1:366–67.

63. An English trick-taking card game popular in the eighteenth and nineteenth centuries. Edmond Hoyle, *A Short Treatise on the Game of Whist* (London: T. Osborne, 1750).

64. Robert Woodworth (1813–70), son of New York Supreme Court judge John Woodworth, graduated from Williams College in 1831, and then studied medicine in Philadelphia, receiving his M.D. in 1834. He was commissioned as assistant surgeon in 1835 and was promoted to surgeon in 1846. He retired in 1867. His last place of residence was Paris, France. Callahan, *List of Officers of the Navy*, 603; Calvin Durfee, *Obituary Report, 1865–1875* (North Adams, MA: James T. Robinson & Son, Printers and Binders, 1875), 2:22.

65. The U.S. naval storekeeper was Robert P. DeSilver, who also served as U.S. consul at Macau from 1849 to 1855. Eldon Griffin, *Clippers and Consuls: American Consular and Commercial Relations with Eastern Asia, 1845–1860* (Ann Arbor, MI: Edwards Brothers, 1938), 362.

66. George W. Parish (c.1830–54) from Hebron, Connecticut, was buried in the cemetery of Gyokusenji Temple in Shimoda. Statler, *The Black Ship Scroll*, 73; Grant Romer, "Near the Temple at Yokushen. . . ." *Image: Journal of Photography and Motion Pictures of the International Museum of Photography at George Eastman House* 29, no. 2 (August 1986): 6.

67. Phineas Taylor "P. T." Barnum (1810–91) was an American showman and businessman remembered for promoting celebrated hoaxes and for founding the Barnum & Bailey Circus. John Howard Brown, ed., *Lamb's Biographical Dictionary of the United States* (Boston: James H. Lamb Co., 1900), 1:200.

68. Garrett R. Barry entered the U.S. Navy in 1824 and rose to the rank of purser in 1826. *Register of Commissioned and Warrant Officers of the US Navy*, 46.

69. In 1811, Captain Vasilii Mikhailovich Golovnin (1776–1831), commander of the *Diana*, was assigned to survey the Japanese-controlled southern Kurile Islands. At that time, the Japanese only allowed foreign ships to enter the port at Nagasaki. As he approached the southernmost island of Kunashir, the Japanese tricked Golovnin into coming ashore. Although he proclaimed his peaceful intentions, Golovnin and

seven other sailors were taken prisoner by the Japanese and held until 1813, when his second-in-command, Pyotr Ivanovich Rikord (1776–1855), negotiated his release. In 1816 Golovnin published his account of captivity, entitled *Narrative of My Captivity in Japan, during the Years 1811, 1812 & 1813, to Which Is Added an Account of Voyages to the Coasts of Japan, and of Negotiations with the Japanese, for the Release of the Author and His Companions, by Captain Rikord.* It was the first description of the Japanese to appear in Russian and only the second European account since German naturalist and physician Kaempfer's *History of Japan* in 1727. Vasilii Golovnin, *Around the World on the Kamchatka, 1817–1819,* translated by Ella Lury Wiswell (Honolulu: Hawaiian Historical Society and University of Hawaii Press, 1979), xix, xxiii, xxvi; *Geographical Dictionary*, 615.

70. Arthur Sinclair (1810–65) was the *Supply*'s commanding officer. He began his career as a midshipman in 1823. He was promoted to lieutenant in 1835 and commander in 1855. He was dismissed from his duties in 1861 to serve in the Confederate navy. He died during the shipwreck of the *Lelia* near the coast of Wales. Callahan, *List of Officers of the Navy*, 499; Margaret Middleton Rivers Eastman, *Hidden History of Civil War Charleston* (Charleston, SC: History Press, 2012), 75, 80.

Chapter Four

1. Succeeding Bettelheim, Rev. G. H. Moreton arrived with his wife and his son Philip on Okinawa in February 1854. Moreton's health failed, and he left Okinawa in October 1855. Francis L. Hawks, *Commodore Perry and the Opening of Japan: Narrative of the Expedition of an American Squadron to the China Seas and Japan, 1852–1854: The Official Report of the Expedition to Japan* (Stroud, UK: Nonsuch, 2005), 498.

2. William Board, apparently while intoxicated, allegedly entered a house and raped an Okinawan woman. The villagers chased him down, beat and stoned him, and drowned him. His body was interred in a small, private Naha cemetery that commemorated Perry's voyages. Peter Booth Wiley and Korogi Ichiro, *Yankees in the Land of the Gods: Commodore Perry and the Opening of Japan* (New York: Viking, 1990), 456–57; Hawks, *Commodore Perry and the Opening of Japan*, 492.

3. John James Glasson (1805–82) started his naval career as a midshipman in 1823. He served in the Mediterranean and the West Indies, and during the Mexican War. In 1837, he was promoted to lieutenant. He commanded the *Lexington*, which carried the presents for the Japanese. He was placed on the reserved list on September 13, 1855. One day later, he was commissioned to the rank of commander on the active list. At the outbreak of the Civil War, he commanded the brig *Perry*, which conveyed troops. From 1861 to 1866, he was stationed at New Bedford, Massachusetts, and the Norfolk Navy Yard. He retired in 1864 and was assigned the rank of commodore in 1867. His death in 1882 was caused by disease of the heart, aggravated by congestion of the lungs. Edward W. Callahan, *List of Officers of the Navy of the United States and of the Marine Corps from 1775 to 1900, comprising a complete register of all present and former commissioned, warranted, and appointed officers of*

the United States Navy, and of the Marine Corps, regular and volunteer (New York: L. R. Hamersly & Co., 1901), 220; *New York Times*, March 13, 1882, 5.

4. A native of Richmond, Virginia, James Willett Spalding (1827–61) was the captain's clerk on the *Mississippi*. He was appointed a lieutenant in Co. H of the 60th Virginia Infantry on 20 August 1861 and promoted shortly after to the rank of lieutenant colonel. A month later, Spalding was killed on scout duty near Sewell Mountain. J. L. Scott, *60th Virginia Infantry* (Lynchburg, VA: H. E. Howard, 1997), 64.

5. Edmund Lanier (1814–72) began his naval career as a midshipman in 1831, and then received a promotion to lieutenant in 1841 and commander in 1861. He retired in 1864 and was promoted to captain in 1867 while on the retired list. Callahan, *List of Officers of the Navy*, 322.

6. James Hemphill Jones (1821–80) entered the U.S. Marine Corps as a second lieutenant in 1847. He was promoted to first lieutenant in 1853, captain in 1861, lieutenant colonel in 1864, and colonel in 1879. Callahan, *List of Officers of the Navy*, 689; Roger Pineau, ed., *The Personal Journal of Commodore Matthew C. Perry* (Washington, DC: Smithsonian Institution Press, 1968), 229; "Col James Hemphill Jones," Find A Grave Memorial # 45915349, *Find A Grave*, http://www.findagrave.com.

7. Located in Zhejiang Province, Ningbo is one of China's oldest seaports. Known to the Portuguese as Liampo and lying on the south side of Hangzhou Bay and facing the East China Sea to the east, it served as a trade city two thousand years ago and a major port in the Tang and Song dynasties. Thomas Allom, "The City of Ning Po," 2010, http://www.chinese-outpost.com/history/thomas-allom-china-illustrated/the-city-of-ning-po.asp; *Merriam-Webster's Geographical Dictionary*, 3rd ed. (Springfield, MA: Merriam-Webster, 2007), 832; Saul B. Cohen, *The Columbia Gazetteer of the World* (New York: Columbia University Press, 1998), 2189.

8. Eli Crosby (d. 1854) began his career in 1849 as a third assistant engineer and was promoted to second assistant engineer in 1851. He served on the *Susquehanna* during the Perry expedition. He probably died of pleurisy. Callahan, *List of Officers of the Navy*, 140.

9. From October 1853 to February 1856, in what became known as the Crimean War, Russia battled and eventually lost to an alliance of France, the United Kingdom, the Ottoman empire, and Sardinia. *Encyclopædia Britannica: A Dictionary of Arts, Sciences, Literature and General Information*, 11th ed. (Cambridge: Cambridge University Press, 1911), 7:450–54.

10. An ancient military fort on the southeastern coast of China, Zhenhai is an administrative unit and outer port of Ningbo on the Hangzhou Bay at the mouth of the Yong River, the thirteen-mile-long river that originates from the Xuedou Mountain. Cohen, *Columbia Gazetteer*, 3531, 3563.

11. Nankeen is a durable brownish yellow cotton fabric originally loomed by hand in China. *The American Heritage Dictionary of the English Language*, 3rd ed. (Boston and New York: Houghton Mifflin Company, 1992), 1199.

12. Sir Harry Smith Parkes (1828–85) served as the British consul at Amoy, China, from May 1854 to February 1855. He accompanied Sir John Bowring on a diplomatic mission to secure a treaty with Siam. Sidney Lee, Leslie Stephen, and

George Smith, eds., *Dictionary of National Biography* (London: Oxford University Press, 1938), 15:296, 298–99.

13. Thomas Hart Hyatt (1809–81) served as U.S. consul at Amoy, China, from March 1854 to May 1861. Gail Unzelman, "Thomas Hart Hyatt: The Man and His Book," *Supplement to the Wayward Tendrils Quarterly* 23, no. 3 (July 2013): 1, 4.

14. Cadwalader Ringgold (1802–67) had taken part in the United States Exploring Expedition of 1838–42 under Charles Wilkes, and in 1853–54 he commanded a surveying expedition in the North Pacific. John Howard Brown, ed., *Lamb's Biographical Dictionary of the United States* (Boston: James H. Lamb Co., 1900), 6:484.

15. Henry Rolando (1820–69) entered the naval service as a midshipman in 1836. He was promoted to master in 1849 and to lieutenant a year later. In 1853 he participated in the Bering Straits expedition under Admiral Ringgold to exterminate the Chinese pirates in China waters. During the Civil War he was given the rank of commander in charge of the Philadelphia Navy Yard. He also was placed in command of the *Keystone State*, which participated in the bombardment of Fort Fisher. After the war he was transferred to the *Florida* and assigned to the West Indies. He retired his commission in 1867. "Death of a Navy Officer in Baltimore," *New York Times*, March 24, 1869, 2; Callahan, *List of Officer of the Navy*, 472.

16. The USS *Porpoise*, a 230-ton, square-rigged-foremast and schooner-rigged-mainmast brig, was authorized by Congress in 1834, built in 1835, and launched from Boston in 1836, with Lieutenant William Ramsay in command. After conducting coastal surveying operations in the summer of 1837, it hunted pirates along the southern coast before resuming survey work in December 1837. With Lieutenant Cadwalader Ringgold in command, it was assigned to the Wilkes U.S. Exploring Expedition Squadron and confirmed the existence of the Antarctic, charted vast areas of the South Pacific, and circumnavigated the globe. In 1842–43 it patrolled for slavers off the west coast of Africa. Between February 1845 and July 1847, *Porpoise* cruised in the Gulf of Mexico, participating in the naval operations against Tampico, Pánuco, and Veracruz during the Mexican War. During the next three and a half years it again hunted slavers along the west coast of Africa. In May 1853 it was assigned to the North Pacific Exploring and Surveying Expedition to chart many of the Pacific islands. While on this expedition, it parted from another vessel on September 21, 1854, between Formosa and China, and was never heard from again. James L. Mooney, *Dictionary of American Naval Fighting Ships* (Washington, DC: Navy Department, Office of the Chief of Naval Operations, Naval History Division, 1959–81), 5:353.

17. A Wisconsin native, John Van McCollum entered the navy as a midshipman in 1841. He was promoted to the rank of passed midshipman in 1847 and served on the North Pacific Expedition and in the Mediterranean Squadron. He was promoted to master on September 14, 1855, and lieutenant a day later. He resigned his commission in 1859. Callahan, *List of Officers of the Navy*, 362; George M. Brooke, Jr., *Big Guns of the Confederacy: The Journal and Letters of John M. Brooke* (Columbia: University of South Carolina Press, 2002), 7.

18. The storeship *J. P. Kennedy* was transferred from Ringgold's U.S. North Pa-

cific surveying expedition to Perry's squadron to protect the American interest in China during the Taiping Rebellion. John H. Schroeder, *Shaping a Maritime Empire: The Commercial and Diplomatic Role of the American Navy, 1829–1861*. Westport, CT: Greenwood Press, 1985, 160.

19. Owned by Reed, Wade & Co. and W. & F. H. Whittemore & Co., the *Shooting Star* was designed, modeled, and drafted by Captain John Wade and built by James O. Curtis, one of the best shipbuilders in Medford, Massachusetts, in 1851. Commanded by Captain Judah P. Baker, it was a 903-ton clipper, 171 feet l.o.a., with a 35-foot beam, and with a full female figure ornamenting the bow. "The New Clipper Ship *Shooting Star*, of Boston," *Boston Daily Atlas*, March 6, 1851; Octavius T. Howe and Frederick C. Matthews, *American Clipper Ships, 1833–1858* (New York: Argosy Antiquarian, 1967), 571–73.

20. Jefferson Finis Davis (1808–69) served as secretary of war under President Pierce from 1853 to 1857. During the American Civil War, he was elected president of the Confederate States of America and served from 1862 to 1865. *Biographical Directory of the United States Congress 1774–2005: The Continental Congress September 5, 1774, to October 21, 1788, and the Congress of the United States from the First through the One Hundred Eighth Congresses, March 4, 1789, to January 3, 2005, Inclusive* (Washington, DC: Government Printing Office, 2005), 928.

21. HMS *Rattler* was an 888-ton sloop fitted with an engine and screw propeller. It was 176 feet l.o.a., with a 32-foot beam, and was launched in 1843 at Sheerness Dockyard. J. J. Colledge, *Ships of the Royal Navy: The Complete Record of All Fighting Ships of the Royal Navy* (Mechanicsburg, PA: Stackpole Books, 2003), 268; Pineau, *The Personal Journal of Commodore Matthew C. Perry*, 140.

22. Robert Milligan McLane (1815–98) was appointed by President Pierce as commissioner to China in 1853 with the powers of a minister plenipotentiary. During his political career, he served as ambassador to Mexico, France, and China; as a member of the Maryland House of Representatives; and as the thirty-ninth governor of Maryland. John A. Garraty, and Mark C. Carnes, eds., *American National Biography* (New York: Oxford University Press, 1999), 15:134–36.

23. Bamboo Town is located on the northern side of Danes Island, or Chang chau. James B. Lawrence, *China and Japan, and a Voyage Thither: An Account of a Cruise in the Waters of the East Indies, China, and Japan* (Hartford, CT: Press of Case, Lockwood & Brainard, 1870), 166.

24. Hamilton Bell received a commission as acting gunner in 1851. He deserted in August 1854. Callahan, *List of Officers of the Navy*, 51.

25. The American consul was William P. Pierce. William G. Beasley, *The Perry Mission to Japan, 1853–1854* (Richmond, Surrey, England: Japan Library, 2002), 87.

26. James Keenan (1823–62) was appointed U.S. consul of Hong Kong in May 1853, but he did not arrive at his post until February 1854. He held the position until 1862. Eldon Griffin, *Clippers and Consuls: American Consular and Commercial Relations with Eastern Asia, 1845–1860* (Ann Arbor, MI: Edwards Brothers, 1938), 361.

27. Monsieur Alphonse de Bourboulon (1809–77) served as the French minister to Canton from 1851 to 1857. Johnston, James D., *China and Japan: Being a Narra-*

tive of the Cruise of the U.S. Steam-Frigate Powhatan *in the Years 1857, '58, '59, and '60 including an Account of the Japanese Embassy to the United States, Illustrated with Life Portraits of the Embassadors and Their Principal Officials* (Philadelphia: Charles DeSilver, 1860), 225; W. F. Vande Walle and Noel Golvers, eds., *The History of the Relations between the Low Countries and China in the Qing Era (1644–1911)* (Leuven, Belgium: Leuven University Press, 2003), 385; George Henry Preble, *The Opening of Japan: A Diary of Discovery in the Far East, 1853–1856*, edited by Boleslaw Szczesniak (Norman: University of Oklahoma Press, 1962), 379.

28. Launched by the Boston Navy Yard in 1850 for service as a steam tug, the *John Hancock* was damaged by a storm in 1851 near Havana, Cuba. It was rebuilt almost entirely and relaunched in 1853, measuring 382 tons, 165 feet l.o.a., with a 22-foot beam and a 10-foot draft, with Lieutenant John Rodgers in command. As part of Ringgold's Northern Pacific survey expedition, it surveyed the waters surrounding the large islands off the coast of Southeast Asia. The *John Hancock* was decommissioned at Mare Island Navy Yard and sold at auction in 1865. Mooney, *Dictionary of American Naval Fighting Ships*, 3:531–32.

29. *Lady Pierce* was the first American vessel to arrive in Japan after the opening of commercial relations between the United States and Japan. Arriving in Tokyo Bay fifteen days after Commodore Perry left, the clipper traveled from San Francisco to Japan via Honolulu carrying supplies that would interest the Japanese. Captained by Silas E. Burrows, it visited Uraga and Shimoda. "Visit of the '*Lady Pierce*' to Japan," *Sailor's Magazine* 27, no. 9 (May 1855): 274; Richard Hildreth, *Japan and the Japanese* (Boston: Bradley, Dayton & Co., 1860), 534.

30. Joshua Follansbie entered the navy as third assistant engineer in 1842. He was promoted to second assistant engineer in 1845, first assistant engineer in 1847, and chief engineer in 1848. He resigned his commission in 1865. Callahan, *List of Officers of the Navy*, 198.

31. The *San Jacinto*, one of the navy's early screw frigates, was laid down by the New York Navy Yard in August 1847 and launched on 16 April 1850. An experimental ship measuring 234 feet l.o.a. with a beam of 39 feet and a draft of 16 feet, it was based on new propulsion concepts. Although plagued by balky engines and unreliable machinery, it recorded an interesting and valuable service until it struck a reef near Great Abaco Island on New Year's Day, 1865. Mooney, *Dictionary of American Naval Fighting Ships*, 6:295–97.

32. The 1,246-ton *Cairngorm* was built in 1853 at Aberdeen by Alexander Hall & Sons. It measured 215 feet l.o.a. with the depth of hold of 20 feet. David R. MacGregor, *Fast Sailing Ships: Their Design and Construction, 1775–1875* (London: Conway Maritime Press, Ltd., 1988), 178; David R. MacGregor, *Tea Clippers* (London: Conway Maritime Press, 1983), 58–60.

33. The longest river in China and Asia, Chang Jiang rises in the Tibetan plateau and flows generally east through central China into the East China Sea at Shanghai. Cohen, *Columbia Gazetteer*, 595.

34. Wusong is the outer port of Shanghai, China, on the Chang Jiang (Yangzi) River at the mouth of the Huangpu River. Cohen, *Columbia Gazetteer*, 3496.

35. Formerly the New York pilot boat *Skiddy*, the USS *Fenimore Cooper*, weigh-

ing 95 tons, was purchased by the navy in 1853. It was commissioned the same year to be used as a tender for the North Pacific exploring and surveying expedition surveying expedition with Master H. K. Stevens in command of the boat. In 1859 it was lost in a typhoon near Yokohama. Mooney, *Dictionary of American Naval Fighting Ships*, 2:401.

36. Alphonse Barbot (1824–c.1884) entered the navy as a midshipman in 1838. He was promoted to passed midshipman in 1844, master in 1852, and lieutenant in 1853. He resigned in March 1861 to be appointed a Confederate States Navy master in November 1861. During the Civil War, he was posted aboard the CSS *Arkansas* and later assigned to the Charleston, South Carolina, naval station. Callahan, *List of Officers of the Navy*, 39; Myron J. Smith, Jr., *Civil War Biographies from the Western Waters: 956 Confederate and Union Naval and Military Personnel, Contractors, Politicians, Officials, Steamboat Pilots and Others* (Jefferson, NC: McFarland & Co., 2015), 17.

37. Chen Alin or Chin-ah-lin was a leader of the Fujian faction of the Small Swords or Dagger, a branch of the Triad Society, during the Taiping Rebellion. After the rebellion, he became a comprador at Siam. Elizabeth J. Perry, *Challenging the Mandate of Heaven: Social Protest and State Power in China* (Armonk, NY: M. E. Sharpe, 2002), 55; John Scarth, *Twelve Years in China by a British Resident: The People, the Rebels, and the Mandarins* (Edinburgh: Thomas Constable & Co., 1860), 219.

38. Count M. Kleskowsky was French minister M. de Bourboulon's replacement who was delayed owing to an accident to the French war vessel that was transporting him. Tyler Dennet, *Americans in Eastern Asia: A Critical Study of the Policy of the United States with Reference to China, Japan and Korea in the 19th Century* (New York: Macmillan, 1922), 239.

39. Bo Hai is the northwest arm of the Yellow Sea enclosed by Liaoning, Hebei, and Shandong provinces and Tianjin municipality of China; its northeast extension is the Gulf of Liaogong. *Geographical Dictionary*, 153.

40. Sir John Bowring (1792–1872) was an English political economist, traveler, miscellaneous writer, polyglot, and the fourth governor of Hong Kong (1854–59). G. B. Endacott, *A Biographical Sketch-Book of Early Hong Kong* (Hong Kong: Hong Kong University Press, 2005), 36–44.

41. Dr. Peter Parker (1804–88) founded the Medical Missionary Society in China in 1838. In 1844, Parker was appointed as the part-time secretary and interpreter of the first U.S. legation to China. By 1847, he continued his work with the hospital in Canton and served as a U.S. *chargé d'affaires*. In 1856, he served as the U.S. commissioner plenipotentiary. A year later he returned to America and became a regent of the Smithsonian Institution. Gerald H. Anderson, ed., *Biographical Dictionary of Christian Missions* (New York: Macmillan Reference USA, 1998), 516; Garraty and Carnes, *American National Biography*, 17:40–41.

42. Walter Henry Medhurst (1822–85) was the Chinese interpreter and secretary to the British minister plenipotentiary in China. United States Senate, *The Executive Documents Printed by Order of the Senate of the United States, Second Session, Thirty-fifth Congress, 1858–1859, and Special Session of the Senate of 1859* (Washington, DC: William A. Harris, Printer, 1859), 325.

43. The negotiations were held in tents pitched for the occasion near the Teen Tsin Hae Kow Forts. Chinese commissioners attending were His Excellency Tsung Lun, the imperial commissioner of the Ta Tsing Empire, his Excellency Wan, the Seuen Fang Tachin, his Excellency Shwang, the chintae, Tseen, the taoutae and Hung, the commandant of the forts. *The Executive Documents*, 340.

44. The southern region of Vietnam, whose capital was Saigon or Ho Chi Min City. Cohen, *Columbia Gazetteer*, 684.

45. About 16 miles southeast of Yangtze cape, Gutzlaff island has a rounded shape and is about 500 yards wide and 236 feet high, with a ledge of rocks off its northeastern side. U.S. Hydrographic Office, *Asiatic Pilot Volume III: Coast of China, Yalu River to Hong Kong with Formosa* (Washington, DC: Government Printing Office, 1910), 308.

46. Founded by Danish navigator Vitus Bering in the service of the Russian Navy in 1740, Petropavlovsk-Kamchatski was a harbor town on the southern tip of the Kamchatska peninsula. From August 29 to September 5, 1854, the Anglo-French forces under Rear Admiral David Price attempted several times to take the city but were repulsed. Cohen, *Columbia Gazetteer*, 2419; Alexis S. Troubetzkoy, *A Brief History of the Crimean War: The Causes and Consequences of a Medieval Conflict Fought in a Modern Age* (New York: Carroll & Graf Publishers, 2006), 271–72.

47. Probably the English paddlewheel steamer *Lady Mary Wood* that was built in 1842. In 1845, the 556-ton vessel, named after the wife of Secretary of the Admiralty Charles Wood, arrived in Singapore as the first mail steamer of the Peninsular & Oriental Steam Navigation Company to dispatch mails to China via Ceylon, Penang, Singapore, and Hong Kong. "*Lady Mary Wood*," *P & O Heritage Ship Fact Sheet*, http://www.poheritage.com/Content/Mimsy/Media/factsheet/93628LADY-MARY-WOOD-1842pdf.pdf.

48. Built c. 1844 at the Washington Navy Yard, sloop-of-war *St. Mary's* was commissioned in the fall of 1844 with Commander Theodorus Bailey in command. She was assigned to the Pacific Squadron. Mooney, *Dictionary of American Naval Fighting Ships*, 6:250–51.

49. Sebastopol is a city and port on the inlet of the Black Sea. It was a major naval base during the Crimean War. The Russians defended the city for 349 days against an allied force of British, French, Turks, and Sardinians. At the cost of heavy allied casualties, the fall of Sebastopol would lead to the Russian defeat in the Crimean War. *Encyclopædia Britannica*, 7:450–54; Cohen, *Columbia Gazetteer*, 2875; Preble, *The Opening of Japan*, 383.

50. On December 7, 1854, the *Mississippi* sailed through a typhoon and received considerable damage to its woodwork and rigging. John Wolter, David Ranzan, and John McDonough, *With Commodore Perry to Japan: The Journals of William Speiden, Jr., 1852–1855* (Annapolis, MD: Naval Institute Press, 2013), 235, 250.

51. Commanded by Commander William King Hall, the 1,057-ton paddle steamer *Styx* was launched in 1841. Measuring 180 feet l.o.a. with a 36-foot beam, it broke down in 1866. Colledge, *Ships of the Royal Navy*, 311.

52. A native of Columbus, Ohio, John Macy Walcutt Jr. (1822–80) entered the U.S. Naval Academy at the age of sixteen. He received a commission in 1840 with a

rank of midshipman. During the Mexican War, he performed coast survey and was promoted to passed midshipman in 1846 and master in January 1855. He retired eight months later and became a merchant ship captain based out of China. He retired from active labor in 1860 and returned to the United States in 1862, where he became a farmer in Kentucky. Callahan, *List of Officers of the Navy*, 564; "John Macy Walcutt, Jr," Find A Grave Memorial #52497972, *Find A Grave*, http://www.findagrave.com.

53. Located southwest of the Philippines and north of Java, Borneo is the largest island of the Malay Archipelago and the third-largest island in the world. Cohen, *Columbia Gazetteer*, 403.

54. Ordinary Seaman William L. Millet (1832–54) was born in Salem, Massachusetts. He was interred on Dane's Island, Canton River, near Whampoa. *Logbooks of the U.S.S. Powhatan,* Record Group 24, Records of the Bureau of Naval Personnel; "Inscriptions on the Graves of Americans on Dane's Island, Canton River, Near Whampoa," *New England Historical & Genealogical Register and Antiquarian Journal* 1, no. 3 (July 1857): 256.

55. The six-gun paddle sloop *Barracouta* was launched in 1851 at Pembroke Dockyard. It served in the Pacific theater of the Crimean War, in the Second Opium War, and in the Anglo-Ashanti wars. Commissioned in 1853, the sloop was 190 feet l.o.a. with a beam of 35 feet and a depth of hold of 20 feet. David Lyon and Rif Winfield, *The Sail & Steam Navy List: All the Ships of the Royal Navy, 1815–1889* (London: Chatham, 2004), 162.

56. Built by William H. Brown of New York, the 1,003-ton *Pacific* was launched in 1850. It measured 225 feet l.o.a. with a beam of 30 feet. In 1861, the vessel sank in the Columbia River near Coffin Rock. By 1863, it was returned to service, and in 1875 it collided with the *Orpheus* near Cape Flattery and sank. John H. Kemble, *The Panama Route, 1848–1869* (New York: Da Capo Press, 1972), 241–42.

57. Tablotype or Calotype is the first negative-positive photographic process, introduced in 1840 by British scientist and inventor William Henry Fox Talbot (1800–1877). Using paper coated with silver iodide, it allowed for multiple copies from a single negative. Jae Emerling, *Photography: History and Theory* (London: Routledge, 2012), 215.

Mezzograph is a halftone made with a grain screen and having a grained surface instead of crossline screen dots. Josef Maria Eder, *History of Photography*, translated by Edward Epstean (New York: Columbia University Press, 1945), 636.

Chapter Five

1. Built by William H. Brown of New York, the *Arctic* was launched in 1850 for the Collins Line of New York. A 2,856-ton ship, it measured 285 feet l.o.a. with a beam of 46 feet. In 1854, it collided with the French steamship *Vesta* near Cape Race and sank. David W. Shaw, *The Sea Shall Embrace Them: The Tragic Story of the Steamship Arctic* (New York: Free Press, 2002), 22–25, 112–13.

2. Robert S. Sturgis served as vice consul at Canton from December 1854 to

September 1855. He arrived in China in 1845, and served as a clerk for Russell & Company. Hoh-cheung Mui and Lorna H. Mui, eds. *William Melrose in China 1845–1855: The Letters of a Scottish Tea Merchant* (Edinburgh, T. & A. Constable, Ltd., 1973), 25.

3. Launched in 1856 by the Norfolk Navy Yard, the 268-foot-long steamer screw frigate *Colorado* had a beam of 52 feet and a draft of 24 feet. With Captain W. H. Gardner in command, the vessel was commissioned in 1858. Mooney, *Dictionary of American Naval Fighting Ships*, 2:144–45.

Launched in December 1855 at the Washington Navy Yard, the wooden steam frigate *Minnesota* measured 264 feet l.o.a. with a beam of fifty-one feet and a draft of twenty-three feet. She served in the East India Squadron and was decommissioned in 1859, remaining in ordinary until the outbreak of the Civil War. Mooney, *Dictionary of American Naval Fighting Ships*, IV: 372–374.

4. Seaman Thomas Schultz. *Logbooks of the U.S.S. Powhatan*.

5. The 700-ton *Vincennes* was launched in 1826 at New York. The 127-foot-long ship had a beam of 33 feet and a draft of 16 feet. During its forty-one years of service, the vessel compiled an outstanding record of achievements in polar exploration, global cartography, and commercial expansion and protection. Mooney, *Dictionary of American Naval Fighting Ships*, 7:525–27.

6. On December 23, 1854, the Ansei Tokai earthquake, with an estimated magnitude of 8.4 on the Richter scale, shook Japan and surroundings. A tsunami more than 20 feet high destroyed most of Shimoda, including Putyatin's ships, with the exception of *Diana*, which was badly damaged and which soon sank as it attempted to sail to Heda for repairs. Tatsuo Usami, "Study of Historical Earthquakes in Japan," *Bulletin of the Earthquake Research Institute* 54 (1979): 416; Daisuke Sugawara et al., "A Huge Sand Dome Formed by the 1854 Earthquake Tsunami in Suruga Bay, Central Japan," *ISET Journal of Earthquake Technology* 42, no. 4 (December 2005): 147–48; Mitsuo Yesaki, *Sutebusuton: A Japanese Village on the British Columbia Coast* (Vancouver: Peninsula Publishing Co., 2003), 6.

7. The frigate *Diana* had an immense battery of four long sixty-eights and forty long thirty-twos. Gideon notes this information in a letter of January 28, 1855 to his wife, Lide.

8. According to the logbook of the USS *Powhatan*, the ship felt a heavy shock of an earthquake at 10:30 P.M. and a slight shock at 11:15 P.M. on January 28, 1855, while anchored in the harbor of Shimoda.

9. According to the USS *Powhatan*'s logbook, two Japanese sailors christianized Peter Japanese and Frank Howard were saved by the American whaler *Isaac Howland* and brought to the *Powhatan* by the French whaler *Napoleon III*.

10. Heda was a village located in the Tagata District within the Shizuoka Prefecture on the Suruga Bay coast of Izu Peninsula on the island of Honshu, twenty-two miles east of Shizuoka. Cohen, *Columbia Gazetteer*, 1259.

11. On February 7, 1855, Russian admiral Putyatin successfully negotiated a Russo-Japanese Treaty of Amity with the Japanese empire. This treaty stipulated the opening of three ports (Shimoda, Hakodate, and Nagasaki), authorized the post-

ing of consuls at Hakodate and Shimoda, provided for reciprocal extraterritoriality, and delineated the Russo-Japanese frontiers. *Kodansha Encyclopedia of Japan* (Tokyo: Kodansha, 1983), 6:340–41.

12. Wilhelm Lobscheid (1822–93) was sent to Hong Kong by the Rhenish Missionary Society in 1848. In 1850, he left for Europe and returned to Hong Kong in 1853 as the medical agent of the Chinese Evangelization Society. With his ability in the Chinese language and some knowledge of Japanese, Lobscheid served as a Dutch interpreter on *Powhatan*'s voyage to Japan in 1855 in order to ratify the U.S.–Japan commercial treaty. In 1861, he left for Europe and again returned to Hong Kong in 1862. *Memorials of Protestant Missionaries to the Chinese: Giving a List of Their Publications, and Obituary Notices of the Deceased* (Shanghai: American Presbyterian Mission Press, 1867), 184; Laura Mason, "Wilhelm Lobscheid," *Biographical Dictionary of Chinese Christianity*, http://www.bdcconline.net/en/stories/l/lobscheid-wilhelm.php.

13. Built in 1852 by Thomas Collyer at Sing Sing, New York, the steamer *Confucius*, commanded by Captain T. D. Dearbourn, had orders to tow vessels up and down the Yangtze-Kiang River. "Once Famous for Shipbuilding," *New York Times*, April 5, 1896, 12; *Shanghae Almanac for the Bissextile or Leap Year 1856 and Miscellany* (Shanghai: "N. C. Herald" Office, 1856), 9; *The Straits Times and Singapore Journal of Commerce*, August 30, 1853, 5.

14. The clipper ship *Wild Duck* was built by George Raynes of Portsmouth, New Hampshire, with a measurement of 175 feet l.o.a. and a depth of 20 feet. The figurehead was an eagle on the wing. In 1856, it ran ashore on the bank of the river Min. Howe and Matthews, *American Clipper Ships*, 702–3.

15. Robert C. Murphy became the first official U.S. consul in Shanghai in March 1854. Johnson, *Congressional Dictionary* (1855), 45; Griffin, *Clippers and Consuls*, 363–64.

16. *Young America* was launched in 1853 from the yard of William H. Webb in New York. The 1961-ton extreme clipper ship had a beam of 43 feet and a draft of 22 feet. In 1883, it sailed under the Austrian flag as *Miroslav*. Howe and Matthews, *American Clipper Ships*, 734, 742.

17. John D. Storm (c. 1828–55) of Schoharie County, Ohio, died on February 2 after a short illness. Gideon, in a letter of February 2, 1855, described him as "one of the largest and strongest men in the ship." "John D. Storm," Find A Grave Memorial# 164030996, *Find A Grave*, http://www.findagrave.com.

18. French frigates *Jeanne d'Arc* and *Constantine*. *Logbooks of the U.S.S. Powhatan.*

19. Guam is the largest, most populous, and southernmost of the Mariana Islands. First visited in 1521 by Ferdinand Magellan, Guam was under Spanish rule until 1898. Cohen, *Columbia Gazetteer*, 1185.

20. In 1852, the Peninsular & Oriental Steam Navigation Company began a Sydney–Singapore mail service with the steamer *Chusan*. It ran every two months by way of the south coast of Australia until the company was forced to abandon the service in 1855 owing to mounting losses. Paul Battersby, *To the Islands: White Australians and the Malay Archipelago since 1788* (Lanham, MD: Lexington Books, 2007), 23.

21. Euchre is a nineteenth-century trick-making card game most commonly played with four people in two partnerships with a deck of twenty-four or thirty-two standard playing cards. It can be traced back to the eighteenth-century French game Triomphe. John W. Keller, *The Game of Euchre* (New York: Frederick A. Stokes, 1887), 9–10.

22. Master's mate John Redman Coxe Lewis (1834–98) co-wrote *Bluejackets with Perry in Japan; A Day-by-Day Account Kept by Master's Mate John R.C. Lewis and Cabin Boy William B. Allen*. "Col John Redman Coxe Lewis," Find A Grave Memorial #16465358, *Find A Grave*, http://www.findagrave.com.

23. According to *Powhatan*'s official logbook, his last name was Westcott.

24. According to the logbook, a boat of ten marines under the command of Lieutenant Lowry was sent to the *Caroline Dow*. Eight of the latter's crew were put in irons and sent to Whampoa.

25. New York native John Dinnen (c.1826–55) was interred in the Macao Protestant Cemetery. Lindsay Ride and May Ride, *An East India Company Cemetery: Protestant Burials in Macao*, edited by Bernard Mellor (Hong Kong: Hong Kong University Press, 1996), 94–95.

26. Washington F. Hickman (c.1823–55) was interred in the Macao Protestant Cemetery. Ride and Ride, *An East India Company Cemetery*, 95–96.

Chapter Six

1. Built at New York City in 1842, the 229-ton *Jacob Bell* was a sidewheel steamer 141 feet l.o.a. with a beam of 21 feet and depth of 8 feet. During the American Civil War, it was commissioned in 1861 with Lieutenant Edward P. McCrea in command and served in the Peninsular Campaign and the North Atlantic Blockading Squadron. Howe and Matthews, *American Clipper Ships*, 289; Mooney, *Dictionary of American Naval Fighting Ships*, 3:483.

2. At 3 P.M. on August 3, 1855, under the command of Commander William Abdy Fellowes, *Rattler* was joined by HMS *Eaglet* and a crew from the USS *Powhatan* in freeing four ships taken by pirates at Ku[h]lan, China. At 8:30 P.M. on August 5, report was made of "an engagement with a Piratical fleet of Junks in Tylo [Ty-ho] Bay which resulted in the capture of 17 Junks with many of the Pirates." An estimated five hundred pirates were killed and another thousand taken prisoner, with the loss of only six British and four American lives. Lincoln P. Paine, *Warships of the World to 1900* (New York: Houghton Mifflin Co., 1997), 145; *Logbooks of the U.S.S. Powhatan*.

3. HMS *Eaglet* was a paddle vessel hired by the British from 1855 to 1857. Colledge, *Ships of the Royal Navy*, 122.

4. Eldest son of Rear Admiral Sir Thomas Fellowes, William Abdy Fellowes (1815–78) entered the British Navy in 1827 as a first-class volunteer. He became a lieutenant in 1840 and was promoted to commander in 1850 and captain in 1856, and retired as a rear admiral in 1874. William R. O'Byrne, *A Naval Biographical Dictionary* (London: John Murray, 1849), 352; Peter Davis, "William Abdy Fellowes, R.N.," http://www.pdavis.nl/ShowBiog.php?id=992.

5. Landsmen Isaac Coe and Joseph A. Halsey and seaman John Pepper were killed. Marine Samuel Mullard, Lieutenant Pegram, landsman J. Pendergast, Lieutenant Rolando, captain of the afterguard William Taylor, seaman Charles Tingwell, marine P. Walderschmidt, marine B. Adamson, marine Frederick Hommell, and seaman Joshua Lewis were wounded. *Indian Mail and Register of Intelligence for British and Foreign India, China and All Parts of the East* (London: William H. Allen & Co., 1856), 14:48.

6. Able Seaman George Mitchell, carpenter's crew James Silvers, gunner John Massey, and private William Oliff were killed. Gunner John Lindsay, gunner David Lloyd, boy first class James Paull, able seaman James Poulter, gunner William Robinson, stoker Richard Clark, and able seaman John Eade were wounded. *Indian Mail and Register of Intelligence*, 14:48.

7. Marine private Benjamin Franklin Adamson was mortally wounded from a gunshot and died on the British hospital ship *Hercules*. Harry Allanson Ellsworth, *One Hundred Eighty Landings of United States Marines 1800–1934* (Washington, DC: History & Museums Division Headquarters, U.S. Marine Corps, 1974), 24.

8. Marine private Samuel Mullard was mortally wounded from burns and died on the British hospital ship *Hercules*. Ellsworth, *One Hundred Eighty Landings of United States Marines 1800–1934*, 24.

9. Lasting from June 30, 1855, to January 3, 1856, the Santal rebellion was a native rebellion in present-day Jharkhand, in eastern India, by the Santal people against both the British colonial authority and the upper-caste zamindari system. Atis Dasgupta, "Some Aspects of the Santal Rebellion of 1855–56," *Social Scientist* 41, nos. 9–10 (2013): 69–74.

10. The USS *Merrimack* was launched at the Boston Navy Yard on June 15, 1855. The 3,200-ton screw frigate was under the command of Captain Garrett J. Pendergrast. The vessel was 255 feet l.o.a. with a beam of 38 feet, a depth of hold of 27 feet, and a draft of 24 feet. In 1857, it became the flagship of the Pacific Squadron. During the Civil War, the U.S. Navy sank the frigate to preclude capture. In desperate need of ships, the Confederates raised the *Merrimack* and rebuilt it as an ironclad ram, commissioning it CSS *Virginia*. Mooney, *Dictionary of American Naval Fighting Ships*, 4:337–38.

11. William H. Porter. *Logbooks of the U.S.S. Powhatan*.

12. Built by George Steers, the *Sunny South* was launched at Williamsburg, New York, in 1854. The 776-ton extreme clipper was 164-foot l.o.a. with a beam of 31 feet and a depth of hold of 16 feet. It had a scary monster as figurehead. The clipper was built to the order of Napier, Johnson & Company of New York and had Captain Michael B. Gregory as its first commander. In 1859, it was sold at Havana, renamed *Emanuela,* and employed in the slave trade. In 1860, it was captured by the British and sent to Mauritius. Howe and Matthews, *American Clipper Ships*, 638–40.

13. George Williams. *Logbooks of the U.S.S. Powhatan*.

Bibliography

Books

Allardice, Bruce S. *Confederate Colonels: A Biographical Register*. Columbia: University of Missouri Press, 2008.

Barnes, James J., and Patience P. Barnes. *The American Civil War through British Eyes: Dispatches from British Diplomats*. Kent, OH: Kent State University Press, 2003.

Battersby, Paul. *To the Islands: White Australians and the Malay Archipelago since 1788*. Lanham, MD: Lexington Books, 2007.

Beasley, William G. *The Perry Mission to Japan, 1853–1854*. Richmond, Surrey, England: Japan Library, 2002.

Beers, Henry P. *Guide to the Archives of the Government of the Confederate States of America*. Washington, DC: Government Printing Office, 1968.

Bennett, Frank M. *The Steam Navy of the United States: A History of the Growth of the Steam Vessel of War in the U.S. Navy, and of the Naval Engineer Corps*. Westport, CT: Greenwood Press, 1972.

Billings, John D. *Hardtack and Coffee or The Unwritten Story of Army Life*. Lincoln: University of Nebraska Press, 1993.

Blake, Richard. *Religion in the British Navy, 1815–1879: Piety and Professionalism*. Woodbridge, Suffolk, UK: Boydell Press, 2014.

Bradford, Gershom. *A Glossary of Sea Terms*. New York: Yachting, Inc., 1927.

———. *The Mariner's Dictionary*. Barre, MA: Barre Publishers, 1972.

Brain, Belle M. *All About Japan: Stories of Sunrise Land Told for Little Folks*. London: Fleming H. Revell Co., 1905.

Brooke, George M., Jr. *Big Guns of the Confederacy: The Journal and Letters of John M. Brooke*. Columbia: University of South Carolina Press, 2002.

Bryant, William Cullen, II, and Thomas G. Voss, eds. *The Letters of William Cullen Bryant*. New York: Fordham University Press, 1992.

Burg, B. R., ed. *An American Seafarer in the Age of Sail: The Erotic Diaries of Philip C. Van Buskirk 1851–1870*. New Haven: Yale University Press, 1994.

Callahan, Edward W. *List of Officers of the Navy of the United States and of the Marine Corps from 1775 to 1900, comprising a complete register of all present and former commissioned, warranted, and appointed officers of the United States Navy, and of the Marine Corps, regular and volunteer*. New York: L. R. Hamersly & Co., 1901.

Casstevens, Frances Harding. *George W. Alexander and Castle Thunder: A Confederate Prison and Its Commandant*. Jefferson, NC: McFarland & Co., 2004.

Clayton, Bruce D. *Shotokan's Secret: The Hidden Truth behind Karate's Fighting Origins*. Valencia, CA: Black Belt Books, 2004.

Coles, David, and David Hartman. *Biographical Rosters of Florida's Confederate and Union Soldiers, 1861–1865*. Wilmington, NC: Broadfoot Publishing Co., 1995.

Colledge, J. J. *Ships of the Royal Navy: The Complete Record of All Fighting Ships of the Royal Navy*. Mechanicsburg, PA: Stackpole Books, 2003.

Cordell, Eugene Fauntleroy. *Historical Sketch of the University of Maryland School of Medicine (1807–1890)*. Baltimore: Press of Isaac Friedenwald, 1891.

Dennet, Tyler. *Americans in Eastern Asia: A Critical Study of the Policy of the United States with Reference to China, Japan and Korea in the 19th Century*. New York: Macmillan, 1922.

Denslow, William R. *10,000 Famous Freemasons*. Whitefish, MT: Kessinger Publishing, 2004.

Dunham, Valgene. *Allegheny to Appomattox: The Life and Letters of Private William Whitlock of the 188th New York Volunteers*. Syracuse, NY: Syracuse University Press, 2013.

Durfee, Calvin. *Obituary Report, 1865–1875*. North Adams, MA: James T. Robinson & Son, 1875.

Dye, Ira. *Uriah Levy: Reformer of the Antebellum Navy*. Gainesville: University Press of Florida, 2006.

Eastman, Margaret Middleton Rivers. *Hidden History of Civil War Charleston*. Charleston: History Press, 2012.

Eder, Josef Maria. *History of Photography*. Translated by Edward Epstean. New York: Columbia University Press, 1945.

Effert, Rudolph. *Royal Cabinets and Auxiliary Branches: Origins of the National Museum of Ethnology, 1816–1883*. Leiden: CNWS Publications, 2008.

Ellsworth, Harry Allanson. *One Hundred Eighty Landings of United States Marines 1800–1934*. Washington, DC: History and Museums Division Headquarters, U.S. Marine Corps, 1974.

Emerling, Jae. *Photography: History and Theory*. New York: Routledge, 2012.

Endacott, G. B. *A Biographical Sketch-Book of Early Hong Kong*. Hong Kong: Hong Kong University Press, 2005.

Erickson, Bruce T. *Encyclopedia of Nineteenth-century Photography*. Edited by John Hannavy. New York: Routledge, 2008.

Freeman, Douglas S. *R. E. Lee: A Biography*. New York: Charles Scribner's Sons, 1935.

Golovnin, Vasilii. *Around the World on the Kamchatka, 1817–1819*. Translated by Ella Lury Wiswell. Honolulu: Hawaiian Historical Society and University Press of Hawaii, 1979.

Griffin, Eldon. *Clippers and Consuls: American Consular and Commercial Relations with Eastern Asia, 1845–1860*. Ann Arbor, MI: Edwards Brothers, 1938.

Gulick, Edward V. *Peter Parker and the Opening of China*. Cambridge, MA: Harvard University Press, 1973.

Hamersly, Lewis Randolph, ed. *The Records of Living Officers of the U.S. Navy & Marine Corps*. Philadelphia: J. B. Lippincott & Co, 1878.

Hawks, Francis L. *Commodore Perry and the Opening of Japan: Narrative of the Expedition of an American Squadron to the China Seas and Japan, 1852–1854: The Official Report of the Expedition to Japan*. Stroud, UK: Nonsuch, 2005.

Heine, Wilhelm. *With Perry to Japan: A Memoir*. Translated by Frederic Trautmann. Honolulu: University of Hawaii Press, 1990.

Hildreth, Richard. *Japan and the Japanese*. Boston: Bradley, Dayton & Co., 1860.

Hinckley, Erik S., and Tom Ledoux, eds. *They Went to War: A Biographical Register of the Green Mountain State in the Civil War*. Victoria, BC: Trafford Publishing, 2010.

Howe, Octavius T., and Frederick C. Matthews. *American Clipper Ships, 1833–1858*. New York: Argosy Antiquarian, 1967.

Hoyle, Edmond. *A Short Treatise on the Game of Whist*. London: T. Osborne, 1750.

Indian Mail and Register of Intelligence for British and Foreign India, China and All Parts of the East. London: William H. Allen & Co., 1856.

Johnson, John M., compiler. *Congressional Directory for the First Session of the Thirty-second Congress of the United States of America*. Washington, DC: Gideon & Co., 1852.

———. *Congressional Directory for the Second Session of the Thirty-second Congress of the United States of America*. Washington, DC: Gideon & Co., 1853.

———. *Congressional Directory for the Second Session of the Thirty-third Congress of the United States of America*. Washington, DC: Gideon & Co., 1855.

Johnston, James D. *China and Japan: Being a Narrative of the Cruise of the U.S. Steam-Frigate* Powhatan *in the Years 1857, '58, '59, and '60 including an Account of the Japanese Embassy to the United States, Illustrated with Life Portraits of the Embassadors and Their Principal Officials*. Philadelphia: Charles DeSilver, 1860.

Jordan, John W., ed. *Colonial and Revolutionary Families of Pennsylvania: Genealogical and Personal Memoirs*. Baltimore: Clearfield Co., 2004. Reprint; originally published 1911.

Keller, John W. *The Game of Euchre*. New York: Frederick A. Stokes, 1887.

Kemble, John H. *The Panama Route, 1848–1869*. New York: Da Capo Press, 1972.

Kemish, S. B. *The Japanese Empire: Its Physical, Political and Social Condition and History*. Japan in English. London: Ganesha Publishing, 2003.

King, Dean, John B. Hattendorf, and J. Worth Estes. *A Sea of Words: A Lexicon and Companion for Patrick O'Brian's Seafaring Tales*. New York: Henry Holt, 1995.

Knoblock, Glenn A. *The American Clipper Ship, 1845–1920: A Comprehensive History, with a Listing of Builders and Their Ships*. Jefferson, NC: McFarland & Co., 2014.

Lamb, Martha J., ed. *Magazine of American History with Notes and Queries*. Vol. 26. New York: Historical Publication Co., July–December 1891.

Langley, Harold D. *Social Reform in the United States Navy, 1798–1862*. Urbana: University of Illinois Press, 1967.

Lawrence, James B. *China and Japan, and a Voyage Thither: An Account of a Cruise in the Waters of the East Indies, China, and Japan*. Hartford, CT: Press of Case, Lockwood & Brainard, 1870.

Lee, Edmund Jennings, ed. *Lee of Virginia, 1642–1892: Biographical and Genealogical Sketches of the Descendants of Colonel Richard Lee*. Philadelphia: Edmund Jennings Lee, 1895.

Linn, John Blair. *History of Centre and Clinton Counties, Pennsylvania*. Philadelphia: Louis H. Everts, 1883.

Lyon, David, and Rif Winfield. *The Sail & Steam Navy List: All the Ships of the Royal Navy, 1815–1889*. London: Chatham, 2004.

MacGregor, David R. *Fast Sailing Ships: Their Design and Construction, 1775–1875*. London: Conway Maritime Press, Ltd., 1988.

———. *Tea Clippers*. London: Conway Maritime Press, 1983.

Memorials of Protestant Missionaries to the Chinese: Giving a List of Their Publications, and Obituary Notices of the Deceased. Shanghai: American Presbyterian Mission Press, 1867.

Millett, Alan Reed, and Jack Shulimson. *Commandants of the Marine Corps*. Annapolis, MD: Naval Institute Press, 2004.

Montez, Lola. *The Lectures of Lola Montez (Countess of Landsfield), including Her Autobiography*. New York: Rudd & Carleton, 1858.

Mooney, James L. *Dictionary of American Naval Fighting Ships*. Washington, DC: Navy Department, Office of the Chief of Naval Operations, Naval History Division, 1959–81.

Morison, Samuel Eliot. *"Old Bruin": Commodore Matthew C. Perry, 1794–1858*. Boston: Little, Brown, 1967.

Morris, Charles. *Men of the Century, an Historical Work: Giving Portraits and Sketches of Eminent Citizens of the United States*. Philadelphia: I. R. Hamersly & Co., 1896.

Morris, Robert. *Congressional Directory for the Third Session of the Thirty-fourth Congress of the United States of America*. Washington, DC: Gideon & Co., 1856.

Mui, Hoh-cheung, and Lorna H. Mui, eds. *William Melrose in China 1845–1855: The Letters of a Scottish Tea Merchant*. Edinburgh: T. & A. Constable, Ltd., 1973.

Nesser, Robert W. *Ship Names of the United States Navy: Their Meaning and Origin*. New York: Moffat, Yard & Co, 1921.

Paine, Lincoln P. *Ships of the World*. New York: Houghton Mifflin, 1997.

Parker, F. Calvin. *The Japanese Sam Patch: Saga of a Servant*. Notre Dame, IN: Cross Cultural Publications, 2001.

Perry, Elizabeth J. *Challenging the Mandate of Heaven: Social Protest and State Power in China*. Armonk, NY: M. E. Sharpe, 2002.

Pineau, Roger, ed. *The Personal Journal of Commodore Matthew C. Perry*. Washington, DC: Smithsonian Institution Press, 1968.

Powell, William H., and Edward Shippen, eds. *Officers of the Army and Navy Who Served in the Civil War*. Philadelphia: L. R. Hamersly & Co., 1892.

Preble, George Henry. *The Opening of Japan: A Diary of Discovery in the Far East, 1853–1856*. Edited by Boleslaw Szczesniak. Norman: University of Oklahoma Press, 1962.

Register of the Commissioned and Warrant Officers of the United States Navy and Marine Corps and Reserve Officers on Active Duty. Washington, DC: Government Printing Office, 1863.

Register of the Commissioned and Warrant Officers of the United States Navy and Marine Corps and Reserve Officers on Active Duty. Washington, DC: U.S. Government Printing Office, 1881.

Register of the Commissioned, Warrant, and Volunteer Officers of the Navy of the United States, including Officers of the Marine Corps and Others to January 1, 1865. Washington, DC: Government Printing Office, 1865.

Representative Men and Old Families of Rhode Island: Genealogical Records and Historical Sketches of Prominent and Representative Citizens and of Many of the Old Families. Chicago: J. H. Beers & Co., 1908.

Ride, Lindsay, and May Ride. *An East India Company Cemetery: Protestant Burials in Macao*. Edited by Bernard Mellor. Hong Kong: Hong Kong University Press, 1996.

Roberts, William H. *Civil War Ironclads: The U.S. Navy and Industrial Mobilization*. Baltimore: Johns Hopkins University Press, 2002.

Sakanishi, Sho, ed. *A Private Journal of John Glendy Sproston, U.S.N.* Tokyo: Sophia University, 1940.

Scarth, John. *Twelve Years in China by a British Resident: The People, the Rebels, and the Mandarins*. Edinburgh: Thomas Constable & Co., 1860.

Schroeder, John H. *Matthew Calbraith Perry: Antebellum Sailor and Diplomat*. Annapolis, MD: Naval Institute Press, 2001.

———. *Shaping a Maritime Empire: The Commercial and Diplomatic Role of the American Navy, 1829–1861*. Westport, CT: Greenwood Press, 1985.

Scott, J. L. *60th Virginia Infantry*. Lynchburg, VA: H. E. Howard, 1997.

Shaw, David W. *The Sea Shall Embrace Them: The Tragic Story of the Steamship* Arctic. New York: Free Press, 2002.

Smith, Myron J., Jr. *Civil War Biographies from the Western Waters: 956 Confederate and Union Naval and Military Personnel, Contractors, Politicians, Officials, Steamboat Pilots and Others*. Jefferson, NC: McFarland & Co., 2015.

Spalding, J. Willet. *The Japan Expedition: Japan and Around the World: An Account of Three Visits to the Japanese Empire, with Sketches of Madeira, St. Helena, Cape of Good Hope, Mauritius, Ceylon, Singapore, China, and Loo-Choo*. New York: Redfield, 1855.

State Street Trust Co. *Some Ships of the Clipper Ship Era, Their Builders, Owners and Captains*. Boston: Printed for State Street Trust Co., 1913.

Statler, Oliver. *The Black Ship Scroll: An Account of the Perry Expedition at Shimoda in 1854 and the Lively Beginnings of People-to-People Relations between Japan*

& America, Based on Contemporary Records, with translations by Richard Lane, Ph.D., and scroll paintings in full color by an anonymous Japanese eyewitness. Rutland, VT: Charles E. Tuttle Co., 1964.

Swann, Leonard Alexander. *John Roach, Maritime Entrepreneur: The Years as Naval Contractor, 1862–1886.* Annapolis, MD: Naval Institute Press, 1965.

Troubetzkoy, Alexis S. *A Brief History of the Crimean War: The Causes and Consequences of a Medieval Conflict Fought in a Modern Age.* New York: Carroll & Graf, 2006.

United States. Navy Department. *Laws, Regulations, Circulars, Orders, Decisions Relating to the U.S. Naval Engineer Corps.* London: Forgotten Books, 2013. Reprint; originally published 1871.

United States Hydrographic Office. *Asiatic Pilot. Volume II—The Japan Islands.* Washington, DC: Government Printing Office, 1920.

United States Hydrographic Office. *Asiatic Pilot: Volume III—Coast of China, Yalu River to Hong Kong with Formosa.* Washington, DC: Government Printing Office, 1910.

United States Senate. *The Executive Documents Printed by Order of the Senate of the United States, Second Session, Thirty-fifth Congress, 1858–1859, and Special Session of the Senate of 1859.* Washington, DC: William A. Harris, Printer, 1859.

United States Service Magazine. New York: C. B. Richardson, 1864.

Valle, James E. *Rocks and Shoals: Order of Discipline in the Old Navy, 1800–1861.* Annapolis, MD: Naval Institute Press, 1980.

Van de Walle, W. F., and Noel Golvers, eds. *The History of the Relations between the Low Countries and China in the Qing Era (1644–1911).* Leuven, Belgium: Leuven University Press, 2003.

Van Dyke, Paul A., ed. *Americans and Macao: Trade, Smuggling, and Diplomacy on the South China Coast.* Hong Kong: Hong Kong University Press, 2012.

Vasile, Ronald S., Raymond B. Manning, and Rafael Lemaire. *William Stimpson's Journal from the North Pacific Exploring Expedition, 1853–1856.* Tokyo: Carcinological Society of Japan, 2005.

Vincent, Francis, ed. *Vincent's Semi-Annual United States Register: A Work in Which the Principal Events of Every Half-Year Occurring in the United States Are Recorded, Each Arranged under the Day of Its Date.* Philadelphia: Francis Vincent, 1860.

Walworth, Arthur. *Black Ships off Japan: The Story of the Opening Up of Japan by Commodore Perry's Expedition in 1853.* Hamden, CT: Archon Books, 1966.

Watson, James. *The Dog Book: A Popular History of the Dog, with Practical Information as to Care and Management of House, Kennel, and Exhibition Dogs; and Descriptions of All the Important Breeds.* New York: Doubleday, Page & Co., 1906.

Wiley, Peter Booth, and Korogi Ichiro. *Yankees in the Land of the Gods: Commodore Perry and the Opening of Japan.* New York: Viking, 1990.

Williams, Frederick Wells. *The Life and Letters of Samuel Wells Williams, LL.D.: Missionary Diplomatist, Sinologue.* New York: G. P. Putnam's Sons, 1889.

Winfield, Rif. *British Warships in the Age of Sail, 1817–1863: Design, Construction, Careers and Fates.* Barnsley, S. Yorkshire, UK: Seaforth Publishing, 2014.

Wolter, John, David Ranzan, and John McDonough. *With Commodore Perry to*

Japan: The Journals of William Speiden, Jr., 1852–1855. Annapolis, MD: Naval Institute Press, 2013.

Wynne, Mervyn Llewelyn. *Triad and Tabut: A Survey of the Origin and Diffusion of Chinese and Mohamedan Secret Societies in the Malay Peninsula A.D. 1800–1935*. Singapore: Government Printing Office, 1941.

Yesaki, Mitsuo. *Sutebusuton: A Japanese Village on the British Columbia Coast*. Vancouver, BC: Peninsula Publishing, 2003.

Reference Works

The American Heritage Dictionary of the English Language. 3rd ed. Boston: Houghton Mifflin, 1992.

Anderson, Gerald H., ed. *Biographical Dictionary of Christian Missions*. New York: Macmillan Reference USA, 1998.

Biographical Directory of the United States Congress 1774–2005: The Continental Congress September 5, 1774, to October 21, 1788, and the Congress of the United States from the First through the One Hundred Eighth Congresses, March 4, 1789, to January 3, 2005, Inclusive. Washington, DC: Government Printing Office, 2005.

Brown, John Howard, ed. *Lamb's Biographical Dictionary of the United States*. Boston: James H. Lamb Co., 1900.

Cohen, Saul B. *The Columbia Gazetteer of the World*. New York: Columbia University Press, 1998.

Encyclopædia Britannica: A Dictionary of Arts, Sciences, Literature and General Information. 11th ed. Cambridge: Cambridge University Press, 1911.

Encyclopedia Canadiana. Toronto: Grolier of Canada, 1977.

Encyclopedia of People of Okinawan History. Naha: Okinawa Bunka-sha, 1996.

Garraty, John A., and Mark C. Carnes, eds. *American National Biography*. New York: Oxford University Press, 1999.

Gaynor, Frank, ed. *The New Military and Naval Dictionary*. New York: Philosophical Library, 1951.

Gillispie, Charles Coulston, ed. *Dictionary of Scientific Biography*. New York: Charles Scribner's Sons, 1970.

Harris, William H., and Judith S. Levy, eds. *The New Columbia Encyclopedia*. New York: Columbia University Press, 1975.

Harvard Memorial Biographies. Cambridge, MA: Sever & Francis, 1866.

Johnson, Allen, and Dumas Malone, eds. *Dictionary of American Biography*. New York: Charles Scribner's Sons, 1958.

Kellogg, Day Otis, ed. *New American Supplement to the New Werner Edition of the Encyclopedia Britannica: A Standard Work of Reference in Art, Literature, Science, History, Geography, Commerce, Biography, Discovery and Invention*. New York: Werner Co., 1903.

Kodansha Encyclopedia of Japan. Tokyo: Kodansha, 1983.

Lee, Sidney, Leslie Stephen, and George Smith, eds. *Dictionary of National Biography*. London: Oxford University Press, 1938.

Logbooks of the U.S.S. Powhatan. Record Group 24. Records of the Bureau of Naval Personnel, National Archives Building, Washington DC.

Louis-Frédéric. *Japan Encyclopedia*. Translated by Kathe Roth. Cambridge, MA: Belknap Press of Harvard University Press, 2002.

Magnusson, Magnus, ed. *Cambridge Biographical Dictionary*. Cambridge: Cambridge University Press, 1990.

Matthew, H. C. G., and Brian Harrison, eds. *Oxford Dictionary of National Biography*. Oxford: Oxford University Press, 2004.

Merriam Webster's Biographical Dictionary. Springfield, MA: Merriam-Webster, 1995.

Merriam-Webster's Geographical Dictionary. 3rd ed. Springfield, MA: Merriam-Webster, 2007.

National Cyclopaedia of American Biography. New York: J. T. White, 1892.

O'Byrne, R. *A Naval Biographical Dictionary*. London: John Murray, 1849.

Onofrio, Jan, ed. *Tennessee Biographical Dictionary*. St. Clair Shores, MI: Somerset Publishers, 2000.

Papinot, Edmond. *Historical and Geographical Dictionary of Japan*. New York: Frederick Ungar Publishing Co., 1968. Originally published 1910, republished 1964, second printing 1968.

Shavit, David. *The United States in Asia: A Historical Dictionary*. Westport, CT: Greenwood Press, 1990.

Tucker, Spencer C., ed. *The Civil War Naval Encyclopedia*. Santa Barbara, CA: ABC-CLIO, 2011.

Webster's Third New International Dictionary of the English Language, Unabridged. Springfield, MA: Merriam-Webster, 1986.

Wilson, James Grant, and John Fiske, eds. *Appleton's Cyclopaedia of American Biography*. New York: D. Appleton & Co., 1887.

Articles

"Alex. Henderson." *Harper Weekly* 49, no. 2301 (January 26, 1901): 97.

Craddock, Stephen Culver. "'To the Honor and Credit of the Country': A History of the Warships Mississippi." *Journal of Mississippi History* 54 (May 1992): 129–48.

Dasgupta, Atis. "Some Aspects of the Santal Rebellion of 1855–56." *Social Scientist* 41, nos. 9–10 (2013): 69–74.

"The Famous Dead of 1870." *Appleton's Journal: A Magazine of General Literature* 5, no. 96 (January 28, 1871): 111–13.

Hughes, George. "The Small Knife Rebels (An Unpublished Chapter of Amoy History)." *China Review* 1, no. 4 (1872): 244–48.

"Inscriptions on the Graves of Americans on Dane's Island, Canton River, near Whampoa." *New England Historical & Genealogical Register and Antiquarian Journal* 1, no. 3 (July 1857): 256.

Morison, Samuel Eliot. "Commodore Perry's Japan Expedition Press and Shipboard Theatre." *Proceedings of the American Antiquarian Society* 77, no. 1 (1967): 35–43.

"Obituary." *American Machinist: A Practical Journal of Machine Construction* 21, no. 10 (March 10, 1898): 193–94.

"Obituary—Prof. S. Wells Williams." *Publishers' Weekly* 25 (1884): 243.

Romer, Grant. "Near the Temple at Yokushen . . ." *Image: Journal of Photography and Motion Pictures of the International Museum of Photography at George Eastman House* 29, no. 2 (August 1986): 1–11.

Schwartz, William Leonard, ed. "Commodore Perry at Okinawa: From the Unpublished Diary of a British Missionary." *American Historical Review* 51 (January 1946): 262–76.

"Some Personal Items." *United States Army & Navy Journal, and Gazette of the Regular & Volunteer Forces* 19, no. 3 (August 20, 1881): 50.

Sugawara, Daisuke, et al. "A Huge Sand Dome Formed by the 1854 Earthquake Tsunami in Suruga Bay, Central Japan." *ISET Journal of Earthquake Technology* 42, no. 4 (December 2005): 147–58.

Towle, Edward L. "Lieutenant Silas Bent's Device to Eliminate Variation Correction in the Magnetic Compass, 1849." *American Neptune* 25 (1965): 93–98.

Unzelman, Gail. "Thomas Hart Hyatt: The Man and His Book." *Supplement to the Wayward Tendrils Quarterly* 23, no. 3 (July 2013): 1–19.

Usami, Tatsuo. "Study of Historical Earthquakes in Japan." *Bulletin of the Earthquake Research Institute* 54 (1979): 399–439.

"Visit of the *Lady Pierce* to Japan," *Sailor's Magazine* 27, no. 9 (May 1855): 274–75.

Newspapers

Boston Daily Atlas
Brooklyn Eagle
New York Times
Richmond Times-Dispatch
Straits Times & Singapore Journal of Commerce
Washington Constitution
Washington Post

Online Resources

Allom, Thomas. "The City of Ning Po." 2010. http://www.chinese-outpost.com/history/thomas-allom-china-illustrated/the-city-of-ning-po.asp. Accessed June 1, 2016.

Davis, Peter. "William Abdy Fellowes, R.N." http://www.pdavis.nl/ShowBiog.php?id=992. Accessed June 1, 2016.

Find a Grave. http://www.findagrave.com.

"*Lady Mary Wood*." *P & O Heritage Ship Fact Sheet*. http://www.poheritage.com/Upload/Mimsy/Media/factsheet/93628LADY-MARY-WOOD-1842pdf.pdf. Accessed June 1, 2016.

Mason, Laura. "Wilhelm Lobscheid." *Biographical Dictionary of Chinese Christianity*. http://bdcconline.net/en/stories/lobscheid-wilhelm. Accessed June 1, 2016.

"New York. Registers of Officers and Enlisted Men Mustered into Federal Service,

1861–1865." Digital images. Ancestry.com. http://www.ancestry.com. Accessed June 1, 2016.

Peebles, Shyama. "Old Protestant Cemetery in Macau." *Gwulo: Old Hong Kong*. October 2010. http://gwulo.com/sites/gwulo.com/files/Gwulo-Macau-Old-Protestant-Cemetery.pdf. Accessed June 1, 2016.

"Pennsylvania and New Jersey, Church and Town Records, 1708–1985." Digital images. Ancestry.com. http://www.ancestry.com. Accessed June 1, 2016.

Pilto, Carrie. "Pilto Family Tree." http://person.ancestry.com/tree/9707512/person/-756253332/facts. Accessed June 1, 2016.

Sauer, M. Patrick. "King Family Tree." http://person.ancestry.com/tree/89897781/person/75004716816/facts. Accessed June 1, 2016.

"Thomas C. Dudley Papers, 1853–1856, 1925." Peabody Essex Museum, Salem, MA. http://phillipslibrarycollections.pem.org/utils/findingaidfull/collection/p15928coll1/id/2579. Accessed June 1, 2016.

"United States. Navy Casualties Books, 1776–1941." Digital images. Ancestry.com. http://www.ancestry.com. Accessed June 1, 2016.

Index

Page numbers in italics refer to illustrations.